THE MODERNITY OF WITCHCRAFT

THE MODERNITY OF WITCHCRAFT

POLITICS AND THE OCCULT IN POSTCOLONIAL AFRICA

(SORCELLERIE ET POLITIQUE EN AFRIQUE– LA VIANDE DES AUTRES)

PETER GESCHIERE

Translated by Peter Geschiere and Janet Roitman

UNIVERSITY PRESS OF VIRGINIA · CHARLOTTESVILLE AND LONDON

The University Press of Virginia

Originally published in French as *Sorcellerie et politique en Afrique—La viande des autres,* © Éditions Karthala, 1995.
Translation and Preface © 1997 by the Rector and Visitors of the University of Virginia
Printed in the United States of America

First published 1997

∞ The paper used in this publication meets the minimum requirements of the American National Standard for Information Sciences—Permanence of Paper for Printed Library Materials, ANSI Z39.48–1984.

Library of Congress Cataloging-in-Publication Data
Geschiere, Peter.
  [Sorcellerie et politique en Afrique. English]
  The modernity of witchcraft : politics and the occult in postcolonial Africa = Sorcellerie et politique en Afrique / Peter Geschiere ; translated by Peter Geschiere and Janet Roitman.
    p.   cm.
  Includes bibliographical references and index.
  ISBN 0-8139-1702-6 (cloth : alk. paper). — ISBN 0-8139-1703-4 (pbk. : alk. paper)
    1. Maka (African people)—Social conditions.   2. Maka (African people)—Politics and government.   3. Maka (African people)—Religion.   4. Witchcraft—Cameroon.   5. Cameroon—Social conditions.   6. Cameroon—Politics and government.   I. Title.
DT571.M35G4613   1997
306.4′096711—dc21   96-46199
                                                                CIP

CONTENTS

PREFACE TO THE ENGLISH LANGUAGE EDITION

In recent years distinguished anthropologists have publicly discussed the possibility, some have even said the likelihood, that anthropology has outlived its usefulness and is about to disappear. We hear that as the servant of imperialism, it exoticized Africans in particular, representing them as very different from ourselves in order to make their continued subordination to Western powers seem appropriate, to confirm an ideology of social evolution, and to incline us to feel good about ourselves as the vanguard of the modern. Though there is much truth to this view, it conceals its own ethnocentric condescension. As independent citizens of the modern world, Africans, we now assume, think about the world as "we" do. No longer obliged to try to understand strange beliefs and institutions lately revealed as anthropological inventions, we are relieved of the burden of intercultural understanding that anthropology thrust upon us and need no longer wrestle with the unease of liberal guilt in the face of African "traditionalism." Every tribe believes that its own habits and values are uniquely reasonable; ours is no exception.

In this forthright study, Peter Geschiere begins by admitting that at the start of his first fieldwork in Cameroon in 1971 he shared this Western condescension toward "witchcraft," "kinship," and other standard anthropological topics. So did I, in Zaire in 1964; we both wanted to study "modern" political relations. It soon became apparent, to him as to me, that almost everybody—peasants, policemen, pharmacists, politicians (especially politicians!)—took seriously the operation of invisible forces, labeled "witchcraft" or "sorcery" in

English, and that this belief was an essential factor in "modern politics" at the national level, not merely in rural hamlets. To be sure, Africans discovered long ago that Westerners did not take such beliefs seriously. On the contrary, Westerners, if in a position to do so, forbade action based on these beliefs, such as accusations against witches. That is now changing; intellectuals, clergy, jurists, chiefs, politicians, and others are increasingly willing to disregard Western opinion in this as in other areas. It is time we listened to them, but to do so it is first necessary to be able to hear in indigenous languages, to liberate ourselves from what Geschiere calls the "moralizing terminology" of "witchcraft" and "sorcery," so that we may begin to understand such concepts as *evu*, *nkong*, and *djambe*.

This is not an appeal for a charitable suspension of rational judgment. The fact is that in the United States we have had, and still have, our own witches and witch-hunts, not to mention our diviners and specialists in the occult, although if we use these terms we put them in quotation marks to show that of course we are not really superstitious. Such beliefs and practices are central to our own national life, on Capitol Hill or Wall Street, where they seem to us uniquely realistic. Consider the weight in American history of the belief in the idea that the human species is divided into a short list of genetically discrete races. Americans are highly resistant to repeated demonstrations that race is a recent cultural artifact, because it is institutionalized to such an extent that its seeming truth is confirmed in daily experience and therefore appears to be a fact of nature. They can also point to a library full of books old and new, written by credentialed scholars, that take this "fact" for granted and argue about how to evaluate the genetic properties of races and their phenotypical manifestations. An anthropologist from some other civilization would be confronted with the traditional and vexing problem of the rationality or otherwise of the natives, whose ideas make no sense to him but are clearly fundamental to their way of life and must therefore be taken seriously.

African beliefs in the occult are highly varied and may have nothing more in common than the word *witchcraft* applied to them by English-speakers. Geschiere focuses on a group of peoples in southern Cameroon, but closely similar beliefs about power are instrumental at the national level throughout the forest areas of West and Central Africa. The witch is believed to "eat" the substance of others and thus to cause them ill health and other misfortunes for his or her own personal profit. But because this occult capability is the nature of power itself, it is also necessary for successful leadership and the defense of collective interests. In the apt phrase of J.-F. Bayart, a political scientist who also writes about Cameroon, "the politics of the belly" refers both to conspicuous greed for material goods and to witchcraft power, located in the belly, that is believed to enable the successful to enrich themselves and to benefit their admiring followers.

A combination of theoretical bias and "liberal" hesitancy has so far prevented many scholars from recognizing local (African) cultural practices and values as the effective political instruments they are. Geschiere demonstrates how well indigenous concepts and practices have adapted in response to new distributions of power and of goods, brought about by the rise of capitalism and state bureaucracy. The idiom of witchcraft is dynamic and effective, not a trait left over from the past; with its talk of "eating" the substance of others, it is not far removed from our own more familiar idioms of "exploitation," "corruption," and "intrusive government." As Geschiere is well aware, similar studies could be made of comparable theories of power in other African countries. He mounts a sustained attack on the view of anthropology that treats its topics as quaint customs irrelevant to the modern world; he shows the utter inadequacy of the traditional/modern distinction (much attacked in theory, still operative in practice) and of the mistaken division between "religion" and "politics." In so doing he calls for a radical rethinking of contemporary African politics.

Wyatt MacGaffey

ACKNOWLEDGMENTS

In witchcraft, one does not say "thanks." But, unlike other recent anthropological studies of the occult, this book is not the story of an initiation. Instead, it stems from an effort to take distance from the vicious circles of witchcraft and sorcery: from the hope, no doubt naive, that showing how these discourses are linked to specific historical and cultural contexts might relativize their self-evidence and weaken their hold over people's minds.

In this effort, the support of two Cameroonian colleagues has been crucial. My long-standing collaboration on these topics with Cyprian Fisiy has been most inspiring. Together, we have published several articles in various journals (see the bibliography). I could never have written the last chapters of this book without his help: it was only thanks to him that I could consult the court files on the witchcraft trials in Bertua discussed in chapter 6; and the comparative effort, central to this book, was only possible due to our long discussions on how ideas on witchcraft affect politics—and especially on how to understand their strikingly different patterns between neighboring regions. Achille Mbembe has read version after version. Even the clumsy language of the first versions could not dampen his visionary capacities. When his eyes started to glow, I knew that a new vista was to be summoned up from the often quite sordid details I put before him. He is, therefore, the *nganga* of this book.

Jean-François Bayart, the editor of an earlier French version of the book, was a source of inspiration that never seemed to run dry—as for so many other projects. Wim van Binsbergen, Phil Burnham, Élisabeth Copet-Rougier, Georg Elwert, Mitzi Goheen, Angelique Haugerud, Daniel Heath, Bogumil Jewsiewicki, Murray Last, Paul Nkwi, Jean-Pierre Olivier de Sardan, Father Eric de Rosny, Michael Rowlands, Matthieu Schoffeleers, Hugo Soly, Patricia Spyer, Michael Taussig, Bonno Thoden van Velzen, Jan Vansina, Jean-Pierre Warnier, and Ineke van Wetering all gave valuable comments at some stage of this long project.

My greatest intellectual debt is to all those persons in various parts of Cameroon who were kind and patient enough to explain the enigmas of *la sorcellerie* to me. John Mayebi from Buea offered his most encouraging support during a long series of interviews with Bakweri elders (Southwest Cameroon) in 1987 and 1988. I owe special thanks to Meke Blaise from Mpalampoam (East Cameroon), who initiated me to "the life of the Maka" in 1971 and who continues to do so. I learned so much from him that it is time for a special countergift. Of course, it would be highly improper for a "son" to try and teach something to his "father." But the complexities of kinship among the Maka are such that I can call him not only "my father" but also "my son." It is in this double capacity that I dedicate this book to him in the hope that a study like this might help break the vicious circles of discourses on witchcraft and sorcery that—in today's rapidly changing circumstances more than ever—threaten to poison human relations.

Pseudonyms are used for individuals mentioned in connection to my fieldwork among the Maka. Real names are retained, however, for public figures.

This book is a translation, partly rewritten, of a French text published as *Sorcellerie et politique en Afrique—La viande des autres*. I thank Robert Ageneau, Jean-François Bayart, Yann Mens, and Jean-Luc Saucet for their help with the French text. For this English version, Janet Roitman contributed her invaluable vigor and inspiration, not only to the English but also to the substance of the text.

THE MODERNITY OF WITCHCRAFT

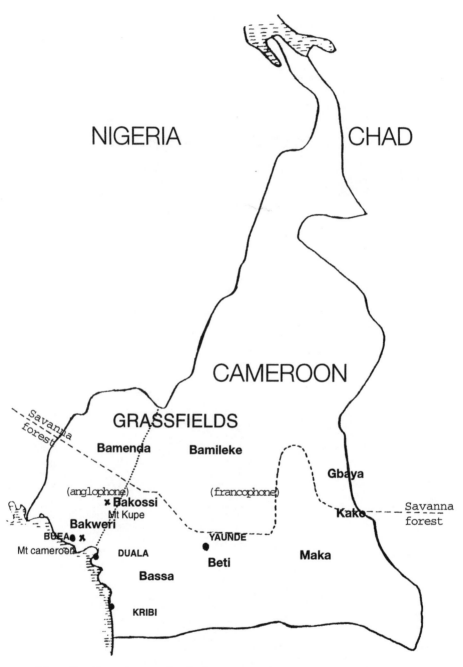

Map 1—Locations of ethnic groups in southern and western Cameroon

INTRODUCTION: WITCHCRAFT AS
POLITICAL DISCOURSE

This book originates from an experience at the beginning of my fieldwork among the Maka in southeast Cameroon in 1971. My car had broken down one night, stranding me in the middle of the forest with my assistant Meke, who was to play a prominent role in my research. I felt ill at ease in the dark, but this was apparently not the case for Meke. He suddenly exclaimed with some excitement, "Oh, if Mendouga was with us. We are like innocent kids. But she would see the witches that fly around here. She has the second sight. She can see what mischief they are plotting." Mendouga was a woman of a neighboring village who regularly visited us. She was also the greatest *féticheur* (healer or witch doctor) of the area.

I found this hardly the moment for Meke's remark, with all the noises of the dark forest around us. But I was nonetheless struck by the clear note of excitement and regret in his voice. Apparently, he regretted—at least at this moment—that he was an "innocent" without special powers. For the first time I understood that *la sorcellerie* (witchcraft/sorcery) was not just something evil to the people among whom I lived but that it also meant thrill, excitement, and the possibility of access to unknown powers.[1] I realized also that I risked overlooking an essential dimension in my research if I continued to neglect the close conceptual link for these people between witchcraft and power. My aim was to study political relations between the villages and the state, and I felt some reluctance about "traditional" aspects like sorcery, witchcraft, or kinship. I wanted to focus on the more modern aspects of village life. Meke's remark made me realize for the first time—maybe because I was oversensitive in the dark with all those noises around me—that, to the Maka, it is hardly possible to talk about power without referring to the *djambe* (sorcery/witchcraft). And, most importantly, I came to realize that this applies not only to local politics within the village but also to modern relations to the state and national politics.

Another of my assistant's expressions turned out to be less clarifying. Initially, he often repeated "where there is electric light, witchcraft will disappear." He had learned this optimistic phrase from the Dutch missionaries for whom he had worked for quite some time. Apparently, he felt that "his" new white man would like this phrase. However, his own experience defied this. Indeed, he was to tell me later how he had been threatened by the occult forces when he worked in town, where there certainly was electricity. After the 1970s, Cameroon was able to expand its electric mains rapidly because of new revenues from petrol. Unfortunately, this has certainly not weakened the obsession with witchcraft. To the contrary, newspapers increasingly "report" presumed nightly escapades of witches, and *Radio Trottoir,* still the most popular purveyor of news, spreads ever more spectacular stories about witchcraft affairs in the highest circles of society.

To many Westerners, it seems self-evident that the belief in witchcraft or sorcery is something "traditional" that will automatically disappear with modernization.[2] But this stereotype does not fit with actual developments in Africa today. Throughout the continent, discourses on sorcery or witchcraft are intertwined, often in quite surprising ways, with modern changes. Nowadays, modern techniques and commodities, often of Western provenance, are central in rumors on the occult.

Characteristic but particularly evocative is the following testimony from Reverend Victor Enow Ayuk (Bethany Baptist Church, Buea, southwest Cameroon):

The testimony that follows tells us what witchcraft is. An old woman (alive), a practising Christian visited me at about 6:00 A.M. sometime ago. She complained of having worked all night. She was very tired, she said, and needed some prayers. I asked her what she might have done all night to be tired—and then she told me the following story:

> I have been driving all night. I drive a plane. We use the plane to transport food, rain and such from places of plenty to the Buea area. Very recently, white people have been attempting to take the plane from us. If I hadn't been so skillful, having piloted the plane for 30 years, they would have long gone with it.

At this point I interrupted. "You mean to say you are a pilot?" I said. "Yes," she said. She went on to explain to me that she has never seen an aeroplane, but she knows how a plane can be built. All planes are in the world of witchcraft, and when the white man gets it from the black man, he then interprets it into real life. As it is with planes, so with televisions, radios, telephones etc."[3]

In light of such syncretist views, it is difficult to maintain that there is a self-evident opposition between witchcraft and modernity. On the contrary, rumors and practices related to the occult forces abound in the more modern sectors of society. In Africa, the dynamism of these notions and images is especially striking: they are the subject of constant reformulations and re-creations, which often express a determined effort for signifying politico-economic changes or even gaining control over them. In many respects, then, one can speak of the "modernity" of witchcraft.[4]

Another example, also from the beginning of my fieldwork among the Maka and equally surprising, at least to me, shows that this obsession with "witchcraft" haunts the elite as much as the rest of the population. On the second Sunday of my stay, I went to see, for the first time, a soccer match in one of the towns of the East Province. However, after half an hour, the match was rudely interrupted when the wife of the town's *préfet* (senior district officer) suddenly appeared on the field and threw herself on the goalie of the visiting team. She shouted that she had to tear his *gris-gris* from him, else her husband's team would never be able to score. Only after the gendarmes had intervened—who indeed frisked the goalkeeper—could the match continue.

In Africa today, such an event is not exceptional.[5] Nearly every soccer match is the topic of persistent rumors that, for instance, the receiving team has "armored" (*blindé*) the field so that the visiting team is bound to loose. Visiting teams often prefer to stay at a mission station—in particular, with European missionaries—because the Christian religion and the "magic of the white man" offers at least some sort of protection against occult aggression. In the beginning of 1993, *Radio Trottoir* of Yaunde announced that the Indomitable Lions of the famous national team refused to work with the *marabout* chosen for them by the head of state himself. This shows that such sorcery experts do not always convince their potential clients but also demonstrates how close the link is between sorcery and politics.

In the example of the dramatic intervention of the *préfet*'s wife on the soccer field, the link to politics was perfectly clear. The *préfet* did his best, for some time already, to have his team promoted to the First Division. Such a promotion would certainly help his political career. Apparently, his wife—who no doubt hoped to get away from this outpost as soon as possible—was not prepared to have this plan ruined by the goalkeeper with his "damned *gris-gris.*"[6]

In the course of my research, I stumbled upon all sorts of interventions of occult forces in modern politics. I also noticed that such incursions could have highly different implications for the course of political processes. From the very beginning of my stay in the village, it became clear that relations between the village and the *sous-préfet* (district officer—the direct representative of the state at the local level) were profoundly marked by *la sorcellerie*. I was, for instance, surprised by the fervor with which this civil servant accused the villagers of using occult forces in order to sabotage government projects. The first time I attended one of his visits to the village, the *sous-préfet* admonished the people in these terms: "It seems that you use your witchcraft to block everything the government is trying to do for you. Well, the persons guilty of this may think that they remain invisible. But I do see them and I shall punish them severely."[7]

Here, references to the occult seem to confirm the stereotype, already referred to, of witchcraft as a "traditional" obstacle to development and the emergence of new inequalities. However, in practice it turned out to be very difficult to ascertain whether the villagers did indeed try to manipulate occult forces in order to oppose state interventions. It seems rather that the civil servants, with their fierce and constant diatribes, rendered *la sorcellerie* into a "subversive" force.

But what is even more confusing is that, alongside such references to witchcraft as a leveling force, which opposes new inequalities and relations of domination, other interpretations emphasize the role of these forces in the accumulation of wealth and power. And it is especially this version of sorcery/witchcraft as an accumulative force that prevails in more modern forms of politics. To the villagers, it is obvious that the ascension of the new elites—in this area nearly exclusively civil servants and politicians—is linked, in one way or another, to the occult force of the *djambe* (a term that the Maka now translate as *sorcellerie*). In the 1970s, for instance, my Maka friends agreed that all efforts by rival politicians to eclipse the *député* (Member of Parliament) in function were of no avail. The reason they gave me was simple: the *député* had assured himself of the services of the best *nganga* (healer) of the area. This made any action against him pointless. It is not only the villagers or the people in the townships who are spreading such rumors. The elites themselves are prone to similar allusions. The *député* concerned, for instance, never missed an opportunity to allude to the extraordinary forces of his *nganga*.

This association of politics with witchcraft was reinforced by the political climate created after independence (1960) by President Ahmadou Ahidjo and his "unified party." The national ideology of the new regime heavily emphasized the need for "unity" and "vigilance" against omnipresent "subversion." But despite all this official emphasis on unity, there was fierce competition between rival politicians and factions. However, in Ahidjo's days, it took place *within* the single party and had to be arranged behind closed doors. Everything was settled by the central leadership of the party, but its decisions were highly abrupt and unpredictable. The consequence was that rumors about *la politique des Grands* were often difficult to distinguish from familiar stories about nightly escapades and confrontations between the witches.[8]

Around 1980, the dealings of the state with respect to witchcraft affairs abruptly acquired a new dimension in the East Province when the regional lawcourts started convicting "witches" often without concrete proof of aggression or confessions. In many of these cases the only "proof" consisted of the testimony of a *nganga* who affirmed that he or she had seen the accused practice *sorcellerie*. These trials are surprising—not to say shocking—because they constitute a dramatic reversal of the preceding jurisprudence. Before 1980, the healers, not the supposed witches, risked being persecuted by the law for defamation and disturbance of the peace. This new role assumed by the courts raises a whole array of questions that are symptomatic of the state's ambivalence toward *la sorcellerie*. Was this new judicial offensive a logical outcome of the Cameroonian state's "hegemonic project" (to borrow a phrase from Jean-François Bayart 1979)? Was it because the regime believed it was threatened by these hidden forms of "subversion" and thus tried to establish its hegemony even in this treacherous domain? Or did the initiative come from below: Was it rather the population that no longer accepted the state's passivity while witchcraft seemed to become rampant? Was the initiative with the people, pressurizing the courts to intervene?

Witchcraft and Modernity

These examples from Makaland are not exceptional. On the contrary, nearly everywhere on the continent the state and politics seem to be a true breeding ground for modern transformations of witchcraft and sorcery. As indicated previously, forms of one-party rule, with their authoritarianism and their tendency to settle everything behind closed doors, created a political climate in which *la politique des Grands* became strikingly similar to stories about witches and their nightly plotting. But the more recent democratization process, as well, is accompanied by a blossoming of rumors on the role of the occult. In Benin, for instance, one of the rare countries where democratization had some success, President Soglo nearly missed his own inauguration because he was supposedly still suffering from a sorcery attack. In the same country, one of the first acts of the new democratic regime was to bring to trial the *marabout* of Kerekou, the deposed dictator.[9] During this trial, this "magician" quite openly threatened the judges with his occult powers. One can cite many similar examples from other countries. For Cameroon, *Jeune Afrique* observes that multiparty politics leads to growing insecurity that in turn makes people "resort to the invisible." [10] According to the *Washington Post,* and many other newspapers, the lifting of apartheid had similar effects in South Africa: in the summer of 1994, it published an article entitled "As S. African Blacks Gain Freedom, 'Witch' Killings Rise Sharply." [11] The problem seems to be that as soon as a new political space is opened, it is overrun by rumors about the use of sorcery and witchcraft.

Western observers might be shocked by this entwinement of democratic tendencies with notions of witchcraft and sorcery; they may even try to ignore it. But for Africa it seems practically inevitable that each political innovation confronts the narrow link between power and the occult. Recently, several authors have emphasized that democracy in Africa can only succeed if it is grafted upon local cultures. If democratization means no more than imposing Western models and institutions upon African societies, it is doomed from the start. In a recent interview, the Cameroonian historian Achille Mbembe insists that more profound innovations are necessary: what is needed is nothing less than the elaboration of "other languages on power" related to African realities, "languages that propose another ethic of power and another political culture. But in order to be rooted in the real . . . they must emerge from the daily life of the people, address everyday fears and nightmares, and the images with which people express or dream them. We must capture . . . the dreams and desires, the moral ideals and imagination of our people by showing that they can be realized." [12]

From this perspective, however, one must inevitably take into account notions of the occult, of sorcery and witchcraft. [13] Nearly everywhere in Africa, discourses on power continue to be marked by these notions. Moreover, often the link between power and witchcraft seems to become tighter instead of weaker. The *imaginaire* of "the politics of the belly"—which according to Jean-François Bayart (1989) dominates politics in Africa—refers directly to this dangerous force that is supposed to live in someone's belly. Witchcraft, this terribly diffuse notion so highly current in Africa, continues to be a key element in discourses on power, despite modern processes of change (or perhaps because of them).[14]

One may wonder whether this is particular to Africa. Are Western journalists right to describe the resilience of such "traditional" notions on the occult as something exotic, the umpteenth proof of the "otherness" of this continent?[15] Recent debates on the paradoxes of processes of globalization suggest that this resilience of tradition in modern contexts is hardly exceptional. The notion of globalization as such, linked as it is with the expansion of capitalism as a world system, may suggest that this expansion leads to inevitable homogenization. However, recently authors of different feathers have emphasized that such processes should be studied not only from an economic or technical angle but also with attention to culture. Through this, all sorts of irregularities and paradoxes emerge.[16] It is true that modern techniques—notably means of transport and communications—now penetrate the remotest corners of the globe. And one cannot deny that peripheral groups are now increasingly involved in the world market not only as producers but also as consumers: new fashions and the latest gadgets turn up everywhere. However, the paradox is that these processes do not lead to increasing cultural uniformity—the global victory of Coca-Cola, so much feared by anthropologists like Lévi-Strauss. On the contrary, the modern world, although often called a "global village," is marked by increasing cultural heterogeneity. Idiosyncratic cultural traits are grafted upon new means of communication and processes of commodification: "traditional," more often "pseudotraditional," traits are reproduced in new forms and on a wider scale. The ease with which witchcraft discourses in Africa incorporate the money economy, new power relations, and consumer goods associated with modernity is a striking example of this paradox, but it is certainly not unique. Elsewhere, also, such "traditional" notions turn up in modern contexts, often with surprising force.

No doubt the tenacity of witchcraft ideas in Africa gives conceptions of power and its exercise special connotations. But this specificity should not be exaggerated. As we shall see, the political implications of witchcraft in Africa conjure up unexpected parallels with feelings of power and powerlessness that mark popular conceptions of politics in Western democracies—the idea that one should have a grip on power and the realization that one rarely can. Witchcraft offers hidden means to grab power, but at the same time it reflects sharp feelings of impotence; it serves especially to hide the sources of power. Is all this so different from the reasons that so many people in the West become disappointed in, or even alienated from, politics? When I listened to my friends' speculations about the hidden role of the *nganga* (healers) and their arsenal of occult tools, which supposedly were decisive factors in regional and even national politics, I was often struck by the parallel with the role attributed to public relations experts in American politics (and increasingly in Europe as well). Like the *nganga,* these experts are supposed to "armor" (*blinder*) the politicians. Their ability to bring success stems from their esoteric, and more or less magical, knowledge. The politicians' gains and losses seem to depend less on the people's support than on the effectiveness of the experts' secret actions. Most importantly, both in Africa and in Europe, the intervention of such experts, loaded with esoteric knowledge, seems to remove power from the people. This is all the more reason to take witchcraft, as a form of political action, seriously.

Three Leading Themes: Ambiguity, Regional Variations, and the Link with Kinship

The aim of this book is to explore, starting from a few Cameroonian examples, how this "modernity" of discourses on witchcraft—their continuities and transformations in new contexts—affects political developments. How are these discourses related to the emergence of new forms of domination and resistance?[17] Three dimensions are central:

- the ambiguity, already noted above, of witchcraft in relation to power
- the importance of regional variations
- the close link between witchcraft and kinship, even in modern circumstances

With respect to the first theme, witchcraft's ambiguity in relation to power, recall the examples above from the Maka region: the *sous-préfet* (district officer) who saw witchcraft as a weapon of the weak against the state and its projects, whereas the villagers themselves saw it as an indispensable support for the new elites. These examples from my Maka studies have more general implications. Elsewhere, these discourses also express, rather surprisingly, both the desire to level inequalities and the ambition to accumulate power and wealth. This ambivalence is certainly not new. In the past, the occult forces were also supposed to both undermine and reinforce power. But this ambivalence seems to be strengthened by the emergence, everywhere in Africa and even within local communities, of new inequalities that are unsettling because of their unprecedented dimensions. New forms of power and wealth seem to rupture old domestic solidarities. That is why they evoke strong sentiments of jealousy and, therefore, hidden aggression. These are all the more dangerous since witchcraft comes "from inside the house." This could be called the "leveling side" of witchcraft. However, it is balanced by witchcraft's "accumulative side." As discussed below, new forms of power and wealth are also easily associated with witchcraft—not only by the people but also by new elites themselves. In the latter case, the occult forces are referred to in order to explain how somebody became so scandalously rich or powerful. It is because of this ambiguity that witchcraft discourses allow for highly different interpretations of the vicissitudes of politics. This "polyinterpretability" might also be one of the main reasons why these discourses still seem to be so easily applicable to explain modern developments.

Yet there are important regional variations—and this is the second theme of this book—in the precarious and constantly changing balance between the leveling and accumulative tendencies of witchcraft in relation to power. The broader importance of such regional contrasts is illustrated in a quite alarming way by the recent ethnicization of Cameroonian politics. Democratization and the installation of a multiparty system—imposed on the Cameroonian regime by strong outside pressure in 1989—came to many as a relief after the long period of one-party authoritarianism. Finally, there was space for opposition and public debate. However, this space was soon filled by ethnicity. Political debate became rapidly dominated by ethnic stereotypes contrasting the Beti of the Center and the South with the people of the West and the Northwest (Bamileke and Bamenda). Characteristically, these stereotypes referred to particular forms of witchcraft: to *famla*, a new form of zombie witchcraft that supposedly explains the success of the Bamileke entrepreneurs, or to the *evu* that makes Beti civil servants "eat the state" in order to appease the jealousy of their greedy kin. These hidden dimensions make such ethnic stereotypes so self-evident but demonstrate also the urgency for research into the background of such notions and the social contexts from which they could emerge. Is it possible to distinguish different regional trajectories in the articulation of discourses on the occult with new inequalities? And can a closer analysis of such different trajectories help rob such ethnic stereotypes of some of their self-evidence?

The third leitmotif of this study, directly related to the themes of ambiguity and regional variations, is the close and persistent link between witchcraft and kinship or "the house."[18] Even in modern contexts—for instance, in the big cities—witchcraft is supposed to arise, first of all, from the intimacy of the family and the home. This is why it is both such a dangerous and unavoidable threat. In many respects, witchcraft is the dark side of kinship: it is the frightening realization that there is jealousy and therefore aggression within the family, where there should be only trust and solidarity.[19]

It is striking, however, that this discourse, so closely linked to the domestic realities of the home and the family, is used at the same time to address modern changes and the increase in scale they imply. In many African societies, witchcraft beliefs seem to be the obvious discourse for attempts to relate new inequalities, produced on an ever larger scale, to the familiar world of kinship and relatives. The discourse is stretched to incorporate new inequalities, which requires a dynamic use of the notions of both witchcraft and kinship. In Cameroon, and certainly not only in this country, people purposely enlarge the scope of these conceptions—they "work" with them—in order to bridge the gap between village and city, between peasants and new elites. In other words, even in modern contexts it remains as difficult to escape from kinship as from witchcraft.

Before discussing these three dimensions in more detail, a few rapid remarks on problems of terminology and approach might be helpful.

Anthropology and the Problems of a Moralizing Terminology

Even though the modernity of witchcraft manifests itself in various walks of life (not only in politics but also, for instance, in sports or business), it has received surprisingly little attention in scientific studies, at least until recently. It is especially surprising that anthropologists paid so little attention to it. For them, after all, witchcraft and sorcery were always favorite topics, not to say hobbies. Yet, for a long time, they seemed inclined to abandon fascinating topics—such as the role of the occult on the football fields or in the arenas of the state—to journalists and other observers. This restraint, regrettable in view of the discipline's rich knowledge about these beliefs, is related to particular trends in the development of anthropological discourse on sorcery and witchcraft. In order not to overload this introduction, this topic is further discussed in the afterword.[20]

Here it suffices to note that anthropologists have long tended to study witchcraft and its implications for power within a strictly local setting (that is, the village). In Africa, the anthropology of sorcery and witchcraft was profoundly influenced by a series of monographs, especially by British authors, from the end of the 1950s.[21] Despite important differences, these authors had the same basic perspective. All studied witchcraft/sorcery as a conservative force within local arenas, focusing on witchcraft accusations that were supposed to serve to maintain the status quo and defend the local order against the undermining impact of new, external influences. It is striking that, among these classical anthropologists and later among many of their followers, a highly moralizing view of the occult forces prevailed. Most anthropologists still tend to reduce discourses on witchcraft to an unequivocal opposition between good and evil, even when the local terminology hardly lends itself to this. At least for the societies studied here, this opposition is not so simple. The local notions now generally translated as *la sorcellerie* rather seem to blur such distinctions. For the people with whom I lived, these forces surely have highly disturbing effects, but they can also be used constructively: to protect oneself or reinforce authority and, more generally, to succeed in life.[22] This ambiguity is crucial to the modern transformations of this discourse. Efforts to appropriate modern resources with the help of occult means are certainly viewed with great suspicion. But we shall see that even such suspect new forms of wealth can be legitimized ("whitewashed"). Then the supposed use of occult means is reinterpreted and seen as "constructive." It is precisely through this ambivalence that discourses on the occult incorporate modern changes so easily.

The need to nuance the distinction between good and evil in this domain emphasizes certain problems with terms like *sorcery* or *witchcraft*. One difficulty is that these terms—like their French equivalent, *sorcellerie*—have strongly moralizing connotations. The diffusion of these terms on a truly worldwide scale seems to demonstrate the success of the Western vision (strongly propagated by missionaries, civil servants, and also anthropologists) of these forces as by definition linked to Evil and opposed to all Good. It is, therefore, all the more important to repeat that these terms are highly unfortunate and even misleading translations of African notions that often have a much wider range of meaning.

It is especially the pejorative tenor of these Western terms that can easily hide the broader and more ambiguous implications of the African notions. A good example is the notion of *djambe* among the Maka of eastern Cameroon, already referred to above. To them, the *djambe* is a force—or even a being—that lives in the belly of a person. It permits its proprietor to transform himself or herself into a spirit or an animal and to do all sorts of other exceptional things. This force can be used to kill and, according to my spokesmen, often is. One could therefore translate *djambe* as "witchcraft." But the same *djambe*, like the *evu* of the neighboring Beti, can also be used in a more positive sense: for instance, to heal or to affirm one's prestige. Sometimes the term is used in such a general sense—for instance, when a guest praises a host by saying that the host's *djambe* makes him such a fine person—that only a vague translation, like "special energy," would be appropriate.[23]

It seems, therefore, that there are clear advantages in translating *djambe* as a more neutral term like "occult force"; this leaves open the question whether the force is used for evil or for good. Indeed, in translating *djambe* as "witchcraft," one reduces a much broader worldview in which the human environment is seen as being animated by spiritual forces to an ugly core—the image of the witches meeting at night and eating each other's kin. Thus the translation of *djambe* as "witchcraft" risks primitivizing a much richer cosmology.

The problem is, however, that the Maka themselves always translate *djambe* as *sorcellerie*. In this respect, they are no exception. Throughout Africa, people have appropriated Western terms like *sorcery* or *witchcraft*, and public debates are now being waged in such terms—for instance, on *sorcellerie* and development. These terms become a kind of panacea blurring all sorts of nuances. One might regret such blurring, as do many anthropologists, who are interested in "authentic" traditions, but this should not make one neglect contemporary uses of key terms like *sorcery* and *witchcraft* by the people themselves.

Thus a serious terminological dilemma arises.[24] In some respects it would be preferable—more "scientific"—to avoid current terms and resort to less loaded terms like *occult forces*.[25] However, in this way, the social scientist would isolate himself from daily discussions in the societies concerned, where one does use diffuse but heavily loaded terms like *witchcraft* or *sorcery*. For this reason, I prefer to retain these last terms. The term *occult forces* seems too anodyne to do justice to the fierceness with which the modern implications of these forces are discussed in Africa. Social scientists cannot permit themselves to withdraw into a purist isolation.

The disadvantages of the terms *witchcraft* or *sorcery* nonetheless remain all too real. For the present study, the most urgent problem is doubtless to escape from the connotations these terms have acquired in anthropological discourse: witchcraft as a necessarily conservative force, as a specter that these societies evoke in order to defend themselves against changes. In their recent study of prophetic movements among the Maroons of Suriname, H. U. E. Thoden van Velzen and W. van Wetering conclude that anthropologists still tend to view local cultures as "backward looking"; even those who are interested in the dynamics of those cultures are often inclined to look for a conservative finality, a basic desire to protect ancient values.[26] However, to understand the resilience of representations of witchcraft and the occult in many parts of Africa, the challenge is rather to explore the possibilities offered by these discourses for attempts to gain control over the modern changes.

Witchcraft and the State in Cameroon

Studies of the relation between witchcraft beliefs and modern politics in Africa may be rare, but there is a pioneering article for Cameroon by Michael Rowlands and Jean-Pierre Warnier (1988) entitled "Sorcery, Power and the Modern State in Cameroon."[27] Interestingly, these authors emphasize that the impact of the occult forces on national politics has become much more manifest over the last decades. In the first years after independence (1960), there was little talk about *la sorcellerie* in the public sphere: the politics of the "young state" were emphatically presented as something new and modern, to be separated from such "traditional" relics as the belief in witchcraft. But since the end of the 1960s, *Radio Trottoir* and, later, the official news media began to refer more and more openly to witchcraft affairs. Rowlands and Warnier note that it became ever more difficult for the state to remain uninvolved. They point out that public opinion in Cameroon, as in other African countries, held that the colonial state protected the witches since, in those days, the authorities refused to apply sanctions against them. Supposedly, this was one reason why witchcraft became rampant to the degree that postcolonial authorities felt obliged to try and contain it. Thus, as the state Africanized itself, the old link between power and the occult was restored. The authors signal that, from the 1970s on, the Cameroonian authorities tried more and more openly to establish their control over the domain of the occult. However, at the same time, this allowed notions on the occult to penetrate and corrupt new relations of power.

Two comments on Rowlands and Warnier's article help define the approach of the present study. First, there is the question of the ambiguity of witchcraft and sorcery with respect to power. These authors emphasize the link between sorcery and accumulation—notably the accumulation of power and wealth. Basing their remarks on a whole series of anthropological studies of various societies in south-central and western Cameroon, they show that, in all these societies, *la sorcellerie* is seen as an inherent aspect of power: *les Grands* are self-evidently associated with *djambe, evu, sem, ewusu,* or whatever terms are used locally.[28] By putting such strong emphasis on the "accumulative" side (as I called it previously) of these notions, these authors seem intent on marking their distance from the emphasis in classical anthropology on the leveling impact of these ideas (witchcraft as a conservative force). In the present study I intend, rather, to highlight the ways in which both sides manifest themselves in modern contexts. It is precisely because of this that witchcraft is such a dangerous force; it is certainly related to the accumulation of power but can also serve to undermine it. Witchcraft is both a resource for the powerful and also a weapon for the weak against new inequalities. It is especially in this last context that the link between witchcraft and kinship—a dimension that is absent from Rowlands and Warnier's study—makes itself felt.

My purpose is to study representations of witchcraft as a precarious balance between "leveling" and "accumulative" tendencies. This conceptual opposition between accumulation and leveling has been an underlying theme in British anthropology since the 1950s (see the afterword below). A Dutch anthropologist, Wilhelmina van Wetering, explicitly related this theme to witchcraft accusations in order to analyze their impact on local politics.[29] She made a typology of societies according to varying forms of kinship organization in order to show that witchcraft seems to encourage accumulation of power in some types and its leveling in others. One might add that the same ambiguity of witchcraft notions manifests itself in their reproduction in more modern politico-economic contexts. One of the central questions in this study is whether this perspective of a precarious balance between leveling and accumulative tendencies can further the understanding of witchcraft's modernity—its all-pervasiveness in modern contexts and the varying interpretations of new inequalities it allows for.

A second comment on the Rowlands and Warnier article concerns the issue, already mentioned, of regional variations. One may won-der whether these authors generalize too easily their own observa-tions for the whole of southern and western Cameroon (that is, the non-Islamized part of the country). They mix their own fieldwork data from the Northwest and the West with descriptions from the southern forest area, even though there are considerable differences between the societies in both areas (especially when principles of hi-erarchy and power are concerned).[30] There is probably a difference of perspective here. It is true that in a country like Cameroon, a kind of interregional "witchcraft culture" is developing most notably around the state and its manifestations in the urban centers. Appar-ently, Rowlands and Warnier wish to give a general picture, seen from the national level. The present study, however, is based on an ap-proach "from below" that highlights the persistence of important regional variations in the articulation of local ideas on witchcraft with modern politics. Moreover, such different regional trajectories di-rectly affect the respective roles of various elites at the national level.

Such variations are not surprising. It is clear that, after the colonial conquest, the articulation of external influences and local power re-lations in the various regions of Cameroon developed according to different scenarios. The exact forms of colonial penetration varied, as did the local structures and the footholds they offered for realizing new forms of *mise en valeur* (the euphemistic French term for the exploitation of the colonies). One of the aims of this study is to relate the multiple transformations of local witchcraft discourses to these different regional trajectories.[31]

Clearly, such a perspective necessitates a comparative approach. But a certain modesty is called for. The link between witchcraft and politics is a highly elusive subject, being permeated with mystery and ambiguity. In the following chapters I start from my studies among the Maka in the forests of eastern Cameroon. But I hope to expand my interpretations through comparative excursions into other re-gions: first to other forest societies, notably the Beti of south-central Cameroon and the Bakweri of the Southwest, whose segmentary forms of organizations correspond to those of the Maka; later, to the more hierarchical societies of the Grassfields of the West (Bamileke) and the Northwest (Bamenda).

The comparison with these latter groups is interesting since it touches upon hot issues in political debates in Cameroon today. Ever since President Paul Biya's rise to power in 1982, national politics have increasingly been dominated by ethnic tensions between the Beti, whose elite is supposed to dominate the state, and the Grafi—that is, the Grassfielders of the West and the Northwest—from whose midst an elite of successful businessmen arose who supposedly control the national economy. It is in relation to these tensions that the ethnic stereotypes mentioned above and their heavy references to different forms of witchcraft play a role. Pro-government pamphlets often contain allusions to the vicious new forms of witchcraft that ostensibly are the "real" explanation for the economic prowess of entrepreneurs from the West and the Northwest. Opposition leaflets, in contrast, refer to the southerners' fear of *evu* and its ferocious egalitarianism, which would explain why these elites, despite strong government support, fail miserably in business, so that they can only "eat the state" to satisfy their greedy kin.

Of course, such tribalist arguments have to be handled with great care. But it is senseless just to ignore them: their impact in politics is all too real. The advantage of a comparative approach, even if only a first attempt, is that it requires an exploration of the historical and cultural backgrounds of such stereotypes and thus might help to demystify them.

The book starts, however, with three chapters on the relationship between witchcraft and politics among the Maka in the East: chapter 2 on central principles of their discourse on the occult; chapter 3 on the precarious balance between leveling and accumulative tendencies in local politics; and chapter 4 on the link with new forms of inequality introduced by the state and the market. This last chapter focuses on the relation between villagers and their *évolués* (that is, the urban elites) as a nodal point in the modernization of the *sorcellerie* discourse and its penetration into the institutions of the state. Between these chapters on the Maka are comparative interstices signaling similarities and differences with developments in other regions of the country. This comparative outlook is further elaborated in the next two chapters. Chapter 5 examines the ambivalent link between witchcraft and new forms of wealth, exploring different regional trajectories that vary from attempts to "whitewash" the suspect new forms of wealth by the Grassfields chiefs to the general panic about the new witchcraft of riches in the South. Chapter 6 looks at new state interventions against witchcraft, notably the judicial offensive that has led to shocking convictions of alleged witches. With these new trials against witches, the state ventures deep into the treacherous terrain of *la sorcellerie*. The question is whether this will indeed force a rupture in these beliefs. Or will the state, instead, be trapped in the vicious circles of these discourses?

The Question of Reality:
Witchcraft, Human Agency, and New Inequalities

Let me end this introduction with three quick remarks that help to define my position in the boggy field of witchcraft and sorcery further.

The first concerns the thorny question of truth. A Western anthropologist who ventures into this field can hardly escape the question of whether these representations correspond to "reality." This is certainly the case when the focus is on power and politics. Here, witchcraft beliefs are mainly expressed in rumors and allusions. Direct accusations and public confessions are rare, and it is often difficult to detect concrete actions. Thus it becomes all the more difficult to avoid the question of the "truth" of these rumors: Do people indeed meet at night in the forest in order to hatch a plot? Do these occult means, to which people refer so often, have a "real" effectiveness?

The experienced anthropologist knows the familiar arguments to dodge such awkward questions: sorcery/witchcraft is a "discourse" that is real to the people who use it. Moreover, when is a discourse real? Even our colleagues from the natural sciences tend more and more to put terms like real between quotation marks. Clearly, the reality of a situation depends on the language and the notions actors use: up to a certain degree each discourse contains its own reality. However, such an academic attitude is difficult to maintain in the face of impatient informants who want to know why the anthropologist poses all the questions. Why is he interested if he does not believe in the force of these powers? Or does he believe in it after all? Back in the West, his Western colleagues want to check if he is not losing his soundness of mind with all these weird stories.

Such questions should not be discarded too easily. They force us to confront the validity of the conceptual opposition between reality and fantasy—between scientific knowledge and local representations, between *etic* and *emic* explanations. Such oppositions still dominate anthropology's general discourse on the Other, but they become especially prominent when sorcery and witchcraft are at stake: the idea that these forces do not really exist continues to mark many anthropological studies.[32]

A very different view can be found in a pathbreaking work that is a source of inspiration for the present study. Éric de Rosny is a French priest who was initiated into the world of the *nganga* "healers" in Duala. His studies of the fierce struggle of the *nganga* against occult aggression in this city are fascinating precisely because he takes such witchcraft threats seriously and refuses to treat them as imaginary. He explicitly attacks the tendency in many Western studies to deny the real existence of the *sorcier*. For him, they are all too real:

> Due to my direct and constant involvement in Duala with victims and sometimes also with accusers, I came to see that evil *sorciers* do exist in flesh and blood. No doubt they are infinitely less numerous than . . . my panicky spokesmen affirmed, but they are nonetheless all too real. They are either people who manipulate others' credulity for their own profit (sometimes even using poison); or persons who are not conscious of their perversity. . . . Aren't there in every society certain perverted persons who—without even knowing it—make their fellow men ill by draining their vital energy from them, thus depersonalizing them—in other words "eating" them?[33]

De Rosny is no doubt right to emphasize that the distinction between what is "imaginary" and "real" is not so clear in this domain. If the belief in the effectiveness of witchcraft is widespread in society, it is indeed highly probable that certain individuals will try to use it. In this respect, witches do exist—that is, men and women who act according to these beliefs in order to hurt others and acquire additional forms of power. Other recent authors, who also had themselves initiated into the local secrets, go even further in this direction. To some, such an initiation seems to lead to an uncritical acceptance of the truth of this knowledge.[34] Such an approach also has its problems: it tends to affirm the reality and the effectiveness of the occult forces. This is certainly not the intention of the present book. In the societies concerned here, we see that the widespread fear that witchcraft is running wild has shocking effects in everyday life—tearing families apart and setting people against each other. Moreover, all this seems to have worsened during the past twenty-five years that I have regularly visited Cameroon. The idea that older ways of protecting oneself are no longer of avail against new transformations of the witches' powers has led to a frantic search for new forms of protection that can have gruesome consequences of their own.[35] This might make one wary of emphasizing too strongly the reality of these beliefs.

Thus the anthropologist seems to be somewhere between Scylla and Charybdis (a platitude that makes some sense in this context). On the one hand, by emphatically denying the reality of these discourses and treating them as pure fantasies, the anthropologist risks becoming side-tracked. Indeed, if one wants to understand the hold of such conceptions over people's minds, one has to overcome the tendency to simply oppose reality and fantasy. As Michael Taussig (1987) has shown most forcefully, one can understand the force of these images only if one "goes along" with them. How can one understand the thrill and the excitement they promise, if one's point of departure is that they are not real and, therefore, should be explained away by reducing them to other terms? But, on the other hand, affirming their reality might mean in practice affirming that monstrous accusations are well-founded. This can become all the more awkward in view of the general panic over the supposed proliferation of witchcraft and the crude sanctions to which people resort in present-day Africa.

The point of departure of this book is to take seriously the discourse on witchcraft—both the fear and the excitement it contains; this means not to try to reason it away by reducing it to other terms.

This seems to be a precondition for trying to contextualize these notions—for understanding under which circumstances people refer to them and what their effects are in everyday life. It is only thus that one can hope to somewhat loosen the vicious circles of witchcraft reasoning from which it appears so difficult to break away. Methodologically, this means trying to relate the discourse, the rumors, and a posteriori explanations to specific contexts and to identify, as much as possible, moments when these notions are translated into concrete actions. Unfortunately, those moments are few and far between since the relation between witchcraft and power is by definition hidden and elusive.

As a consequence—and this is a second general remark—the study of witchcraft and sorcery raises somewhat uncomfortable questions as to the nature of human action and, more specifically, the plausibility of methodological individualism that, since Weber, has become a kind of premise in the social sciences. The relation between witchcraft and action is fraught with paradoxes. On the one hand, the secrecy of the discourse serves to conceal the actors involved behind a veil of rumors and mystery. By definition, witchcraft is practiced in secret; it is therefore often very difficult to know who did what. Yet it is also a basic tenor to these discourses that they explain each and any event by referring to human agency.[36] Thus, they tend to personalize the universe: all sorts of events, especially those that Westerners call "natural" disasters or chance, are seen as direct consequences of human acts—either individual initiatives or, more often, collective conspiracies fomented by shadowy gangs.[37] These are, therefore, representations that heavily emphasize human action but that, at the same time, hide the actors and their acts from view. This raises the problem of how to account for the effects of actions that are very hard to discern.

To give an example (to which I return below): when discussing the ups and downs of the career of the Maka politician who dominated regional politics in the years of independence—his electoral successes, his abrupt fall, but also the fact that he only spent a few months in prison—my spokesmen invariably referred to his occult powers. The exact interpretations varied, but everyone I talked with was convinced that he had used occult means in many ways. The old politician himself clearly encouraged such rumors by all sorts of allusions. However, in practice, it was nearly impossible to determine what he had done "in reality." People also referred to the powerful witchcraft of his "Pygmy" wife—in those days, it was very rare for a Maka man to have a fixed relation with a Pygmy woman—and there was also a lot of talk about his *nganga,* who supposedly "armored" the politician. But for these allies as well, it was impossible to know what they "really" had done. Yet it was clear that such rumors strongly influenced people's perceptions of political developments and thus their political actions. In brief, it was impossible for me to verify what really had happened, but I could not deny the very "real" effects of these mysterious actions.

In Africa, this vagueness is no doubt reinforced because of people's inclination to refer constantly to the occult forces. This is all the more reason to underline that there is no absolute difference in this respect with political processes in the supposedly "disenchanted" Western world. In the West, as well, the "real facts" of crucial political events—for instance, the Kennedy murder—are obscured by a proliferation of rumors on secret conspiracies. Despite—or, rather, due to—extensive newspaper attention and a long series of inquiry committees, it is still difficult to know what really happened. The whirlpool of insinuations and interpretations can obscure the "real facts" as effectively as witchcraft discourse. And, as noted before, there are intriguing parallels between the role of witchcraft beliefs and that of modern public relations machines in blurring the course of the political process.[38]

When studying the link between witchcraft and politics, then, one stumbles constantly—despite the direct references to human action (or, rather, because of them)—upon the limits of methodological individualism and the one-dimensional Western image of the person as a clearly defined actor. In witchcraft/sorcery discourse, in contrast, human action is by its very nature related to uncertainty, ambiguity, and hidden dimensions. The question is whether the study of the political implications of these discourses can give some insight into different conceptions of human agency.

Finally, it is important to state that the exploration of such topics is not just an academic pastime. The strong presence of witchcraft and sorcery in the more modern sectors of society, in Cameroon as in other African countries, is not an exotic curiosity. To the contrary, it has its own meaning. To many Africans, this seems to be the preferred discourse to relate the familiar context of home and the family to the modern changes that have so deeply affected domestic relations. As emphasized above, witchcraft/sorcery still is, in many respects, the reverse—one might say the dark side—of kinship.[39] The discourse is still closely linked to the family, even in urban contexts. But it is also a language that "signifies" the modern changes: it helps one to understand new inequalities, unexpected and enigmatic as they are, as seen "from below"; it promises unheard-of chances to enrich oneself; and it can serve as a guide to find one's way in the networks of modern society, reproduced on a much wider scale than the familial relations at home.

The Cameroonian historian Achille Mbembe, already quoted above, has recently contested, with his usual eloquence, any possibility for offering general explications for Africa's present "crisis."[40] The emphasis on international *dependencia,* however real it may be, soon turned into a panacea. And the same might happen to the notion of "the politics of the belly"—which Jean-François Bayart, quoted above, characterizes as a specific form of *gouvernementalité*—if it is applied too generally.[41] Mbembe insists that, for Africa, such interpretations in macro terms must be linked to variations at the most micro level of society, at the level of the family and the house. A fundamental factor in the present crisis in Africa is that much of the control over labor and its exploitation still resides there, at the bottom of society, inside the family. To Mbembe, problems of "unproductive accumulation," or the pressure of the politics of the belly, can only be understood in relation to the variable and constantly changing forms of familial control over labor. The great challenge is to relate macro analysis to the humble level of kinship relations and their highly variable transformations, which are often concealed by an apparent continuity.

It is from this perspective that one can try to understand why witchcraft and sorcery remain so terribly important in modern contexts in present-day Africa. Indeed, it is this discourse that bridges, for the people themselves, the gap between these levels—between the familiar realities of the domestic community, on the one hand, and, on the other, the large-scale processes of change that opened up unprecedented possibilities for enrichment but that also imposed new forms of dependency that are all the more frightening since they appear to be impersonal. Witchcraft is still the flip side of kinship. But it is also a discourse that incorporates new inequalities: it can serve to personalize these shocking inequalities, to relate them again to kinship frameworks, and hence to dynamize kinship. A crucial question is how—and to what degree—this discourse facilitates the apparently easy passage from local relations to the broader frameworks of the modern world, and vice versa. It is especially due to the incorporative faculty of these discourses that the link between witchcraft and politics remains as self-evident to many Africans in modern circumstances as in the past.

A FULL BELLY: THE MAKA AND THE *DJAMBE*

Discourse on witchcraft and sorcery, being ambiguous, lends itself to myriad interpretations. This is especially so when its relationship to power is at issue. Anthropologists have a tendency—perhaps driven by the desire to affirm scientific pretensions—to systematize what are in fact rather mutable and unsettled beliefs. This certainly reinforces the coherence of their descriptions, but it can push the limits of excessive systematization. When changing and unstable representations acquire a certain rigidity, it becomes difficult to explain how they can so easily incorporate modern changes.[1] There are, then, good reasons to be weary of aggressive systematization. Nonetheless, even if ideas are unstable and often hardly systematic, certain principles can be discerned in local discourses about witchcraft and sorcery that have specific implications for political processes. This chapter attempts to identify the principles underlying knowledge about *djambe* (witchcraft) among the Maka of eastern Cameroon.

The event that marked the beginning of my stay with the Maka—the car breakdown, described previously, during the night in the middle of the forest, my assistant regretting his not possessing the power of a *nkong* (healer) to "see" the witches prowling around us—constituted, in some way, a turning point in my research. After this mishap, I had a hard time avoiding witchcraft. For every theme I studied, *djambe* emerged like a shadow. Even case studies on village politics (for instance, a long dispute over the succession of a chief that I thought I had examined in an exhaustive manner) suddenly presented a false bottom: from underneath the conflict that unfolded in the light of day emerged parallel and often more dramatic scenarios in the nocturnal world of *djambe*. Whatever subject I chose—agriculture, bridewealth, education—I always came up against witchcraft. *Djambe* threatened to become a sort of quagmire not only for the people with whom I lived but also for myself. Hence I decided to try to extricate myself by searching for at least some fixed principles that might serve as beacons.

The Maka and the Germans:
A Segmentary Society against State Authoritarianism

The specific characteristics of discourse on *djambe* and its implications for everyday life in Maka villages can be understood only with reference to the historical relations that established the specificity of this region. Two points are of particular importance:

- the continuous weight of leveling forces in village life, a legacy of the old segmentary principles of organization
- the precarious equilibrium established between the segmentary order and new forms of authority imposed by the state subsequent to colonial conquest (1905–10)

In this region, the state adopted quite authoritarian practices, in sharp contrast to the local order. However, this contrast did not establish a radical opposition. Instead, it was negotiated by the people through hybridization, which involved creative combinations of the two registers, often producing quite surprising results.

The ethnic prestige of the Maka in Cameroonian society today is fairly mediocre. In Yaunde, the country's capital, the East Province generally has a reputation for being "backward." And the name *Maka* is associated with other characteristics that carry even more pejorative connotations. A standing jest put to Europeans who venture into this region is to ask if they are not aware that the Maka eat whites. Ancient practices of anthropophagy are invariably referred to whenever the Maka are mentioned, apparently in order to signal their

ferocity. Moreover, they themselves play on their reputation as cannibals. This was brought to my attention the first time I invited the
village elder to eat at our house. To my consternation, he began the
meal with a discourse as brief as it was shocking: "It's good. Before
we ate whites. Now we eat with them." I was dumbfounded and
thought I had not understood. But my assistant and a few other villagers who were present were overcome with laughter. For them, the
elder's statement represented the epitomy of good humor.

The Maka's ferocious reputation has a historical basis: their fierce
resistance to the Germans, the first colonizers of Cameroon. Until
their subjugation (1905), the Maka social order exhibited all aspects
of what anthropologists call segmentary, or "tribal," societies con-
sisting of small, autonomous family villages, in this area probably
of approximately one hundred inhabitants. There were all sorts of
exchanges between these villages—most notably between kin-
linked villages—but there was no central authority. Each village was
formed around a patrilineal segment, often supplemented by matri-
lateral kin or clients (*melwa*).[2] Inside the village, the elders exercised
strict authority over the women and youth, who depended on their
mpaanze (palaver house). A village was normally made up of several
mempaanze (pl.); the elders of each *mpaanze* formed the village
council that "carried" the *milesu* (affairs) of the whole community.

During the eighteenth and nineteenth centuries, the Maka were
subject to invasions by the Beti and Bulu, who penetrated the forest
from the northern savanna. The Maka elders still insist that the
Ngumba, who now live close to the Atlantic coast, are their "brothers," and in fact it seems that they are able to understand each other's
language.[3] In the past, they lived together along the Nyong River,
but they were eventually separated by the Beti and the Bulu, who
pushed the Maka upstream, toward the east, and the Ngumba down-
stream, toward the coast.[4]

The last phase of this long historical process was marked by confrontations with the Mpang (or Omvang) and the Yebekolo at the
end of the nineteenth century. This conflict has a central place in
Maka oral tradition. When asked about their history, the elders first
recount the great battles against the Beti "generals," the redoubtable
Nkal Selek of the Mpang and Evina, the great Yebekolo chief. It was

only then that European products made their way from the trading houses along the shore to this remote part of the forest. The Mpang and the Yebekolo, being closer to the coast, thus acquired rifles before the Maka. And this, no doubt, is one of the reasons for the failure of Maka resistance. Another significant factor might be the more centralized forms of sociopolitical organization known to the Yebekolo and the Mpang. Oral tradition seems to indicate that the Mpang and Yebekolo chiefs even attempted to impose regular controls on Maka villages. They demanded tribute instead of dispersing or incorporating subjected villages, thus introducing the beginnings of political centralization into the region. But the arrival of the Germans after 1900 nipped this development in the bud.

The colonizers met with great difficulties in subduing the population of the region. The swampy forest was difficult to access. But the most daunting problem was the dispersed social organization of the local communities: there was no central authority with which to conclude treaties and conventions. The villages had to be subjugated one by one. Moreover, the Germans considered the Maka to be *die Primitivsten aller Primitiven* (the most primitive of all the primitives), especially in view of their *Mangel an staatenbildendem Sinn* (lack of sense for forming a state). Indeed, "pacification" demanded considerable effort. The first direct contact with the Maka goes back to 1905, but the region was not fully subdued until 1910.

The climax in tensions between the Maka and the Germans was precipitated in 1910 by the murder of a young German rubber merchant, Arno Brettschneider. The young man had wandered too far off the main road. He was taken by surprise in the marshy region to the north of Angossas by an ambush of a few Maka men who killed him along with his cook, his concubine, and two of his porters. According to oral tradition and numerous witnesses, whose testimony constitutes an impressive file at the colonial archives in Potsdam, their bodies were cut into pieces and eaten, which was customary practice for the Maka when dealing with foreign (i.e., nonkin) warriors.

This event aroused much emotion in Germany. The father of the unfortunate merchant wrote a furious article in the *Dresdner Zeitung:* "My son was eaten by ferocious cannibals." And the Berlin newspaper, *Die Tägliche Rundschau,* provided details of the horrible scene: "The innocent boy was dragged to the village. . . . His porters had already been hacked into pieces next to the fire when his hands were cut off, which are valued as particularly good morsels." And in typical fashion, the newspaper added: "With the present rise in the price of rubber, we cannot remain indifferent to the inaccessibility of the most important region for the purchase of this product, due to a rebellion."[5]

The government decided that energetic measures had to be taken. Dominik, the swashbuckler of the colonial army who remains a mythic figure in Maka imagination, was entrusted with the direction of a large-scale expedition (he already had led a more modest expedition in the Maka region in 1905–6). He ordered the entire region to be combed, and so the villages and fields were burned and all the inhabitants, including women and children, were arrested. Contemporary sources speak of a *Vernichtungsstrategie* (strategy of destruction).[6]

These apocalyptic scenes were played out against the backdrop of the quest for wild rubber, the "black gold of the forest." The Germans were particularly interested in this inaccessible region because it was rumored that especially abundant sources of rubber could be found there—the most abundant in all of Africa. At the time, the demand for rubber was rapidly on the rise in the West due to the development of the automobile industry in particular.

The consequences of this quest for wild rubber were dramatic for Maka country, especially since the region was sparsely populated and had hardly been engaged in the market economy before that time. Suddenly, an enormous need for labor arose. Indeed, *Die Arbeiterfrage* (the problem of labor) dominated German colonial policy until 1914. Workhands were lacking for the harvesting of rubber in the forest and, more critically, for porterage along the roads toward the coast since the tsetse fly made the use of pack animals impossible. The local population was forced, in every way, to work for the rubber merchants. Their food reserves were pillaged to feed the caravans, and the rubber trees were exploited in a devastating manner. So urgent was the desire to profit from the new demand for rubber that the trees were cut down instead of being tapped. Already in 1906,

Dominik, who one can hardly suspect of sentimentality, was appalled by the distress brought on by the terror: "But I saw with my own eyes the misery of a land where the struggle for this gold of the forest has taken place. The desire to get rich as quickly as possible and the fear of competitors outdo any feeling of shame[. . . .] It is lucky for the country that the wave rolls on when rubber has begun to run out. But then come the caravans that cross the country, food is scarce and that brings new violence."[7]

Maka narratives reflect the population's dismay in the face of the "rubber hurricane" and the consequent German military expeditions. One of the oldest of my informants—who, incidentally, had great admiration for Dominik despite the atrocious things the old man said about him[8]—offered me the following story:

> Dominik arrived here in the village. He called for my father, Angus, who was the elder of the village. He became angry because there were not enough men to carry the soldiers' baggage. He said that my father was disobedient and called a soldier to kill him. But Angus said, "Wait, don't kill me yet; I will tell you a story."
>
> > One day a man had a surprise visit from his in-laws. He said, "What should I do? What can I offer them to eat?" He went into the bush to check his traps and he found an antelope. He killed the animal, skinned it, and set the skin aside. He went to find some leaves to wrap up the meat, but when he returned, the antelope stood up trembling and ran away; the skin remained with the man. In the forest, the antelope met a buffalo who, after one look, stamped and then left. The antelope met another antelope, who also avoided the animal. The antelope cried out, "Ay, what should I do? I don't have any skin anymore, my body is covered with blood. When I see my brothers they flee. I'm ashamed. It would be better for the man to take me."
> >
> > The man was still sitting next to his trap. "What misery! What am I going to do? If I go back to the village with this skin, everyone will laugh at me. What can I offer my guests?" Just then the antelope without skin came back and laid in front of the man: "Do as you wish." The man cried out with surprise. He killed the antelope and cut it up.

And Angus concluded his story for Dominik: "I am the ante-lope. If you kill me, it is both your shame and mine. I followed your orders. I helped your soldiers when they came through here. I am like the antelope without skin who is shirked by his brothers. Do you want to kill me now?"

Angus had good reasons for asking this rather desperate question. The same informant, in order to illustrate "how tough the Germans were," told me that the Germans used the Maka's own ideas about cannibalism to interrogate people. One day Dominik wanted to force the elder of a neighboring village to eat the flesh of a rebel who had been killed. The elder refused and was executed on the spot under the pretext that this refusal "proved" that he was a kin, and hence an ally, of the rebel. This story implies, then, that Dominik knew of the prohibition that prevented the Maka from eating their own kin.

Above all, though, it was the scale of the German operations that frightened the Maka. According to my informants, Dominik gave all women who had been captured in Maka villages to his Yekkaba aux-iliaries, who had contributed largely to the German victory.[9] Some added that the Yekkaba also left with baskets full of human flesh. Such accounts reflect the profound impression the German inter-lude, no matter how brief, left on the Maka. Its traces endure today.

For the Maka, the dramatic events of the German period were a cruel taste of things to come: they provided a rude initiation to state authoritarianism and also established the Maka's reputation as "sav-ages," which haunts them to this day. What is important for the pres-ent discussion, moreover, is that anthropophagy was a key element in the founding of this reputation since it makes direct reference to sorcery and witchcraft.

This explosive mixture, combining the exploitation of rubber, German oppression, and Maka "savagery," recalls the images that Michael Taussig (1987) evokes with respect to the "rubber terror" in the Amazon at the end of the nineteenth century.[10] Taussig inter-prets the atrocious stories that were spread about the barbarity of the local people—in which cannibalism also represented a sort of culmi-nating point—as in fact projections of the colonial imagination, be-ing haunted by its own obsessions. For him, these terrifying images play a determining role in the effusion of colonial terror. In the Cameroonian case as well, it was surely no accident that the Maka became the very prototype of the savage in the colonial imagery of the Germans ("the most primitive of all the primitives"). In this rubber-rich region—a sort of promising paradise in economic terms, soon transformed into hell by rapacious exploitation—the colonizers needed more than anywhere this image of a savage population in order to justify colonial terror as the ferment of "civilization."

But contrary to Taussig's rendering of Amazonian history, for the Maka region it is hazardous to simply view anthropophagy as a colonial projection. There are strong indications that it was practiced by the Maka for quite some time. To my oldest informants, of whom several were born before the arrival of the Germans, the idea that one once ate strangers—that is, people from villages outside their kinship network (*bjel*) and especially defeated warriors—was quite normal. Thus I often heard the comment, "In such and such village, we couldn't eat." I first interpreted this expression as a prohibition against eating together. But the real meaning turned out to be quite different: my interlocutors wanted to make me aware that the village in question was part of their kin network and that thus they could not eat its inhabitants. Evidently, restrictions on cannibalism—the formal interdiction against eating kin—constituted a sort of map of the region, permitting one to distinguish between kin-linked villages (potential allies) and others.[11]

For the Maka, then, the fact of having eaten a German is not really a novelty. But it seems that anthropophagy was expanded on an unprecedented scale subsequent to German military action. My informants' narratives about Yekkaba warriors, the auxiliaries in Dominik's army who supposedly returned home with "baskets full of human flesh," are not the only signs to this effect. A German historian, Cornelia Essner, recently located in the archives of the German army in Fribourg extended documentation of a polemic, in 1910, between Schipper, the *Hauptmann* (captain) at Dume, and Dominik, because the latter would have allowed his Kako (or Kaka) auxiliaries to eat defeated Maka.[12]

One of the most enduring contributions of the German period was the founding of the Maka's reputation (and that of other com-

munities of the eastern region) as hardened cannibals and their consequent location in the sphere of witchcraft and sorcery. The Maka
themselves may establish a sharp distinction between the eating of
one's own kin, which witches are reputed to do, and the eating of
nonkin, which is a manifestation of past states of war between villages. But elsewhere in Cameroon and in Africa more generally,
the association between anthropophagy and witchcraft seems inevitable.[13] This is one reason why Maka country, and the East Province
in general, is always thought to be teeming with sorcerers. As discussed below, more recently, this somber reputation has had dramatic consequences for the role of the state vis-à-vis occult forces in
the region.

The French Period and the Emergence of a New Maka Elite

The French, who conquered this eastern part of the German colony
in 1914, proved to be no less authoritarian than their European rivals. But they placed a different emphasis on economic problems. In
their reports, French administrators complained incessantly that the
mise en valeur (exploitation) of this thankless region was going no-
where. After 1913, the market for wild rubber, so lucrative during
the German era, collapsed in the face of competition from the plantation rubber from Southeast Asia. The French searched desperately
for alternative products to revitalize commerce, but all attempts
failed. This was, in part, due to close collaboration between the government and the colonists in order to reduce prices paid to local producers as much as possible. The French, however, attributed this
stagnation to the *douce inertie* (mild inertia) of the Maka—or, more
explicitly, to their "sloth" and their "aversion for work." The only
solution, at least to the government, seemed to be to *force* the Maka
to make a bigger effort. Thus the "obligation to work" became the
central tenet of governmental policy. Up until the end of the Second
World War, the administration operated, for the most part, as one
immense coercive apparatus in its attempt to increase the productive
efforts of the Maka: "forced labor," "forced cultivation," and draconian methods of tax collection (which drained the little money the
villagers earned out of the village) were all enacted under the strict
and continuous supervision of the gendarmes.

In order to execute this entire gamut of coercive measures, the French completely reorganized the region (a project that had already begun with the Germans). Families once living in autonomous villages were obliged to leave the forest and settle with other, often unrelated, groups in larger villages that stretched along the new roads. Through relocation, the population was to be better *encadrée* (regimented). In addition, the administration created a new type of chief, whose authority extended over dozens of villages. This was a true revolution for the Maka. Against this background, the title of *chef coutumier* (customary chief), which the French gave to these chiefs, is somewhat strange.

These chiefs played a starring role in my informants' stories about French coercion. They were, in fact, extraordinary characters. Armed with heretofore unfathomable resources—the support of the government and its gendarmes—they rapidly built pseudotraditional positions of authority, characterized by ostentatious exaggerations of the habitual signs of prestige. Polygamy was one of these signs. But while in the past eminent heads of Maka families mostly had no more than five wives, the colonial chiefs accumulated dozens, with the number sometimes amounting to more than one hundred.[14]

My informants recall the brazen manner in which these chiefs executed official orders. One chief was nicknamed Old Machete because of his zeal and the cruelty with which he recruited forced labor for the French. But the villagers' stories recount, above all, the abuses of power perpetrated by these colonial chiefs for their own gain. Consider the following account:

One day, my father was wearing a new *boubou* [shirt]. He was very proud of it and everyone admired its colors. But then the Paramount Chief came through with his men. He ordered my father to take off the *boubou* and give it to him. My father hesitated. So the chief became angry: "What? You, a simple villager, you want to wear a *boubou* more beautiful than mine?" His men threw my father to the ground, pulled off the *boubou,* and gave it to the chief.

That was how it was with the chiefs in the time of the French. We had to hide all the pretty women from them. If he saw a woman who pleased him, the chief said: "Give me that woman"—

and he didn't even pay the bridewealth. How do you think they were able to accumulate so many women in their compounds?

As one might expect, such stories are always accompanied by allusions to the extraordinary magical forces possessed by the chiefs. Kamanda, the paramount chief of Dume during the interwar period, is said to have been able to transform himself into a panther. But he did not have just one panther like ordinary mortals; he had several. Moreover, his panthers would still wander in the forest. Another chief is said to have been the first Maka to buy "lightning" from the Hausa. In this respect as well, then, "customary chiefs" surpassed the traditional limits of power.

It was not until after 1946 that relations became more relaxed. The most burdensome forms of forced labor were abolished, thus reducing the power of the chiefs. At the same time, prices paid to the peasants for their products (especially cocoa and coffee) were increased. Under these conditions, the Maka were more willing to make greater efforts for the market, regardless of the pessimistic prophecies of the colonials. After 1946, the villagers rapidly expanded their cocoa and coffee plantations without government pressure to do so.[15] Maka country became the richest in the East.

Relations in the villages gained new dimensions with these developments. Long-standing inequalities based on age and sex—the authority of the elders over women and juniors—retained their significance. But new inequalities emerged alongside them. A small group of cocoa and coffee farmers demarcated themselves from the other villagers by virtue of their new wealth. More important was the emergence of a new educated elite of *évolués,* as locals used to call them. Toward the end of the 1950s, some young Maka men who had received diplomas took advantage of decolonization and the Africanization of the state bureaucracy in an unexpected manner. Several of them made brilliant careers, being carried by the flux of vacant posts. In spite of their new positions in the city, most of these officials still maintain ties with their native villages. And they do have a new kind of prestige among the other villagers. But their wealth, which largely surpasses the old norms, also incites new degrees of jealousy.

The emergence of richer farmers and a new administrative elite expanded the villagers' contacts with the outside world. But relations with the government changed very little, even after independence. The state remained a decidedly authoritarian institution. After a brief interlude (1958–60), during which elections that had true political significance were held, the new president Ahmadou Ahidjo established a highly bureaucratic regime. Under his one-party system, elections and political institutions retained only symbolic significance, and civil servants, who inherited their authoritarianism from their colonial predecessors, once again dominated relations with villagers. During the 1970s, the people in the villages still referred to the office of the *sous-préfet* (district officer) as *le pays des Blancs* (the white man's land). And civil servants compared themselves to instructors whose task was to reinstate discipline among the villagers, those unruly pupils. This authoritarian and bureaucratic system made no room for the articulation of interests from below, at least not through formal channels. Moreover, it concealed the foundations of power and the reasons for its decisions from the eyes of the population. All this encouraged the association of modern politics with the world of witchcraft and sorcery. The *renouveau* (revival) of 1982, proclaimed when Paul Biya succeeded Ahidjo, harldy inspired changes at the village level. It remains to be seen whether the blaze of democratization that has overtaken Cameroon since 1990 will have a more profound effect. Until now, that has been difficult to discern in Maka villages. To be sure, people are more disposed to political discussions, but the influence of the regime's party in the region does not seem threatened.

One constant factor in the flux of all these changes in Maka country is the close rapport between *djambe* and power. There is remarkable continuity that unites, despite all their differences, the modern politicians with the colonial chiefs and even with Nkal Selek, the Mpang general who terrorized the Maka at the end of the nineteenth century: the invincibility of all of them is always explained by their being so well armored (*bien blindé*) by the *djambe*. Evidently, it remains to be seen whether the notion of the *djambe* remained identical through all these transformations. Nonetheless, it is clear that these conceptions still greatly influence the discourse of those who engage in modern politics as much as that of those who are subject to it. To better apprehend these changes, then, we must explore this idea of the *djambe*.

The *Djambe* and the "Hazards of the House"

What is this *djambe* about which the Maka talk so much?[16] When I asked people to describe it, their answers were often evasive. After all, openly demonstrating that one knows "too much" about the subject can be risky; this might signify that one is a witch. Everyone agreed, however, that the *djambe* is a small being that lives inside the belly of its possessor. Some compared it to a grey mouse, others to a crab. The most detailed response came from our good friend Mendouga, the famous healer mentioned above. Evidently, given her status, she had to show that she knew more than most. She was sorry that I had not come to question her earlier, because she once had a "photo" of the *djambe* that she unfortunately lost. She remembered the precise moment she had seen the *djambe*. The whites had operated on a woman in the Presbyterian hospital and had taken the *djambe* out of her belly. They closed the *djambe* up in a cage: it was a small, ferocious beast with mean teeth that snapped at the flies that flew around its cage.

Others recounted a well-known story about the way the *djambe* spread among people. This narrative—a true myth that lends itself to all sorts of interpretations about the relationship between sorcery and society—was told to me in several versions. The most elaborate was the following:

> One day, a hunter found the *djambe* between the roots of a giant tree, deep in the forest. The *djambe* said to him, "Give me a little meat."
>
> The hunter gave him some. On this day, he killed many animals. And this continued. Every day, the hunter gave a little meat to the *djambe,* and he returned with a well-endowed game bag.
>
> His wife suspected something. One day she followed him in secret. She saw him speak to the *djambe*. When he left, the wife approached the *djambe* herself, and asked him, "Who are you?"

The *djambe* answered, "Do you really want to know? Then crouch down here, spread your legs, and I will show you. I will make you rich, too." The woman, being jealous of her husband's success, crouched down, and, hop, the *djambe* entered into her belly. Thus the woman brought the *djambe* to the village.

From this day on, the *djambe* in the belly of the woman demanded meat to eat. The woman gave it all the meat her husband brought back from hunting, but it was not enough. The *djambe* forced her to kill all the animals in the compound, but it still was not enough. Finally she had to give him her own children, one by one.

Thus the *djambe* came to live amongst humans thanks to the covetousness of women.

Later, *djambe* spread to men as well.[17]

This seemingly simple story evokes so many implicit themes and associations that one risks getting lost in them. It contains the idea of a fatal threshold, a frontier that must not be crossed. All goes well so long as the *djambe* remains in the forest; there, it is a source of wealth. But as soon as it enters the village, things go awry, and the *djambe* becomes a source of catastrophe.[18] The story of the *djambe* also lends itself to a gendered reading that makes it even more sexist than the parallel myth of Adam and Eve. Man knows how to use the *djambe* in a constructive manner and becomes rich (it should be noted that the *djambe* is evidently susceptible to positive uses); it is only woman and her lust that leads the *djambe* to become destructive and make people kill their kin.

This narrative also suggests more complex associations. It establishes a direct link between covetousness and killing. Sometimes the fact of killing is justified: man goes off to hunt and kills game in abnormal quantities thanks to the *djambe*. In this instance, the *djambe* offers wealth and prestige. For the woman, however, cupidity leads to atrocious carnage: the *djambe* forces her to devour her own children. And yet these two acts of killing, that which is justified and that which is not, are both inspired by the *djambe*. The narrative, and discourse on the *djambe* in general, thus raise a crucial question: who kills rightly and who kills wrongly?

Another central theme of this story that is fundamental to the *djambe* is the devouring of kin. The close connection between the *djambe,* kin, and anthropophagy is a true obsession for the Maka. An instinctive drive pushes the *njindjamb* (possessor of the *djambe*) to participate in nocturnal feasts with other witches. To have access to these banquets, he or she must sacrifice his or her parents. Hence the *djambe* introduces treason into the most reliable space in Maka society, the *njaw,* or circle of kin that constitute a "house."

The crucial question to put to someone to test if he or she is a *njindjamb* (witch) is whether he has brought out (*wos*) his *djambe*— that is, if he has transformed himself into a *djim* (phantom) or any other frightful apparition. During the night, when the owl calls, the true *minjindjamb* (pl.) leave their bodies. Like pale *mindjim* (pl.), they fly off into the night along the spider webs (*taande*) of the *djambe* toward the *shumbu* (witches' "sabbath" or nightly encounter) to meet with their acolytes. This *shumbu* is an image that obsesses the Maka. They speak about it with horror, but also with curiosity and even excitement. It certainly takes courage to go to the *shumbu* since the world of witches is full of treacherous ambushes and violent confrontations. But the *shumbu* also has its temptations. The sorcerers organize grand orgies there. And the culminating point is an anthropophagic banquet where the witches eat the hearts of their kin. Their victims fall ill the next day; without the help of a *nkong* (healer), they die a certain death.

The most striking aspect of the Maka's exalted stories about these nocturnal rendezvous is that they divulge in so many ways an inversion of everyday relationships. At the *shumbu,* men make love with men, and "even" women with women. For the Maka, this reversal is utterly shocking: homosexuality is always bound up with witchcraft. The cannibalistic practices of witches constitute an inversion of the same order. We saw that the idea of cannibalism in itself is not scandalous; old histories are full of it. But witches eat their own kin, and this practice is strictly forbidden.[19]

If one wants to understand the implications of these notions for politics, an important question concerns their consequences for the concept of human action: do they refer to a particular concept of the person as an agent? A basic idea in discourse on the *djambe* is that, in principle, all humans have a kind of double within them and can learn to double themselves. This notion of doubling oneself *wos*, ("go out" in Maka) is fundamental. As long as the *djambe* remains in the belly of its possessor, it can reinforce the latter. But when one makes one's *djambe* "go out," things get complicated. One has access to special powers but becomes extremely vulnerable as well. Someone's double, *djim* (phantom), can go out to attack other *mindjim* (pl.), or even innocent victims. But once it is out, the double is exposed to new dangers: it can always fall into ambushes itself.[20] If this occurs, the possessor of the double falls ill and dies, unless he receives the aid of a healer endowed with greater powers than the witches.

The idea that everyone may have a double, and the emphasis placed on the possibility of doubling oneself as an essential moment, seem to give an added dimension to human action. Indeed, *djambe* discourse gives central place to human action. Almost all that happens—most notably sudden events, whether fortunate or unfortunate—is explained with reference to the interventions of either one or several people. The Maka believe, moreover, that witches are quite aware of the deeds perpetrated by their doubles: in general, they are thought to more or less control the acts of their doubles, for which they are held responsible.[21] In this sense, this is an individualizing discourse. But it is also a discourse that blurs the contours of the person. Human actors remain hidden behind the mysteries of witchcraft. Above all, the very idea that everyone has a double renders human actions unpredictable. There is an invisible dimension to their actions. It is no wonder that discourse on *djambe* mostly serves to explain events retrospectively: for the Maka, interpreting by witchcraft is almost always a case of reconstruction a posteriori.

Such interpretations are inspired, no doubt, by particular conceptions of the person and human action. But the difference between these and Western concepts should not be exaggerated, and simplistic dichotomies between "their" and "our" ideas should be avoided. As we shall see, all sorts of correspondences can be established that play an important role in the modernization of witchcraft. From this point of view, the individualistic tenor of *djambe* discourse is significant. As noted above, this notion refers to individual actions. Those who make their *djambe* go out remain responsible for its acts. Indeed, one is supposed to try to develop one's *djambe* in keeping with personal ambitions. Narratives about *djambe* are in this sense surprisingly similar to capitalist themes. The Maka speak of their witches as entrepreneurs who are always on the alert and ready to appropriate new riches or powers. Witches' confessions often contain the idea that a person was pushed by his or her *djambe* to carry out a particular action. But these confessions are also reminiscent of authentic capitalist tales, such as Charles Dickens's *The Christmas Carol*, which portrays Scrooge's obsession with earning more money. In fact, an important theme is "indebtedness." Witches who can no longer acquit themselves of debts owed to other witches of the band (for instance, because they are unable or unwilling to "give over" kin) can only sacrifice themselves. These aspects of *djambe* allow for surprising and variable articulations between notions of witchcraft, on the one hand, and new modes of accumulating wealth and power introduced by the state and the modern market, on the other.

Even in the modern context, one always reverts back to the close link between *djambe* and kinship. It is doubtless the central motif that emerges from the rapid outline above of Maka notions of witchcraft. As said, *djambe* is the dark side of kinship. It introduces the possibility of treason where there theoretically should be no discord. Discourse on *djambe* expresses the frightening awareness that there is in fact inequality, and thus jealousy, in the interior of the family—that is, between people with whom one must live and work. According to the Maka ethos, one can trust only one's kin; one hardly has a choice since they are the only reliable allies. To use the terms of one of my Maka friends, "I must trust my brother. If he is jealous of me and if he wants to kill me, what can I do?" For the Maka, *djambe* discourse raises a fundamental problem: how can one trust those with whom one lives when there are good reasons for jealousy and hate? But this discourse also indicates how one can maintain familial relationships in spite of this terrible threat that comes from within. Éric de Rosny (1992, 114) cites a Duala proverb from the Cameroonian coast that could easily apply to the Maka: "One must learn to live with one's sorcerer." For the Maka, the same *djambe* that seems to undermine domestic relations can equally serve to repair them.

This close but contradictory relationship between *djambe* and kinship is essential for an understanding of its political role. Discourse on *djambe* seems to express the fundamental doubts of the Maka with respect to power as such. Like *djambe,* power is at once suspect and indispensable. The old notables could not manage village affairs and maintain their authority unless they were *blindés* (armored) with *djambe*. In certain instances, this link between *djambe* and power seems to justify even the sacrifice of kin. One says, for example, that, in the past, the *nkong* (healer) could be initiated only after such a sacrifice; only then could the *nkong* have access to the forces necessary for healing. We return, then, to the central question raised by the myth on the origins of *djambe:* who kills rightly and who kills wrongly? That the answers to this question are always relative and equivocal is, no doubt, characteristic of this segmentary society. Tenacious rumors about the excursions of so and so through the *djambe* can lead to open accusations, and such accusations imply that the general opinion is that the "witch" killed wrongly. But the same kinds of rumors might also reinforce the respect accorded to that person. This is especially the case when the rumors involve a prestigious notable of the village, a successful politician, or, in the past, a famous war hero. Which interpretation prevails seems to depend on the balance of social relationships at a particular moment.

Djambe discourse indicates, above all, that power constitutes an essential problem for these societies. It translates both profound distrust and an impassioned lust for power.

The Vicious Circles of *Djambe*

A case study illustrates the play of these concepts in everyday life.

The compound of Old Tsjume[22] was struck by a rapid series of misfortunes. First, one of the kitchens collapsed. Then Tsjume became ill: he had long suffered from rheumatism, but the symptoms suddenly became much worse. Then his third wife— his favorite, who was still fairly young—died abruptly. Everyone thought it was witchcraft, and people sought the guilty party, as usual, within the house itself. Rumors mostly pointed at Nanga, the first wife of Tsjume, who had always been jealous of other women and who, moreover, had quarreled with her husband because he was very severe with their only son. It was said that she was so angry that she had given her co-wife over to the witches of her band so that they could eat her.

After a few days, Nanga became sick too. She quickly became emaciated and no longer got up from her bed. This was generally interpreted as a new sign of her guilt. According to some people, she was tortured by her conscience. Others said that she had fallen ill for fear of being attacked, herself, by her acolytes, because that is how things work in the world of *djambe*.

Two days later, Nanga was transported by her son to her native village; she died a few hours after arriving there. After that, the roles were reversed. The brothers of Nanga openly accused Tsjume of giving his wives over to witches and refused to cede the corpse of their sister for funeral rites. They wanted her to be buried in her own village and not in her husband's compound since he had treated her so badly. Nanga's burial in her native village ended with a violent brawl between her brothers and Tsjume's family.

But even after the burial, Tsjume's problems did not end. A few weeks later, his second wife, who had already been ill for some time, also died. Furthermore, Tsjume's state of health continued to be of concern. Finally, Tsjume began accusing Meguya, another woman who lived in his compound. Meguya had remained untouched until now because she had a very good reputation. She was very active in the church and had come to live with Tsjume after refusing to stay with her husband—of the same family as Tsjume—who drank too much and spent the little money Meguya earned on his pleasures. Moreover, Meguya displayed exemplary behavior during the whole affair. She cared for all of Tsjume's wives and had even tried as much as possible to maintain their farms. In spite of these burdens, she had brought an impressive amount of food to the church for a reception held for important visitors.

Nonetheless, Tsjume appeared one day in front of the catechist's house and declared loudly, so that everyone could hear what he was saying: "This woman, Meguya, is crazy with fear. She already gave my three wives to the witches. Now she is desperately seeking other victims for fear of being eaten herself by her colleagues." The sole reaction I heard from Meguya, a stoic woman, was a brief but effective commentary: "People who know so well what the witches do are the first to leave their bodies in the night." She thus accused Tsjume, but in a manner sufficiently implicit so that he could hardly respond.

After several days, Tsjume's health recovered little by little. His son still refused to move or speak to anyone. He sat on a chair in front of the house, his eyes wide as if in a trance. From time to time, he murmured in a menacing tone that he would go to Bertua to consult a great *nkong* (healer). The *nkong* would tell him who was behind these events and would help him to avenge his mother, Nanga. But one week later, he participated in a large work party organized by a friend. After several weeks, people hardly spoke about all that had happened. And my neighbor concluded, "Apparently, the witches settled the whole affair among themselves."

This tragic episode underlines certain key points in *djambe* discourse. First, there is the close relationship between *djambe* and kinship or, more specifically, the "home." For the Maka, the *djambe le njaw* (witchcraft of the house) is the most dangerous since witches have a hold over their intimates. The rapid series of deaths in Tsjume's house could be explained only by witchcraft, and it was obvious that the guilty party had to be found within the house. Tsjume himself was not beyond suspicion. The elderly are especially thought to have learned how to defend themselves through *djambe,* and this was surely why he tried so energetically to put the blame on others (first Nanga, then Meguya).

Tsjume's accusations were based on the central motif of *djambe:* he implied that the witches had left their bodies during the night to fly to a meeting with their counterparts at *shumbu* (nightly encounter). There, they would have given over the other women of the house. As a Maka proverb says: "A witch has neither father nor mother, neither brother nor friend." Once people take the *djambe* road, they are ready to betray anyone.

But this episode also demonstrates how *djambe* presents risks for anyone who ventures down its road. Such is the flip side: *djambe* gives new powers, but it also engenders deadly threats. If a witch can or will no longer give up kin, he or she will be the next victim of the band. This is why Tsjume claimed that Meguya was "crazy with fear"; she was supposedly obliged to deliver the people of her house to her colleagues to avoid being eaten herself.

In this manner, *djambe* discourse inscribes vicious circles that are almost impossible to break. When old Zila died, one of his grandsons explained that the old man had been bewitched and that he went to the *nkong* (healer) when it was already too late. But a man who had always had problems with Zila made it clear to me that Zila was himself a great witch and that his witchcraft had turned on him. He had transgressed the prohibitions that his *djambe* teachers had imposed on him and then suddenly died; or another sorcerer might have surprised him and killed him. In such a case, one can also suppose that the dead had refused to continue delivering his kin to his counterparts and that he had to sacrifice himself as a sort of martyr. People then speak with a certain pity of the absolute solitude and panic that overcomes the witch who knows he or she has no more allies and hence must confront single-handedly all the other witches. The proverb that speaks of no father nor mother nor brother has a flip side: the witch who has betrayed kinship is left completely alone in the face of the terrifying dangers of witchcraft. *Djambe* seduces because it promises unparalleled powers, but it also brings utter vulnerability.

The story of old Tsjume underscores in yet another manner the circularity of discourse on *djambe*. Meguya countered Tsjume's insinuations by stating that those who see *djambe* everywhere are the first to go out at night themselves. The Maka say that such a person is like the owl who calls the witches to the *shumbu* (nightly encounter). The simple fact of seeing what witches do implies that one has *miesj meba* (a second pair of eyes), which is a sign of a highly developed *djambe*.[23] Thus accusations can easily take on a boomerang effect, falling back on those who "see" witchcraft so clearly. Those who adventure into *djambe* expose themselves to unknown dangers—this is the maxim that Mendouga, the healer, made me understand in her own particular manner:

> During the 1970s, Mendouga was a woman of a certain age; she was very sure of herself and knew how to confuse people. After a long discussion with her, during which I had asked innumerable questions about *djambe*, she abruptly moved to a counterattack: Why was I asking so many questions about *djambe?* Did I want to make mine go out in the night? She giggled in her way and looked at me mockingly, but she seemed to be quite serious all the same.
>
> When she saw that she had confused me, she became sweet again and reassured me. She had evidently already "seen" that my belly was empty—that is, that I had not developed my *djambe*—and that she had nothing to fear from me. If I wished, nonetheless, to know what happened during the night, she could put a salve in my eyes to give me this second pair of eyes about which people talked so much.
>
> I hesitated (I had little confidence in Mendouga) and said that I would come back later. After much thought I finally decided that if I wanted to become an anthropologist, I could not miss such an opportunity. I returned to Mendouga's house the next day and asked her to please treat me. But she had changed her mind: "If I give you a second pair of eyes, you will not only see what the witches do, but they will see you as well. Then they can attack you, and if they do you harm the *sous-préfet* [district officer] will blame me. You came here with his authorization, and I don't want any difficulties with the *ngomena* [government]." At the time, I attributed her refusal to her capricious character. But later I learned that she indeed had encountered problems with the authorities not long before (there had been a complaint against her for slander).

Those who adventure into *djambe* become visible and hence accessible to all the other witches, even those outside the family. The Maka also believe that it is more difficult to kill an "innocent" person with witchcraft. Someone who is not involved with witchcraft will first become ill if attacked, and will die slowly. On the other hand, witches immediately "see" their attackers and then engage in a battle to the death.

The final characteristic aspect of *djambe* that is highlighted by Tsjume's affair is the absence of an unambiguous conclusion. In the end, the accusations did not have a concrete effect in the daytime world. Even Nanga's son did not carry out his threat to consult a *nkong*. It is noteworthy that the Maka have few concrete sanctions against *djambe* in the diurnal world.[24] The surest way to protect oneself against *djambe* or to avenge oneself involves recourse to the *djambe* itself. Hence the circularity of these representations is reinforced once again.

Some people say that, in the past, witches were publicly executed, especially during funerals. A burial is always full of tension. It is the moment to pronounce accusations, most often against the wives of the deceased. If a woman is not supported by a strong retinue from her own family, her position is quite tenuous. If certain informants are to be believed, in the past, the wife could be killed on the spot by the descendants of the dead. However, I was unable to locate a well-documented case of such an execution.

But I do know of two instances in which young boys were accused with such insistence that they thought it was best to temporarily exile themselves from the village (several of them returned after a few years).[25] Sometimes, when accusations become so acute that they upset the entire village, a large palaver takes place during which the village chief and the elders are entrusted to clear up the affair. In the past, these palavers often resulted in the scission of the village. In those cases, the ardor of the accusations indicated that trust between segments of the patrilineage had been severely undermined. If the palaver did not succeed in reestablishing unity, one of the segments could opt to found an autonomous village elsewhere. Since the colonial "pacification," this sort of solution is no longer possible, and large palavers over witchcraft usually end in a vague conclusion. The discussions are generally extremely violent. The accusations and counterattacks are theatrically dramatized. Sometimes some of the old men will grumble that similar accusations led, in the past, to the breakup of the village. But today the notables limit themselves to asking the parties involved to go consult a *nkong* to see who is right or wrong. In practice, the parties rarely do so; if they do, they often obtain quite equivocal answers from the *nkong* (see Geschiere 1982, 423).

It is relatively rare that the vortex of accusations and rumors of witchcraft has a clear effect in the diurnal world, especially if one takes into account their great frequency.[26] In Maka country, the most obvious retort to witchcraft is counterwitchcraft. If the victim is still alive, he or she must go to the *nkong*. If the victim has died, the descendants must take revenge by *djambe*, eventually with the support of the *nkong*. It is symptomatic that the *nkong* can furnish only protection or vengeance because he or she has a very developed *djambe*.

The figure of the *nkong* plays a central role in discourse on *djambe*. It attests to the fact that *djambe* is not always evil and can lend itself to constructive uses as well—as long as it is "controlled." The *nkong* is also the best example of how precarious it is to distinguish between the positive and negative expressions of *djambe*.

In the story of Tsjume, the *djambe* only manifests itself as a force of evil. But this episode touched upon other intrigues, where different implications of *djambe* appeared. The catechist, for example—to whom Tsjume complained about the voracity of Meguya and the devastation she had brought upon his house—spoke to me about *djambe* in an entirely different sense. He told me how he became a catechist by a sort of miracle. One night he saw a small flame dancing behind his house. He was not afraid; he pursued and trapped it. It was a *djim* (phantom). He struggled with the *djim* all night long. When dawn came, the *djim* made a last-ditch effort to liberate itself, but the catechist did not let go. Finally, the *djim* said, "Tell me what you want, and I will give it to you." He responded, "Make me speak Ewondo tomorrow so that I can become a catechist." (Ewondo is the language of the Catholic mission.) The next day he spoke Ewondo fluently, and the very same year, he was named a catechist.

The catechist in question was highly considered in the village not only due to his position but also because of his dignified manner. Nonetheless, his story establishes a direct link between his success and the *djambe*. Surely certain elements of this narrative are borrowed from the Biblical combat between Jacob and the angel. But others—the *djim* in the shape of a dancing flame—issue from the imagery of *djambe*. Yet this link did not affect the catechist's prestige;

instead, people saw it as a good example of a constructive use of the
djambe. The very same week, I noted a story about a person thought
to have received the *djambe* of his dying father. In response to my
innocent question whether this was grave, people replied that, to the
contrary, it was very good. Generally speaking, *djambe* can be bad,
but in this instance it was clear that the father had given his *djambe*
to his son so that the latter could make good use of it.

From this, it follows that *minjindjamb* (witches) do not constitute
a distinct, homogeneous category to the Maka. When asked how one
acquires a *djambe,* people respond variously. Some say that the
djambe is inherited—in the masculine line for boys and the feminine
line for girls. Others describe how old people can make their *djambe*
enter newborns by secretly blowing in their mouths. Still others suggest that, in principle, everyone has a *djambe,* but only some develop
it in stages with the help of the most experienced *minjindjamb,* thus
becoming truly dangerous witches. But even if these viewpoints differ somewhat, their implications are similar. For the Maka, *djambe* is
not the reserve of a special group of people. They are prepared to
admit that, theoretically, each and every person is disposed of a
powerful *djambe*. Above all, the elders (men as well as women) are
thought to have acquired strong support in the occult world during
the course of their long lives.[27]

The first question is not whether someone has *djambe,* but, rather,
what he or she does with it, and this is revealed in practice. The Maka
distinguish between different forms of *djambe*. Aside from *djambe le
njaw* (the betrayal of kin), they speak of more positive forms, like
djambe le doomb (war), which armored warriors of the past, or
djambe idjuga (power), which permits the elders to dominate the
kaande (village council). But these distinctions are not absolute. One
is never sure of the way in which someone who has developed his
djambe will make use of this dangerous force. To better understand
this ambiguity, we must return to the enigmatic figure of the *nkong*.

The *Nkong* and the Precarious Equilibrium of the *Djambe*

The *nkong* (healer) is above all the person who can protect against
the *djambe*. But as we have seen, the *nkong* is only able to do so

because he or she possesses a highly developed *djambe*. The Maka claim that the *nkong* is "a witch who has beaten all the records." Since their own *djambe* is so well developed, the *onkong* (pl.) can "see" what is making their client ill; it is this same force that allows them to "go out" of themselves (*wos,* the primary characteristic of a witch) to surprise evildoers and force them to lift their spells. The *onkong* always insist that they can use their powers only for healing and that their "professor" would kill them on the spot if they used their *djambe* in evil ways. But the Maka are never entirely convinced of this. *Djambe* can have different angles, more positive or more negative, but it remains whole. One never knows how someone who has learned to develop his or her *djambe*—like the *nkong*—would use it in practice. The *nkong* is hence an intrinsically ambiguous figure.

Great *onkong* are few and far between. During the 1970s, there were only three renowned specialists in the canton where I lived (which had about ten thousand inhabitants), but they drew clients from the entire region, and even from Yaunde.[28] The *onkong* are women as well as men. They differ in age, and there are even some relatively young *onkong*. They often appear as marginal figures. Some combine masculine and feminine attributes. Some prefer to live in the forest, far from the village. From old narratives, one can deduce that, in former days, the *onkong* did not really belong to one lineage group. They could circulate between villages in spite of hostilities, and their encampment was a refuge for people of different lineages. Today, it is still rare for *onkong* to play a conspicuous role in the politics of their own village.

Onkong must constantly prove their power, since the basis of their renown is always unsteady. The witches are supposed to give the *nkong* a mandate or *dju* (command, order), but they can always try to revoke it. The Maka have difficulty explaining this mandate that the witches could revoke. Sometimes it is assumed that this mandate was appropriated by the *nkong* after he or she had caught and "bound" the witches. But on other occasions the Maka seem to refer to a pact between the *nkong* and the witches. Sometimes they speak of the *nkong* as an intermediary: for instance, a *nkong* asks his or her clients to kill a sheep. With this meat, the *nkong* can persuade the witch to lift the spell. But other times the *nkong* is thought to organize such schemes by himself or herself. The *nkong* collaborates with the witches so that people become ill, thus drawing clients; the *nkong* then splits the fees received for his or her services with the witches.

The *onkong* practice their profession in different ways. Some put on spectacular dances, dressed in ancient warrior garb as well as feminine wear, such as wrappers and scarves. They sing to ask for the assistance of their professor and the *mindjim* (phantoms, or spirits of the witches and the dead). Others work in their homes with herbs and *midu* ("charged" objects). Some *onkong* are specialists of *lundu* (oracles), which helps them expose witches or thieves.

The great *onkong* draw clients from afar, even from other provinces. The new elites are among their clients, including eminent persons such as civil servants, high-ranking politicians, or ministers. These *onkong* have compounds big enough to lodge clients for weeks and even months. If their health permits, the clients often work in the *nkong*'s fields. They must also reimburse the *nkong* for services rendered, sometimes in kind but more frequently in cash as well.

A *nkong* owes his power to the lessons of a "professor," with whom he stays regularly "to restore force." This professor teaches the *nkong* to control and develop the *djambe* in his belly. He puts the *nkong* in contact with the *mindjim* (phantoms or dead), but also imposes prohibitions concerning secrets that have been taught. If the pupil transgresses these interdictions, the professor immediately punishes the *nkong*. The most serious prohibition, as noted above, is the use of these powers to kill. But in other domains as well, the relationship between the *nkong* and the professor is fraught with tensions. A Maka proverb says: "*mpwim adebe nkong anene*" (the pupil becomes a great *nkong*)—that is, the pupil will supplant his or her own master. For this reason, the student must live far from the professor. Almost all the Maka *onkong* whom I knew had a professor from another ethnic group (e.g., Djem or Badjué), at distances of more than sixty miles.

Theoretically speaking, everyone can become a *nkong* as long as he or she finds a good professor. If there are signs that someone is predisposed with a lively *djambe*, a training period with a professor is in order. In the neighboring village, for instance, a *nkong* had a ten-year-old girl as a student. He had "seen" that she had a dangerous *djambe* because she had "eaten" all the children born to her mother after herself. He accepted her as a pupil in order to channel her ferocious *djambe*. It was also clear, however, that he had taken on the young girl because of her gift for dancing. This *nkong* was a large, athletic man, and his therapy consisted of long nighttime dance sessions. From then on, he always danced with the girl. The rapid hip movements that he executed, barechested, were repeated by the little girl, which made for a rather exciting show. Another woman was said to have had what it takes to become a great *nkong*, but her husband forbade this. This woman often complained of severe pain in her belly, which was a sign that she had a lively *djambe* that wished to manifest itself. Had she completed training sessions with a *nkong*, she would have learned to channel her *djambe* in a creative way.

In everyday life, the *onkong* behaved, for the most part, like others. They seemed, above all, very sure of themselves. Some tried to show that they were preoccupied by things that common mortals do not see: they would shake your hand firmly while staring at something in the distance, behind you; or they would grab at some invisible thing before your face. The story of our friend Mendouga, the famous healer mentioned previously, illustrates these general remarks:

When I came to live with the Maka in 1971, Mendouga was about forty-five years old and was at the height of her renown. She was the second wife of an older man who had been an elder in the Presbyterian church. She had two sons, the older of which had been sent home from the army after being accused of malversation. For the most part, she owed her reputation to her spectacular success against a new form of witchcraft, *gbati*. In two villages, she had been able to uncover a band of boys who made the women and the fields sterile and, even worse, had tried to kill their parents.

Mendouga did not dance. She received her clients in her home. The compound she lived in was vast but somewhat poorly appointed; none of the structures had aluminum roofs. When referring to her, people often cited a proverb that says that the *djambe* "enjoys without sweat"—which means that the wealth acquired

by *djambe* does not last. According to them, a *nkong* rarely becomes rich. Mendouga dressed normally, in wrappers, but sometimes she wore beautiful dresses. She had undeniable allure due to
her clear eyes and her piercing look. Her most remarkable attribute was a ring with a very large black stone. She explained to me
that she had received it from her professor: she fled into this ring
when the witches attacked.

She told me that she went to search for *midu* (charged objects)
with a great *nkong* "because of her anger." Her son was in the
army and was driven crazy by his own brothers (i.e., boys from the
same village). She had "seen" everything (she already knew, then,
how to use her *djambe*), but she could do nothing. So she went to
a *nkong* in the village where her husband's sister lived. This *nkong*
sent her to a more powerful *nkong* in the region of Messaména
(seventy-five miles southeast).

When she arrived, the *nkong* asked her, "Why did you come
here?" (even though he knew very well why she came to him). She
explained everything, and he made a mixture of cocoyam, pepper,
and salt with his own saliva. She swallowed it all and thus took the
power (*djambe*) of her professor. The saliva of the *nkong* was so
strong that, without the cocoyam and the salt, she never could
have gotten the medicine down.

Then the *nkong* put her in contact with the *mindjim* (the
dead).[29] One night he told her to lie down. He tapped for a long
time on her back and then had her swallow medicine. Her body
remained recumbent as if she were dead, but her soul (*shishim*)
flew up toward the *mindjim*. Mendouga always became enthusi-
astic when she spoke of her encounters with the dead: it was a
fabulous world. The *mindjim* are pale like white people. They live
underground in vast and rich palaces. They dance the "tango"
(i.e., modern Cameroonian dances) much better than anyone
here. The *nkong* told her to find her mother there, but, to her
surprise, she found that in the world of the *mindjim* your own
parents avoid you. She was finally able to catch her mother, who
gave her a lot of medicine (*biang*, an Ewondo word). On her way
back, Mendouga met her sister, who had just been killed by her
husband. She gave Mendouga medicine for jaundice.

Mendouga met many other people she knew while with the *mindjim*. She even saw Jean Mabaya, the well-known deputy who had represented the region at the National Assembly. Evidently, she had to laugh when she found him with the *mindjim*. She told him, "Now I understand what you meant when you said that the phantoms in the forest will vote for you if we don't." [30]

For her first training session, Mendouga stayed with this *nkong* for several months. She paid him 30,000 francs CFA ($75 at the time). Later, she went to Nanga Eboko, in the region of the Bamvele, to complete a session on *gbati* for 35,000 francs CFA ($85). She was the only *nkong* in the canton who was not surprised when *gbati* first appeared; the others did not know how to combat it. Finally, she did another session at Kribi for 10,000 francs CFA ($25) in order to learn how to cure sterile women. Mendouga mentioned the precise amounts paid for these training sessions with great emphasis. Evidently, it was important to underscore how much she had paid; this proved her expertise.

Before treating a client, Mendouga interrogated him or her with the help of a "mirror" she had received from her first *nkong*. The vital question was to know if the client had engaged in witchcraft or sorcery; that is, if the client had made his or her *djambe* "go out" (*wos*).[31] Mendouga saw in her mirror if the client was telling the truth. This mirror was a narrow bottle containing five sticks and a viscous liquid. Her *nkong* had first shown her the bottle, then the sticks. Afterward, he had made her sleep deeply. When she had woken up, the sticks had been inside the bottle. When she interrogated a client, Mendouga made the liquid pass between the sticks: if it passed, the client had not "gone out"; if a drop remained, the client had lied. A client who admitted immediately to his or her nocturnal escapades could still be cured. But if a client continued to lie, Mendouga had to send him or her away because she could do nothing more. Then, the client became easy prey for witches in pursuit. It is clear that the client would be forced to confess even simple thoughts or whims. Under such pressure, dreams or even hidden thoughts inevitably take on terrifying proportions.

Mendouga's treatments offer stark examples of the contradictory rapport between *djambe* and kinship, and the dual capacity of *djambe* to strain as well as renew familial ties. Mendouga almost always looked in the close circle of kin for the instigator of hidden attacks against her clients. These insinuations often served to revive family tensions. But she generally refrained from specifying her accusations and normally only vaguely indicated that she had "seen" a threat coming from within the "house" and that she was capable of neutralizing it. Apparently, she tried both to reassure her client and to implicate the entire family in her treatment. She often repeated that her role was not to disturb relations but to reestablish peace in the family.

When I returned two years later, Mendouga's reputation had declined significantly. Her courtyard was often empty, and rumors about her failed treatments were more and more frequent. People had less confidence in her, especially after her failure in a *gbati* affair that had affected a neighboring village. Mendouga herself told me that she had been taken by surprise by the "gbaticians" while resting for a moment. If her dog, who "saw" witches, had not howled to warn her, the witches would have certainly "bound" her. She fled from the spot and never returned to this village, even though she had already received 2,000 francs CFA ($5) to neutralize the *gbati*. According to some villagers, the witches had decided during one of their nocturnal encounters to no longer obey Mendouga. They supposedly turned to another *nkong* who lived in a village farther away and who did resolve the *gbati* affair.

Mendouga appeared to keep her calm under all this pressure, but she did try to draw attention to herself in all sorts of ways and to show that her occult forces were still intact. For example, she spread the rumor that she was pregnant, although people believed her to be too old for that. According to her, it was a particularly odd pregnancy: she had "seen" that the baby was "placed badly." Later she said that she had terminated the pregnancy because she "saw" that the baby was a "mongolian."[32] The last time I saw her, she told me that she would soon leave on a trip. Her friend, the *préfet,* had asked her to come because he was having difficulties with his higher-ups in the capital. She was to "settle the affair." In spite of her efforts to regain attention, people's confidence in Mendouga was not rekindled. When I returned in 1980, she had died. People were reluctant to speak of her death; some implied that witches settle their affairs among themselves.

Once again, the circularity of discourse on the *djambe* is evident in many different ways in this story. The main protector against *djambe*, the *nkong*, is profoundly implicated in this same *djambe*. But Mendouga's story also illustrates the tendency of the *djambe* to both aggravate and resolve conflict in the family. The *nkong* seeks the witches who have attacked the client within the "house" but will also use the *djambe* discourse to reestablish family relations. Furthermore, the client, by going to the *nkong*, becomes automatically incorporated into the world of the *djambe*. We saw that the first question asked is whether the client has made his or her *djambe* "go out." This puts the client under acute pressure: if the client lies, the *nkong* must abandon him or her to the witches. The Maka often say that it takes a lot of courage to go to a *nkong* because one thus admits to being engaged in the *djambe*.

Djambe: Ambiguities and Inconsistencies

As my research continued, I was struck not only by this circularity but also by the highly unsystematic, if not inconsistent, character of discourse on *djambe*. Above, I emphasized the dangers inherent in the oversystematization of these conceptions. Numerous anthropologists base their analyses of this domain on clean classificatory schemes and binary oppositions. But there is a real danger that such an approach congeals these highly unstable notions. And it is precisely this fluidity that allows for the easy adaptation of these discourses to contemporary transformations.

The distinctions that the Maka themselves establish within *djambe* discourse are always precarious. It seems rather that *djambe* tends to erase all distinctions. Indeed, through this pliability it lends itself to all sorts of interpretations, becoming all the more difficult to refute. This ambiguity is quite evident when one considers the good/evil opposition, the standard point of departure for so many anthropologists and Western observers of sorcery and witchcraft. We saw that, in spite of its utterly terrifying nature, the *djambe* can be put to many uses, both good and bad. But even when distinctly positive uses are at stake, one can never quite separate out the somber core of representations of the *djambe* (i.e., the image of witches flying in the night to the *shumbu* to eat their kin). Even for those who, like the *onkong*, have completed extensive training to learn how to control their *djambe* and use it in a constructive manner, the destructive tendency always threatens to surface.

My Maka friends' discourse, in all its ambivalence, can be summarized as follows. In itself, the *djambe* is certainly bad. But given its omnipresence, one has to participate in it in one way or another—in order to protect oneself, or even to have access to these supplementary powers. Without any hidden support, it is hardly possible to achieve success in any realm whatsoever. My informants used an array of expressions that designate an "innocent," or someone who has not developed his or her *djambe*. This person has "an empty belly," "a fish in the belly," or a "*djambe le muda*" (a woman's *djambe*, which is "weak like a woman"). These characteristics are certainly not positive; rather, they express a certain contempt: an innocent is weak; if you know nothing of the *djambe*, many things escape you. When the Maka speculate about what happens in the world of *djambe*, the good/evil distinction is usually of secondary importance. The interminable accounts of violent confrontations between witches, their ruses and deceit, are more often punctuated by questions about efficacy. Who won? How does one manage to surprise an adversary? If one starts from a good/evil opposition, as so many anthropologists have done, it becomes difficult to understand why the Maka are so fascinated, even excited, by what happens in this nocturnal world.

Another reason why conceptions of *djambe* are so hard to systematize is their indeterminate nature. Maka discourse continually integrates foreign terms. Rumors about new forms of sorcery and witchcraft introduced by outsiders spread throughout the region like true epidemics and create real panic since locals do not feel protected against such novelties. When I came to the region in 1971, people everywhere were afraid of the *gbati*, a new form of witchcraft that was unheard of until then. This epidemic was followed by several others, creating similar states of panic.

More modern influences are integrated just as easily. Riches coming from the West have become a constant element in these representations: "Our witches have airplanes like you. In one night, they fly toward Paris." Or, "Their palaces are bigger than that of De Gaulle." *Djambe* discourse even borrows "magic" methods from the West. In the 1970s, for example, the "star of Madame Mylla" or "the ring of Brother Bernard," sold by correspondence by European enterprises, were greatly feared precisely because they were novelties. This interest in borrowings and novelties is hardly surprising given the general attitude of the Maka with respect to occult forces. The world of *djambe* is a true arena of ongoing confrontations and ambushes. A new procedure has considerable tactical value; it can serve to surprise the adversary and evade or undermine his *blindage* (armor). On the whole, the continuous innovation of *djambe* is a veritable leitmotif in Maka discourse.

These borrowings and innovations certainly do not reinforce the coherence of *djambe* discourse. But did it not always contain inconsistencies? It is striking that, for the Maka, each situation inspires an array of explanations by *djambe*. Seemingly contradictory maxims are combined and adapted to produce certain interpretations. Consequently, all outcomes can be explained by *djambe,* and thus the discourse itself becomes irrefutable.

A good example is the case, cited above, of the death of poor Zila, which involved me in long, long discussions with the people of our courtyard.

The grandson of Zila told us that his grandfather had been the victim of the witches. Later, I asked my assistant if that meant that Zila had been a witch himself. He had died suddenly, and I had always been told that "innocents" were less easily killed by witches. But my assistant patiently explained that this reasoning did not apply in this case. The witches had doubtlessly used *kule-kwak* (a new form of witchcraft) and thus were able to kill poor Zila brutally, even though he was innocent.

My neighbor, to the contrary, made it clear that Zila was himself a witch. He had already "given" several of his kin but finally had to sacrifice himself since he had no more family members to offer to his band of witches. Thus they killed him. I retorted that there were very few recent deaths in Zila's family. But my neighbor said that this was logical: most of Zila's kin lived close to the Presbyterian mission and were hence protected against *djambe*. I tried to continue our debate by citing the case of another man who died inside the Presbyterian camp, but who nonetheless was pronounced a victim of witchcraft. But my neighbor cut me off, saying that this was an entirely separate issue because the man in question had collaborated with a famous *nkong*. No doubt there had been a quarrel between the two.

These types of discussions become interminable, as I would experience all too often. But what is noteworthy in their ceaseless flow is the facility with which people explain apparent deviations from maxims about *djambe* by evoking other rules and alternative interpretations.

When people speak about *djambe*, I often have the impression that they constantly trace new circles that can then be combined in all sorts of ways. The circularity of *djambe* is inescapable because the distinction between more positive and more negative expressions is always relative, but also because sanctions are only found within the domain of *djambe* itself. Perhaps these vicious circles are characteristic of segmentary societies, where power is always relative and no one institution is clearly removed from *djambe*. From this point of view, certain contrasts with other regions of Cameroon, which are explored in the following pages, are interesting. For the Maka, this circularity is, above all, what makes *djambe* a vortex that is so difficult to escape.

COMPARATIVE INTERSTICE 1: THE VARIABLE FACES OF SORCERY AND WITCHCRAFT

Western readers might be struck by certain parallels between Maka conceptions of *djambe* and European discourse on sorcery and witchcraft: the idea of a nocturnal "sabbath," witches who fly away into the night, the owl that calls them. To be sure, I sometimes wondered if these were appropriations.[1] A closer look, however, reveals profound divergences. The devil, who has become a central figure in Western images of the witches' sabbath, is absent from Maka discourse, aside from certain instances of direct and conscious borrowings.[2] Sexuality, which is essential to the Western *imaginaire* (imaginary), is again less central to Maka representations of these nightly meetings. In contrast, there is a heavy emphasis among the Maka (and many other African societies) on eating—especially eating one's kin—as the most compelling urge of the witches.[3] And the direct relationship between witchcraft and kinship constitutes another specificity. Evidently, the sociopolitical context is also entirely different. I later return to the comparison with the West (and the way in which historians have studied the great witchcraft trials in the sixteenth and seventeenth centuries), but it seems preferable to begin with less adventurous comparisons, starting with the Maka's neighbors, with whom contact has steadily increased from colonial times through the present national context. In fact, these contacts directly influence conceptions of the relationship between *djambe* and politics, and it is in this context that a new interregional discourse on witchcraft and politics is being generated.

In the Cameroonian context, Maka representations of *djambe* are certainly not exceptional, especially if one compares them to other people of the forest in southern Cameroon. Close parallels exist with discourse on *evu* of the Beti, the Maka's neighbors who live in the region of Yaunde, the capital, and who hold a preponderant position today in the state apparatus.[4] In the past, the social organization of the Beti was profoundly influenced by segmentary logics, as in the case of the Maka. *Evu* is an Ewondo term, one of the principle languages of the Beti, which has spread as a sort of lingua franca through all of southern Cameroon; it serves as the language of the market as well as that of the Catholic church. The notion of *evu* has thus met with a certain regional success, becoming the general term for "witchcraft" and "sorcery" throughout the forest zone. The Maka, among others, often use the word *evu* instead of *djambe*.

Indeed, there exists a clear correspondence between *evu* and *djambe*. *Evu*, like *djambe*, is described as a small, ferocious beast (a crab, a frog, an animal endowed with fearsome teeth) who lives in one's belly. Its characterstics are the same as those of the *djambe*: a second pair of eyes, the capacity to leave the body and fly toward the sabbath of the witches, the obligation to give over kin for an anthropophagic feast. The *evu* man or woman also has a double (*nkug*) who is an assistant, like the *mindjim*, and who is in contact with the dead. *Evu* is also as ambivalent as *djambe*: the eating of kin is at its center and is no doubt very evil, but one can likewise learn to control one's *evu* so as to use it in a constructive manner. The forces of *evu* are indispensable to those who wish to accumulate wealth or power.[5]

Philippe Laburthe-Tolra (1977, 1019) describes with some humor an experience he had while doing research in the Beti region, which reminds me of the impatience I exhibited when faced with the difficulty of determining whether *djambe* was evil or not. Laburthe-Tolra recounts how some of the elders he wished to interview surprised him by proposing that he and his assistant submit themselves to a sort of oracle to see if they had *evu* in their bellies. They had to choose between two horns; if the one selected was empty, they had no *evu*. They accepted the proposition after some hesitation and were utterly relieved when their horn proved empty.

As Laburthe-Tolra continues, in his flowery style: "At the very moment of triumph, to my great surprise, the elders were taken with consternation and distress: 'But if you have nothing, if you have no *evu*, what can you understand? We cannot tell you anything: you are children. . . .' We found ourselves to be discredited as 'failures' because we had nothing in the belly . . . How could one then support the idea that *evu* had only a purely negative value? Is it good, is it evil? Our first attempt to define *evu* appears to have resulted in hopeless embarrassment" (1977, 1027).

The author finally concludes that *evu* in itself is evil. Yet he also insists that the very same force is also a condition for all forms of success. Apparently, the Beti confirm even more explicitly than the Maka that an individual cannot live without *evu*. Denying someone his *evu* amounts to killing him. If, for example, during birth, the *evu* risks coming out of the woman's belly, it must be pushed back immediately (1027).

There are also differences. It seems that Beti oral tradition refers more frequently to executions of witches, especially females. Poison ordeals that put the "guilty" to death also appear to have been more common. In the past, the funeral of an old family head often led to summary executions. According to Laburthe-Tolra (1977, 1273), such occasions could sometimes become veritable scenes of butchery during which the nephews (the sons of the sisters of the deceased) terrorized all other participants. These males might execute the widows and even the sons of the deceased on the spot.[6] In general, though, the Beti share Maka ideas about sanctions. For them as well, there is no question of eliminating *evu* as such. To the contrary, one must teach the individual to control his or her *evu*. At the very worst, if someone's *evu* continues to cause trouble, it must be neutralized. The *evu* must be "healed"; it must "shine" and be without scars. It thus becomes an indispensable support in life. (Laburthe-Tolra 1977, 1015, 1078; Mallart 1981 and 1988).

The specialist who must heal or eventually neutralize the *evu* is called *ngangang,* and this person's profile closely corresponds to that of the Maka *nkong*. The *ngangang* can only heal because of his or her own developed *evu* and is, then, a somewhat suspect figure. The Beti also believe that, in principle, the *ngangang* must deliver a family member to his or her professor in order to be initiated. Someone who is treated by a *ngangang* is automatically implicated in *evu* since the first condition of healing is, as for the Maka, confession of all one's nocturnal escapades. For the Beti as well, the main protection against *evu* is found with the *ngangang*—that is, in *evu* itself. As Laburthe-Tolra (1977, 1115) summarizes in a concise formula, "the antidote is of the same nature as the evil." Hence discourse on *evu* acquires the same circularity as that of the Maka on *djambe*.

Élisabeth Copet-Rougier offers a similar image of witchcraft for the Kako (or Kaka), who live to the northeast of the Maka on the frontier between the forest and the savanna.[7] The central notion in this instance is *lembo,* from the same Bantu root as the Maka term *djambe. Lembo* also lives in the belly. It is a hideous creature, armed with a terrifying mouth, who is afflicted with an insatiable desire to eat human beings. As is the case for the Maka, witches are thought to attack their own kin.[8] Apparently, here as well, it is difficult to clearly separate what is bad from what is considered acceptable in this domain. Copet-Rougier underscores that *lembo* is potentially "the worst of all evils" due to its tendency toward vampirism. But the Kako also speak of the *lembo* of wisdom or intelligence. Copet-Rougier notes that it is essential for all leaders to have support in this invisible world.

The Kako almost never have recourse to concrete sanctions against witchcraft in the daytime world. Accounts are settled during the night. It is especially the *ngan* who is charged with forcing the witches to lift their spells or with avenging a victim who is already dead. The profile of the *ngan* is again highly reminiscent of that of the Maka *nkong* (or the *ngangang* of the Beti). Among the Kako also, the *ngan* is a figure who is at the margins of society. According to Copet-Rougier, the *ngan* is a stranger who roams the country and avoids practicing in his own area. As with the Maka or the Beti, the *ngan* searches for the witches among the victim's kin, taking care to avoid being too specific and thus rupturing familial relations. When the *ngan* dances before the fire in the night, he always tries to assemble the family around him and to include them in the therapy. Another common trait identified by Copet-Rougier is that the Kako also believe that the *ngan* can heal only because he is a witch himself.

The Kako even think that, in order to become a *ngan,* one must eat a series of one's own kin: "the power of his healing capabilities matches the number of victims he previously killed and ate: the more voracious he was, the greater his power." The *ngan* can "reveal publicly his witchcraft so as to neutralize its maleficent effects, or even to transform it into an anti-witchcraft struggle." But he remains an ambivalent and even suspect figure. This is why he is always on the move. The Mkako are hardly pleased when a *ngan* overstays his welcome in their village, "for fear that he returns to his first misdeeds." [9]

Further to the west, in the forest zone, similar elements are manifest. *Ngina* and especially *ewusu,* terms used by the Duala of the coast to designate witchcraft, correspond to the *evu* of the Beti (Bureau 1962; de Rosny 1981). The Duala notion of *lemba,* or that of *liemba* among the Bakweri of the slopes of Mount Cameroon in the anglophone region, derive from the same Bantu root as *djambe.* [10] Among the Duala and the Bakweri, similar traits recur. Witches are said to transform themselves in the night, fly to sabbath, and eat their own kin. But it seems that narratives on what happens during these nocturnal meetings are less detailed, and that the imagery of occult forces is less fraught with ambiguity. [11] For instance, the Bakweri sometimes link *liemba* to a more constructive use of occult forces by the *nganga* (healer); this is, however, rare. The emphasis is more often placed on the bad intentions of all those who develop their *liemba.* In these societies, stories of the past about the executions of witches, most notably females, are clearly more numerous. According to Edwin Ardener, each Bakweri village had its tree for hanging witches. The first German expedition, against Buea (one of the most important Bakweri villages) in 1891, was motivated, at least officially, by the hanging of two witches. The older Bakweri still refer to the town of Limbe, the oldest missionary center in Cameroon, as *fo* (the place of the witches) since "in the past, we sent our witches to the missionaries." Here, it seems that sanctions were more regularly applied to witches in the daytime world.

In this region, already touched by European commerce long before the colonial conquest, ancient and very basic notions like *liemba, ewusu,* or *ngina* appear to have been overrun by new notions of witchcraft (*ekong, nyongo*) directly linked to the modern market economy, to which we return in chapter 5. In relation to these new forms of witchcraft supposedly exercised on a greater scale, occult associations formed that surpassed the family domain. The relationship between these new associations and the old, basic notions is not entirely clear. Altogether it seems that discourse on occult forces is more compartmentalized in this area: different concepts referring to different aspects of the occult are used alongside each other, and there are no notions that have such an overarching status as *djambe* among the Maka or *evu* among the Beti. This conceptual compartmentalization—the effort to separate different aspects of the occult—has important consequences: it nuances the circularity that characterizes discourse on all-pervasive notions like *evu* or *djambe*.

One encounters a more distinct discontinuity when the comparison is extended to the Grassfields of the West (the region of the francophone Bamileke) and the Northwest (among the anglophone Bamenda). Here, one finds a very different cultural space. These societies were extremely hierarchical well before colonization. They comprise a large number of chiefdoms that vary from a few thousand to over a hundred thousand inhabitants (the largest chiefdoms being Nso and Bamun). The chief (*fon* or *fo*) is everywhere the nerve center of local society and even holds certain authority over the new urban elite—the "sons of the realm" who have made their careers in the cities elsewhere in the country. The question is whether the link between witchcraft and politics is of another order in these more hierarchical societies.

At first glance, discourses on sorcery and witchcraft are not very different in the Grassfields from those previously described. The basic elements of discourses on *evu* or *djambe* recur: the second pair of eyes, vampirism, the owl, and nocturnal meetings where witches betray and devour their intimate relations.[12] But closer inspection reveals significant differences: the circularity of these discourses seems less pronounced, there are more categorical distinctions between positive and negative expressions of occult forces, and specific institutions are responsible for dealing with witchcraft and sorcery.

The *fon* (chief) and the associations of notables of the court play a key role in these societies' attempts to classify and control occult forces. Demonstrative examples of this are found in a fascinating recent study by Miriam Goheen (1996), who worked among the Nso.

During the nineteenth century, successive Nso *fon* conquered vast territories in the Grassfields over which they imposed a hegemony of remarkable coherence. The subjugated chiefdoms were integrated into the Nso hierarchy through a concerted mix of co-optation, military coercion, and ideological constraint.

In her analysis of this imposing hegemony, Goheen attributes a central place to the notion of *sem*, or occult power.[13] This term cannot simply be equated with witchcraft since *sem* has a much broader meaning. There is always the possibility that *sem* can degenerate into witchcraft (which, for the Nso, also refers to the mastication of human flesh). But in other contexts, *sem* connotes a more positive power: wealth and power are automatically associated with it. However, it is always a dangerous force that must be controlled or "domesticated," or it may become noxious. This general characteristic is surely reminiscent of Maka *djambe*, as are some of *sem*'s other attributes. Goheen states that *sem* is associated with *kibay*, which lives in the belly (or liver) of its possessor; anthropophagy, the mark of evil *sem*, is also directed primarily against kin.

It is especially the *fon* who is responsible for the control and domesticatation of *sem*. During the night, he is able to transform himself into a lion, and accompanied by his leopards—his notables—he prowls the country to combat witches and sorcerers. In the past, people suspected of practicing sorcery against the *fon* were regularly executed. Apparently, it was up to the *fon* to determine whether the *sem* of a subject was bad or acceptable. As discussed later, the *fon* still plays this role in relation to the somewhat suspect novel forms of wealth, accumulated by the new elites abroad. The *fon* does not necessarily have *sem* himself, but he must be surrounded by notables of the associations of the court—most notably, the *ngwerong*—who do have it. Without it, he could not rule. But Nso discourse seeks to distinguish him emphatically from bad *sem*.[14]

This discourse operates therefore on the basis of clear distinctions. The issue raised by Maka discourse on *djambe* ("Who has the right to kill and who does not?") is no longer a real question here: the *fon* determines whether or not one abuses *sem*. He himself is associated with *sem* (in his own person or through his notables), but no one contests his right to execute witches who direct their *sem* against him.

The power of the *fon* and his associates is conceptualized outside the bounds of witchcraft: his *sem* is by definition in contrast to *sem arin* (bad *sem*—that is, witchcraft). Hence he is capable of distinguishing social *sem* from evil *sem* and legitimating sanctions that are external to the domain of witchcraft. In such a discourse, the field of action of witchcraft is more clearly circumscribed; at least certain institutions are clearly separated from it. The tendency toward a conceptual compartmentalization of the occult, already noted above for the Bakweri and the Duala, is more strongly institutionalized in the Grassfields, where it seems to allow for a breakthrough in the circularity of the discourse on the occult. The *fon* and the institutions of his court are conceived in principle to be outside witchcraft and have, therefore, the authority to punish it.[15]

The question remains as to the extent to which such conceptual distinctions can be maintained in practice, even in the Grassfields. In the case of the Nso, for instance, it seems that discourse on *sem* is nonetheless marked by all sorts of ambiguities. Miriam Goheen (1996, 57) observes that this notion indicates the moral ambivalence of all forms of power. We see below that, characteristically, this ambivalence is today highlighted in people's mixed reactions to the *fon*'s efforts to "socialize" the suspect wealth of the nouveaux riches and to coopt them into the traditional hierarchy.

Apparently the societies of the Grassfields have also not been able to completely vanquish the ambivalence at work in the relationship between witchcraft and power. Nonetheless, here, the circularity of these discourses appears to be less ineluctable. Efforts are made, more than in the societies of the forest, to devise sanctions outside of the domain of witchcraft that can control and domesticate these occult forces. The question to which we later return is how such differences influence contemporary relations of power and the integration of new socioeconomic inequalities.

WITCHCRAFT AND LOCAL POLITICS:
THE DIALECTICS OF EQUALITY AND AMBITION

3

To the Maka, the *djambe* discourse certainly does not speak only about power and politics. The examples above indicate under what conditions rumors about witchcraft tend to emerge: illness, death, accidents, and other unhappy events. Witchcraft helps explain unexpected misfortune. Moreover, it indicates possibilities for acting against misfortune since, characteristically, *djambe*—like other witchcraft discourses—tends to explain the unexpected by referring to human agency: it personalizes adversity and thus makes it possible to act against adversity.

Yet it is precisely because of this personalizing tendency that even apparently apolitical manifestations of the *djambe* refer to what people in the West call "politics"—to human action, power, and inequalities. Witches are supposed to be motivated by jealousy or ambition, which links the *djambe* automatically to social inequalities. In this sense, *djambe* is by definition a comment on power relations such that politics are always present in rumors on *djambe*.

Moreover, *djambe* does not serve only to explain misfortune; *djambe* rumors also concern conspicuous successes like sudden enrichment or a spectacular victory. As indicated above, a basic ambiguity of *djambe* is that it can serve to level inequalities as well as to confirm the accumulation of power and riches. And it is especially in relation to this accumulative tendency that the political tenor of the *djambe* discourse comes to the fore. Yet even in those cases, its leveling side is still there as some sort of underside.

This chapter discusses the impact of the *djambe* on village politics in Makaland. In this region there is still a clear gap between local politics and the new political space created around the state. Even though this gap is increasingly bridged by all sorts of informal, clientelist relations, it still highlights the contradiction between the old tribal order of the Maka and the authoritarian principles imposed by the state after the colonial conquest. And the political role of witchcraft in this society is also to be understood in relation to this tension.

Village Politics and State Politics among the Maka: Different Styles of Political Action

The aim of my research among the Maka was to study the interaction between village and state—between national and local politics. However, a first problem was that it proved to be quite difficult to find an equivalent in Maka language for the notion of *politics*. My informants, after some hesitation, gave the term *kwani*, but this turned out to have quite negative connotations. People say, for instance, that a woman is doing *kwani* when she is constantly harassing her husband to give presents to her own family. The aim of her "politics" is, of course, to keep her family satisfied so that she can always fall back on them in case of quarrels with her husband. The informants who gave me this example of what *kwani* means were all men, so one can be sure of the negative connotation of this notion. Others shrugged off my questions by saying that they had nothing to do with politics: this was *l'affaire des Grands,* of the officials and politicians around the state.[1] To them, the term *politics* was apparently related to the new brand of authoritarianism the state had imposed upon the Maka communities. In general, the villagers make indeed a strict separation between, on the one hand, the vicissitudes of village life and its politics (such as the confrontations between families, the fierce competition for the position of village chief or for other titles, and the great palavers) and, on the other hand, national politics, formally the domain of the "unified party" but in reality controlled by the bureaucracy.

Or course, there were all sorts of links between the two spheres. The elections for the position of village chiefs were, for instance, openly manipulated by the *sous-préfet* and the regional party bosses.

The same *sous-préfet* intervened regularly with his gendarmes—that is, very directly—in village politics. And the representatives of the then single party had the task of mobilizing the villagers around the national political ideology—for instance, by organizing "formation seminars" at which the local party dignitaries had to explain a paragraph from the party's charter. The emphasis on exegesis made such seminars surprisingly like church services. The difference was, however, that the villagers showed much less interest in attending these party meetings.

The villagers from their side tried to bridge the gap with the state institutions via informal, clientelist networks via *originaires*—sons from the village who had made careers in the city. In Makaland, most of them had made their careers in the civil service. Using all sorts of means, the villagers tried to force these *évolués* into some sort of broker role: they were constantly reminded of their obligations to use their contacts and their access to state institutions in order to further the interest of the village as a whole and their relatives in the village in particular.

The distinction between local and national politics was therefore less complete than my informants would have had me believe. But it was, and is, clear that strikingly different political styles prevailed at these two levels. In the large village council completely different ways of behaving (of presenting and defending oneself) were required than with respect to the *sous-préfet* and other state authorities; and the ways in which the latter approached the villagers differed even more. Yet one should add that both the villagers and the urban elite switched with apparent ease from one register to the other.

The central political institution in the village is doubtless the *kaande* (council)—the great village palaver led by the village chief and his old notables, the *lesje kaande* (those who speak in the *kaande*). In the village where I lived, the *kaande* met normally on Sundays, after the various church services had finished, in front of the chief's house, around his *mpaanze milesu* (house of palavers). However, when there was an urgent case, the palaver could also meet at another time or place.

The formal organization of the *kaande* is quite simple. The chief and his notables sit on chairs or little stools in front of the *mpaanze*.

The audience forms a large circle around them. Most remain standing, but some bring their own stools with them. In principle, a palaver is completely public: everybody can attend, even someone who
happens to pass by. Women also attend and mark their presence by
loud comments or shrill cries when they do not agree. They can also
speak in front of the palaver but normally remain somewhat in the
background, such as under the overhanging roofs of the surrounding
houses.

The *kaande* can meet for all sorts of reasons. The chief can con-
vene it when he has received an order from the *sous-préfet* or in order
to deal with a general problem in the village. In most cases, however,
the *kaande* will meet to "cut" a case—that is, to sit and judge a
complaint from a villager. This is why the villagers now translate
kaande in French as *le tribunal du village*. Any villager, including
young men or women, who thinks he or she has been treated un-
justly can lodge a complaint with the chief. The latter asks for a small
remuneration—some palm wine, a chicken, or a few hundred francs
CFA that he will share with his notables—and convenes the *kaande*.

Normally, a palaver is opened by the chief, who briefly announces
the topic. Then the complainant and the accused expound their respective versions of the case. They can also call in witnesses. The notables interrogate both parties and their witnesses; they can call in
other witnesses as well. The general public also participates most actively. At any moment, people from the audience may intervene in
the discussion. If all goes well and some sort of consensus emerges,
one of the notables summarizes the debate and gives a final pro-
nouncement. In exceptional cases, the chief and his notables may
retire for a consultation behind closed doors.[2]

This summary might suggest that the *kaande* proceeds in a formal
and orderly fashion. In practice, however, the contrary is the case.
For the parties concerned, and also for the general public, the palaver
is the preferred place to show one's rhetorical prowess. The complainant and the accused each put forward their case with dramatic
ostentation, and the witnesses often add to this. Sometimes the notables ask all people involved to reenact the scene, which is often
done with such passion that the parties risk coming to blows once
more. Moreover, anybody present can intervene in the debate whenever he or she sees fit. It is certainly not only the notables' prerogative

to ask questions or state an opinion. Anyone in the audience, including young men or women, can interrogate the witnesses in order to demonstrate that their statements are inconsistent or to show their own cleverness by giving a different interpretation. It is quite common that several people will be speaking at the same time, all raising their voices in order to make themselves heard and to add to the strength of their argumentation. Thus a palaver can quickly develop into a tumultuous gathering that gives the impression—at least to a Western researcher—of complete chaos.

This impression is reinforced by the tendency of all participants—complainants, accused, witnesses, bystanders, and even the notables themselves—to pile up all sorts of accusations. Often the link with the original complaint is not at all clear. To me, this apparent lack of a clear line in the palaver was especially frustrating. In the beginning, I dutifully attended the palaver every Sunday with my notebook and my assistant to help me understand the more difficult speeches. But many Sundays, the whole happening gave me a headache not only because of all the noise and drama but also due to the frustration of not being able to make sense of it all.

Later on, I came to understand that this apparent confusion was essential to the palaver. One of the notables made me understand this in his eloquent way during a very complicated palaver. For me, the palaver began to derail immediately after it started since people kept bringing in new accusations involving completely different persons than those implicated in the original complaint. Then, a young man, a student spending his holidays in the village, stood up and said with some irritation that the witnesses should finally limit themselves to the case at hand and stop confusing the palaver with other grievances. This was exactly what I had wanted to say all along. But one of the notables reproached the young man severely: "You are wrong. A palaver must proceed like the women when they are fishing in the stream. They stamp and shout and make all sorts of noises in order to make the fish come out of their holes. It is better to bring out all sorts of accusations into the open during a palaver. Only after everything has been discussed can we try to bring people together again."

All this may indicate why the task of a *lesje kaande* is not an easy one. The village chief—often relatively young because of the government's preference for a chief who can read and write—presides over the meeting. But when a palaver is underway, the chief often can hardly make himself heard. Only the old notables can then take matters in hand. The strongest notable of the village where I lived was Mr. Mpal (who gave the memorable speech at our house, saying that formerly people ate the white man while now they were eating with him). He often showed in a quite spectacular way how a true *lesje kaande* can control the council.

In 1971, Mpal was about seventy-five years old. He told me that he was about ten years old when the first German came to his village (this must have been in 1905). At first sight he made a rather poor impression. Since he suffered from leprosy, he often walked barefoot and put a wrapper around his hips. He could look very tired and old with a dull gaze. But all this changed when he stood up in the palaver. Then he had a piercing look and a penetrating voice. Normally he began speaking quite softly but gradually raised his volume, accelerating the speed of his argument. His greatest asset was, however, showing off his knowledge of ancient traditions. He often punctuated his words with explicit references to the secrets the elders of olden days had taught him in order to make him "invincible" in the *kaande*. As he told me himself: "My elders made me 'eat the *kaande*'; this is why nobody can contradict me in the council."

It is mainly through their personal ascendancy that the notables can try to direct the debates in order to arrive at some sort of a conclusion. Sometimes a notable tries to close the debate by relating an ancient parable or singing a song he learned from his elders, in order to indicate where the solution lies. A notable will do so especially when the palaver concerned is so serious that it threatens the unity of the village—that is, when it is imperative to humor both parties. Such a demonstration of ancestral knowledge profoundly impresses people and shuts up even the noisiest ones. But, and this might be characteristic, such allegories often lend themselves to highly different interpretations: it is not uncommon that the parties involved draw opposite conclusions.

The first time I heard Mpal tell such a *kanda* (parable) was at a particularly fierce palaver on a topic that often raised problems in the villages: a widow who administered the cocoa plantations left to her by her husband. This time it concerned Mpot, the widow of Nkwud who had died without leaving any children. Formally, Mpot should have been taken in levirate by Dama, Nkwud's younger brother, but for all sorts of reasons this had not taken place. On his deathbed, Nkwud had made his brother promise that one of his sons would marry as soon as possible with the help of the money of Nkwud's plantations (that is, Nkwud's cocoa money was to be used to pay the bridewealth). The first son of this marriage was to be named after Nkwud so that his name would live on even though he had left no children himself. Only after this were the plantations to be divided among his widow, Dama, and his other patrilineal kin. However, none of Dama's sons was in a hurry to get married. Dama did not do anything and just left the whole affair hanging.

This changed, however, when Mpoam, an old man from another family in the village, moved in with Mpot, Nkwud's widow. He did all sorts of small jobs for her, and she fed him. But the old man also had himself inscribed as *planteur* with the new cooperative, even though he himself had no cocoa plantations. This was reason enough to suspect him of trying to appropriate Nkwud's plantations. For Dama, it was also reason enough to lodge a complaint with the village chief.

The palaver took place the next Sunday. Initially, it proceeded quite calmly. Dama made his statement in a straightforward and collected manner. But the affair began to "heat up" when Mpot began to speak. She piled up all sorts of accusations: Dama and his sons had been glad about Nkwud's death (an allusion to witchcraft); they had always neglected her; and so on. She went completely berserk when the village chief declared that, in his opinion, the solution was simple: the inheritance should be divided as quickly as possible. This drove the widow into a frenzy of protest: Nkwud's last words were sacred; the plantations could not possibly be divided before a bridewealth had been paid for one of Dama's sons and Nkwud's name had been conveyed to his grand-

son. This threw Dama into a frenzy of rage. He started to shout
that the woman had always been a nuisance, that he had enough
of her.

In this confusion, Mpal took the floor in order to "cut" the
case with a *kanda* (parable). Like all the elders' stories, this was a
very long one. In this context, it is only possible to summarize it:

> A man had two wives. At first he took good care of both of
> them, but eventually he started to neglect his first wife. He did
> not give her any share of the bushmeat he had killed on his
> hunting trips, and he did not even clear a new field for her in
> the forest.
>
> One day the woman said to him, "Should I still call you my
> man? You never sleep with me any more. Will anybody believe
> that I have a man in this village if they see my poverty? I shall
> summon the notables and ask them whether I still have a man
> in this village."
>
> But the man refused. He told the woman to stay in her
> kitchen and asked her to heat up some water for the night (a
> sign that he would sleep with her). After nightfall, the man
> came indeed, sat next to the pot of water and said, "Come
> here, I shall wash you." He squatted before her, took her right
> foot and washed her leg up to her crotch; then he did the same
> with her other leg. That night he slept with her.
>
> The next morning it was the man who summoned the no-
> tables. He said, "I have called you to ask you why my wife is
> complaining so often." The notables called the woman and
> asked her to explain herself. She started to reiterate her story,
> going on about how the man had neglected her. When the el-
> ders asked the man if this was true, he only answered, "I tell
> you that I take better care of my wife than all of you. You say
> that you are good to your womenfolk. But who of you has ever
> washed his wife's feet? Yesterday I not only washed her feet,
> but even her legs up to her crotch."
>
> Everybody was astonished, the notables included. They told
> the woman to stop complaining, because no man took such
> good care of his wife as her husband.

This was the end of the *kanda* (parable) and also the end of the
palaver. People left, highly satisfied with Mpal's performance: he

had once more demonstrated that he was a true *lesje kaande* (speaker).

I was indeed impressed that the whole audience had listened to Mpal's *kanda* in deep silence—to me a real relief after all the noise and excitement produced by Mpot, Dama, and the others. The old Mpal had once again given an impressive performance. But to me the exact implications of the parable in relation to the issue before the palaver were far from clear: the end especially seemed to lend itself to all sorts of interpretations.

To my surprise, the villagers were also quite uncertain about what Mpal really wanted to say with his parable. Some explained to me that Mpal wanted to admonish Mpot, the widow: with this parable, he sought to warn her not to bother the notables with trifles, like the woman in his story. But others insisted that Dama was like the man in the story trying to deceive the notables with his strange behavior (washing his wife's feet and legs). Yet another interpretation was that Mpal wanted to reproach both Mpot and Dama for bothering the notables with problems they should solve among themselves.

Finally, I found the courage to ask old Mpal himself what he meant with his story. But he reacted with obvious irritation: his grandfather had taught him this story, everybody had heard it, and people should decide for themselves what they thought of it.

The parable certainly did not help to solve the conflict between Mpot and Dama. When I left the village eighteen months later, old Mpoam still lived with the widow without their relation having been formalized in one way or another, while Nkwud's plantations still remained an open issue. However, in other respects the parable had been quite effective. Mpal had succeeded in restoring some sort of peace after violent disagreements: unity had been reestablished, albeit precariously. Apparently, this was the primary aim of Mpal and his *kanda*.

Another favorite tactic of the notables is to try to reconstruct— one could even say "discover"—kinship ties between the complainant and the accused. The Maka use kinship terms in a very wide sense. My spokesmen, mocking my bewilderment about their complicated reckonings of kinship, often told me, "The African family is large, yes, very large." Thus it is possible to incorporate all sorts of relations into the networks of kinship. A striking example of this was a palaver initiated by a man who complained that a woman had maltreated him with her umbrella. She claimed that he had molested her. On this occasion, the notables succeeded in reconstructing actually three different kinship links between the two. They told the complainant that the woman's father was "really" his mother's brother; moreover, they said that the woman's husband was "really" the son-in-law of the complainant; finally, they told the complainant that the woman could even be called his daughter. The complainant was unable to withstand so many arguments. He replied that "blood covers the truth"—that is, he indicated that he accepted that the conflict be treated as an affair among kin. The elders are so keen—in this and in many other cases—to translate a conflict into kinship terms, since then it is no longer necessary to impose a punishment or fix a compensation. It becomes an affair between kin, and solidarity can be reestablished through proper exchanges between persons in different kinship positions.

Clearly, one of the characteristics of this *tribunal du village* is, therefore, the ambiguity of its judgments. In this respect, it hardly corresponds to the Western idea of a tribunal. The notables are reluctant to designate one of the two parties unequivocally as the guilty party or to impose a one-sided punishment. As Mpal said during another palaver, "We must not divide the village and embitter the hearts." The notables will try, rather, to admonish both parties, telling them to respect each other more and exchange the proper gifts.[3] Restoring unity is more important than punishing. After all, the notables' authority depends on their personal powers of persuasion. In practice, this so-called tribunal does not dispose of concrete means to impose punishments.

The crucial test for the old notables is the funeral palaver. This "palaver of death" is of special importance since it concerns the vital question of whether death was "just" or "unjust."[4] Funerals are the occasion for the expression of all sorts of tensions, contradictions, and therefore witchcraft accusations. Such accusations will burst into the open at the very moment that the body is put into the grave.

Most often, they will be directed against the daughters-in-law—that is, the women who married into the patrilineage of the dead and who are, therefore, relative outsiders.[5] But sometimes, and this is considered to be more serious, the accusations are directed against another branch of the patrilineage. In such cases, the very unity of the village is at stake.

A funeral constitutes a key political moment for the Maka, especially if the deceased was a prominent elder. His death means that an important link in the network between related lineages disappears. Therefore, it is crucial to reemphasize these links, and this is what the funeral rites do, with dramatic ostentation. The daughters-in-law, supported by the sons-in-law, dance all night to mock the patrilineal descendants of the deceased for their loss. The descendants, in contrast, have to mourn and weep. The nephews—that is, the sisters' sons, who are in an ambivalent position since they are blood relatives but belong to lineage of their own father—terrorize the deceased's camp. A first climax is the *kombok:* the daughters-in-law and the sons-in-law "steal" the body; the elders of the deceased's family must "buy it back," through strenuous negotiations, by paying a considerable sum of money. At the moment of the burial itself, the mother's brothers have to be paid for digging the grave; once more, this requires long negotiations punctuated by fierce rhetorical confrontations.

The deceased is supposed to rejoice over the aggressive behavior of his affines because this is proof of the vitality of the relations he forged, during his long life, with other groups. These demonstrations of aggression and ostentatious competition serve, indeed, to highlight the importance of the ties between the lineages concerned.[6] Thus funerals become key moments in the reproduction of political relations between autonomous family groups that constitute Maka society.

These are also crucial moments for the old notables to prove their prestige. The elders of the different lineages confront each other as true champions during the successive negotiations with ostentatious rhetorical display. However, it is clear as well that it is their ultimate task to reestablish unity and contain the tensions between the lineages involved. Often, the leading part is played by an elder who does not belong to the deceased's family and who, because of this distance, will be more capable of maintaining control over things during moments of great tension.[7]

Yet it is not at all certain that the elders will indeed be able to reestablish unity among the various groups at "the palaver of death." The most precarious moment is when the body is put into the grave since, as noted above, this is the moment for publicly expressing witchcraft accusations. In the past, such accusations were the most common reason for splitting the village: often, the accused group would leave and establish its own village elsewhere in the forest. But since colonial "pacification," such fission has become impossible. Nowadays, people look for other ways to resolve the tensions expressed by such accusations.

Certain aspects of the *kaande* (village council) are clearly new. For instance, the village chief is a colonial creation, even though he is called "customary chief" in the administrative jargon. Prior to the Germans' arrival, the villages were formed by a patrilineal segment under the authority of one, or more often several, elders. However, as indicated above, the Germans, and after them the French, forced the families to live along the new roads where they resettled several families in larger villages under the authority of one *chef de village* (in German, *Häuptling*). Since then, each village is constituted by several *grandes familles* (which used to form independent units). That one chief was supposed to command over several, often unrelated, families was completely novel to the Maka. Initially, these chiefs were simply appointed by the colonial government, but since the end of the colonial period, they are now elected by the villagers themselves. In other respects as well, the position of the village chief has become more and more rooted in local society. This is, for instance, quite clear from his prominent role in the *kaande*.

Other aspects of the *kaande* clearly continue ancient themes, such as the open and apparently egalitarian character of the discussions: everybody can take the floor, and even the chief cannot stop them from speaking (at least not formally). Yet, in practice, the organization of the *kaande* affirms the ascendancy of the elders, another traditional trait. They know the wisdom of the ancestors and their secrets. This allows old notables like Mpal to play first fiddle in the *kaande*.[8]

However, and this is crucial for understanding politics among the Maka and in many other segmentary societies, the elders' authority is never self-evident; it must constantly be proven. When I tried to discuss notions like power or authority with them, my Maka informants always emphasized the distinction between *idjuga* (commandment) and *gume* (prestige). An elder has only *idjuga* over the people of his own *mpaanze,* that is, his descendants; indeed, they must obey him unconditionally. But in the *kaande,* the same elder has only *gume,* and this always depends on his powers of persuasion at that particular moment.

In the relations with the *sous-préfet* and other state officials, a completely different political style prevails. In contrast to the notables, the *sous-préfet* does possess means of coercion that are highly concrete: the omnipresent gendarmes. I found it often quite shocking to see with what ostentatious humility a man, who only yesterday had delivered a fiery speech in the *kaande,* behaved in front of the *sous-préfet.* Here, there is no occasion for flowery figures of speech or parables that must convince the audience. Before the state officials, a completely different behavior is required: villagers must be as brief as possible; if they take too much time to express themselves, they will be rudely interrupted.

The *sous-préfet,* for his part, does not try to convince the audience; he simply insists on his capacity to command. Any objection, no matter how humbly formulated, is pushed aside. And in case of *insubordination répétée,* the *sous-préfet* will order his gendarmes to put such unruly elements in a lorry and take them off to the station. This latter possibility inspires a holy fear among the villagers, since it is generally rumored that anybody brought into the gendarmes station will receive a "warning"—that is, a thorough whipping—to begin with. Consequently, the *sous-préfet*'s sessions are marked by a general climate of authority and repression that is in sharp contrast to the flamboyant and dramatic style of discussions in the village *kaande.*

In chapter 4, I return to the new relations of domination imposed by the state and explore to what extent the *djambe* has penetrated these relations as well. The rest of this chapter concerns the question of how the *djambe* affects the precarious balance between equality and ambition in village politics.

Djambe and the Balance between Equality and Ambition

Anthropologists often tend to label societies like the Maka as "egalitarian." Unfortunately, this term has been taken over by colleagues from other backgrounds—for instance, in general debates about development—resulting in quite simplistic oppositions between supposedly egalitarian societies and hierarchical ones. This label of egalitarian may be confusing, notably when one wants to understand different patterns of articulation between these societies and the state (or modern politics in general).

It is true that the local order among the Maka had, and still has, strongly egalitarian overtones. As emphasized above, in the *kaande* anybody, including youngsters or women, can take the floor; nobody can prevent someone from speaking. Even the old notables cannot command the *kaande;* they can only try to convince and persuade.

However, these egalitarian accents go together with an ostentatious show of ambition and a personal striving for supremacy that hardly correspond to what Westerners mean by "egalitarianism." The performance of a notable like Mpal in the council is characterized, rather, by an insistence on inequality and personal ascendancy. Mpal did all he could to give his words more weight. He made ample use of his personal rhetorical talents. But often, notably when the case at hand seemed to be particularly difficult, he started his speech by summing up all his merits. He sometimes talked about the *kaande* as a battlefield where he would "crush" his opponents. And he boasted of how his elders had made him "eat the *kaande*" so that nobody could resist him.

Moreover, the notables are certainly not the only ones who put on such a show of personal valor. In this apparently egalitarian society there is a true obsession with titles of honor. A good example of the strength of this obsession is offered by the new working groups of men that were formed in the 1950s when the cultivation of cocoa and coffee spread, requiring a more regular input of male labor. One of the reasons for the popularity of these working groups seemed to be that they created a whole array of titles, from "chairman" to "vice-server of the palm wine." In the village where I lived, one of these groups had been inactive for several years because of a conflict between two men about the title of "server of the food." The majority of these titles had little practical meaning since these *fonction-naires* had no real function to perform. But the fierce competition for these honorary positions corresponded to the general obsession with titles. As my neighbor said to me one morning, "I must become village chief, even if I will die the next day. I must have this title."

When it concerns a title like vice-server of the wine, such an obsession might seem somewhat comical. But this obsession with titles as such relates no doubt to an old and deeply rooted attitude. In the old stories, the protagonists invariably adorned themselves with challenging surnames: "I, the caterpillar slippery as saliva" or "Me, the leprosy that spares no one." In former days as well, there was heavy emphasis on exhibiting one's personal merits and exploits—what Parsonian sociologists tend to call "achievement." Such a preoccupation with achievement might seem surprising for a society where kinship plays a key role. After all, in Parsonian sociology, kinship was often equated with "ascription"—that is, ascription of social status on the basis of the given of social life (for instance, descendance). From this perspective, achievement is seen as the opposition of ascription. In kinship societies, there would be, therefore, little scope for personal achievement: rather, someone's social status would be ascribed—that is, fixed by the lines of descendance and kinship.

Elsewhere (Geschiere 1982), I tried to show that this equation of kinship and ascription can be misleading. Among the Maka, kinship terms have such a wide meaning that the kinship configuration leaves all sorts of choices: a relation between two persons often lends itself to various interpretations in kinship terms, and one person can often have different options as to which group he (or she) wants to belong. Social status is not fixed by kinship; it depends, rather, on personal performance. A position of authority, for instance, is not automatically inherited or attributed; it has to be conquered and then confirmed by showing off one's personal talents. The old family heads were, in many respects, "big men" who succeeded in one way or another in increasing the number of their dependents (for example, due to their success in bridewealth negotiations or by attracting young men from impoverished lineages). One never becomes a notable automatically by virtue of one's age or on the basis of one's descendance. Rather, a real notable is someone who knows how to convince people of his superiority through his personal performance.[9]

To the Maka, all men are, in principle, equal. Hereditary inequalities are not very important.[10] But it is precisely because of this basic equality that any form of ascendancy has to be won personally, and that the tendency to boast about one's personal achievements is so pronounced. In practice, this unresolved tension between equality and ambition constitutes a fertile breeding ground for the *djambe*.[11]

The prototype of a true leader in the stories the elders told me about the Maka and their history was the great war hero of the Mpang, Nkal Selek.[12] Even though he was a Mpang and not a real Maka, he was integrated into Maka history. Indeed, his descendants—very numerous, as is fit for a great chief—have become assimilated more or less to the Maka.[13]

Nkal Selek's epic highlights the basic principles of Maka political culture. He did not owe his success to any hereditary position. On the contrary, in the beginning of the epic he was reduced to slavery. His rise as a great leader was due to his personal qualities. Typically, the occult forces played a key role in this. The young Nkal Selek succeeded in rising above his humble position only because he cleverly deceived his chief and appropriated the magical forces meant for the latter. Thus "armored," he became invincible and could accumulate power on an unprecedented scale. However, all his armoring did not constitute a definitive guarantee. His sudden and unexpected death on the battlefield proved that any leader, no matter how well armored, remained vulnerable. One can even say that it was precisely the *djambe* that made him extravulnerable.

The following is one version of the Nkal Selek epic, as told to me by a Maka elder from the region of the Ndjonkol:

Evina,[14] the great Yebekolo chief, attacked a village of the Mpang. The Yebekolo killed all the men and took the women and the children as slaves. Nkal Selek and his brother Viang Selek, still boys, were taken as well. Evina saw that they were beautiful and strong. He said, "No. I killed many men, but I will not kill these boys. I will hand them over to my women, and they will raise them."

The women took good care of the boys. When they grew up, Evina included them among his *bwane mpaanze* (his pages; literally, the "children of his house"). They had to accompany him when he went to make war, but they also had to work in his compound. One day, Evina told them to go and cut poles for the new *mpaanze* (palaver house) he wanted to build. All the pages left, but not Nkal Selek.

Viang Selek said to his brother, "What is this Nkal? Aren't we going?"

But Nkal refused: "*Itombang* [cry of rage]. Should I cut poles? Should I carry them on my shoulders?"

Viang tried to persuade him: "What do you want? Our father is dead. Our mother is dead. Do you want to die as well?"

But Nkal did not accept. When he showed his hands they were white like those of him over there [the author]. Finally Viang went. He cut twice as many poles, enough for both of them. And he carried all of them to the compound.

Evina asked his pages to go and collect raffia near the pool for the roof on his *mpaanze*. All the boys went. But once more Nkal refused: "*Itombang*. What is this with raffia? Its thorns will wound my hands."

And Viang pleaded again: "Nkal don't do this. Evina has massacred our village. You are only a boy. Why do you take yourself for a big man?"

But Nkal insisted: "No, I refuse. I am Nkal Selek. If this is death, I must die."

And once again, his brother went to the pool and made two packages of raffia, enough for both of them. Thus Viang saved the life of his brother Nkal.

Some time later, Evina heard about a woman among the Mpele[15] who could make warriors invincible by her fetishes. He told his women, his children, and his pages that he wanted to go there; they had to follow him. They marched for a long time through the forest: "*via, via, via.*" Finally they found the woman sitting in front of an old hut. She was alone; her man had died. She sat there, dirty and hungry since no one looked after her. But she had the basket with *bubuwa* (war fetishes) that her husband had left her. The basket was full—full of *bubuwa*.

The old woman saw them coming. She said, "No, don't come further, you beautiful men. I am too dirty. What did I do to you that you come to see me in this state?"

But Evina and Nkal went up to her and sat on the ground.

The old woman turned her back on them. "No I do not want this visit. My husband is dead; he left me here to die as well. I am here, and no one protects me any more. You have come to kill me? What did I do to you? Let me wait here for my death by myself."

But Evina said, "Mother."

She replied, "What is this? Am I your mother?"

He said, "We did not come to kill you. We came to see you."

She said, "Do you want to see me like this, all dirty?"

He replied, "If you are dirty, I feel dirty as well. It is you who brought me into this world." [16]

She still did not trust him. "If it is like this, if you are my son, don't you see my shame? Don't you see my misery? I will see what you can do."

And Evina said, "You will see. All this will change."

Evina went back with Nkal to where he had left the women and the other pages. He told his pages to take their cleavers, cut poles, and collect raffia. They cleared a piece of land and constructed a nice house. They made doors in it and beds. Evina told his women to go and fetch water and wash his new "mother." They braided her hair and rubbed her with *kong* (red powder) so that her skin was shining again.

Finally, the old woman called for Evina. "I see all you have done for me. Well, what do you want me to do for you?"

He leaned forward and took her hand. "Mother, *sague me doomb* (literally, "make me the war"): make me invincible on the battlefield, make that when I cry out, *heeeye,* a flame will come from my mouth, that my enemies will flee, that I spring on their backs to kill them."

She said, "Is this what you came looking for?"

He replied, "It is this."

She said, "Then I can satisfy you."

She went and took her basket. She placed it on the ground between them. She asked once more, "So you want the *bubuwa?*" And he said, "Yes, that is what I want."

Then the old woman made him the *bubuwa*. But Nkal Selek was there and saw everything. Nkal was only a slave. But because he was a slave, he could be there to see how the old woman made the *bubuwa* for Evina.

She took the *mpenje* (bamboo splinters) from her basket and burned them in the fire. Then she told Evina to swallow them. She took the basket and placed it in front of him. Then she said, "So, give me." [17]

Evina told her to wait. He took Nkal aside and told him to go rapidly to the village of Kokdombo and to come back with eight boys and eight women. Nkal ran off, "*bou, bou, bou,*" and arrived at Kokdombo. He took ten boys and ten women. "The chief told me to come and look for you. Let's go."

They went, "*lik, lik, lik,*" and arrived in the land of the Mpele. Nkal took two boys and two women and hid them in the forest. He took the others to Evina. Together they went to the old woman.

Evina said, "Mother."

She replied, "Chief, you came?"

And he said, "Yes, I am here."

She asked, "So what do you have to say?"

And he said, "I am Evina, your son. Nobody will harm you as long as I live. These boys will clear your fields and construct houses for you. Those women will work in your fields; they will fetch you water, harvest your food, and prepare it."

She was satisfied. "Thank you. You did well."

She went to fetch her horns and her *bubuwa* and gave all of them to Evina. She covered him with saliva (benediction) and told him, "Go and make war; nobody will be able to resist you."

Evina and Nkal began the journey home: "*wou, wou, wou.*" When night fell, Evina preferred to sleep on the road and continue the next day. Nkal accepted. But in the night, when Evina slept, Nkal got up without any noise. He said to himself, "*Itombang,* will I return empty-handed? This will not happen. I'll go back to see the old woman."

He went to try his luck in his turn. It is like you, Pierre [the author]: you come to us and then you leave, taking the stories we told you with you.

Finally, Nkal arrived at the old woman's place.

She asked him, "Young man, why do you come back? You were here with your father, weren't you?"

He said, "That is true, but I came back. Make me the war—for me also."

She said, "I did make the war already, for you and for your father."

But he insisted, "No, you did it for my father. I want you to do it for me."

She said, "*Ho*, is it like this?"

And he continued, "Yes, it is like this. Don't talk to me any more, just make me the war now. It is me, Nkal Selek, who speaks to you."

So the old woman took her basket again and her horns to make the *bubuwa* for Nkal. She took the bamboo splinters from her basket and held them in the fire. Nkal swallowed them. Then she put the basket and the horns before him and said, "So, give me."

Nkal went to fetch the two young men and the women he had hidden in the forest. He said, "Old woman, take those."

But she did not accept. "You have to add."

Nkal said, "If I have to add, I give you my father Evina."

She accepted, gave him the basket, the horns, and her blessing, in the same way as she had given it to Evina: "Go, you will see that the war is yours."

Before dawn, Nkal was back where Evina slept. Together they went back to the village.

Nkal became a great warrior. He went from left to right, destroying all the villages. But Evina lost his strength and stayed at home. Throughout the region people cried Nkal's name. Sometime later, death took Evina.

The last lines of the story are crucial. They indicate that Nkal Selek had become so close to his new "father," Evina, that he could deliver

Evina to the witches just like a real kinsman. Evina had killed Nkal's father and had enslaved Nkal. But he had also integrated Nkal into his house and made the boy his *mwane mpaanze* (the child of his house). Apparently, this created enough intimacy to give Nkal a hold over Evina in the occult world. A basic theme in this story is the link between witchcraft and kinship.

Another basic theme, also emphasized above, is the ambiguity of these occult forces. The old woman had the *bubuwa* that made a man invincible in war. This is central to the story and, to the Maka, certainly a positive expression of the occult forces. But, in a more hidden way, the story also indicates that she was a dangerous witch who participated in the nightly cannibalistic practices of the witches; this is why she asked both Evina and Nkal for people in exchange for the *bubuwa*. Moreover, the story suggests that Nkal himself participated in this dark side of the *djambe* world. He delivered his "father" Evina to the witches in order to get the war fetishes. And, indeed, the whole expedition of Nkal, going back to the old woman in the dark of the night, smacks of *djambe*.

The result of Nkal's treason was Evina's death, as a victim of the witches. Thus, the end of the story illustrates a third theme mentioned above: that of the *djambe*'s basic insecurity. *Djambe* promises extra powers, but at the same time it makes people extra vulnerable. Evina had hoped to become invulnerable through the old woman's *bubuwa*. But her occult forces turned against him, exposing him to new dangers that became fatal.

During our next session, the same elder told me what happened after Evina's death.

On his death bed, Evina told Nkal that he had to take his place.[18] But the Mpang refused this: "No, the man who massacred our village and who led us into slavery is dead. Nkal, if you really have the power, you must bring us back."

At first, Nkal refused. But his companions forced him to swallow the *mempu*—powerful herbs that oblige you to respect a promise. So Nkal had to accept. At night they left secretly. When they arrived at the river, they lay in ambush on both sides.

The next morning, the Yebekolo discovered that Nkal Selek had left with his Mpang. They hurried to pursue them. They ar-

rived at the river. When they were in the middle, the Mpang attacked them from both sides. For a long time, the battle surged to
and fro [it remained undecided]. But finally, Nkal Selek threw
himself into the heat of the fight. He cried, "*Itombang,*" and a
flame sprang from his mouth. The Yebekolo panicked and fled.[19]
From then on, Nkal Selek and his Mpang terrorized the region.
They attacked the villages of the Mboans like those of the Ebessep
[two Maka groups], and even the Kaka villages far to the north.

The various versions of Nkal Selek's epic continue with stories about
subsequent confrontations between the Mpang and the Maka. The
main emphasis is on the terror inspired by Nkal Selek. In certain
stories, he risks being beaten; but even in difficult circumstances, he
succeeds in saving himself due to his superior war magic. Clearly,
Nkal Selek made a profound impression on the Maka. To them, it is
self-evident that such superiority can only be explained by a particularly strong *djambe le doomb.*[20]
    However, the story of his death indicates, again, the flip side of the
coin. It is much shorter than the epic of his rise:

> Nkal Selek did not die with us. One day, he went to make war with
> the Mpele, toward Nanga-Eboko. But it was his last expedition.
> He was killed, and the people danced around his body.

Moreover, several elders gave this last story a surprising twist. They
insisted that Nkal Selek had been killed by a woman. Even this hero,
the best armored of all warriors, could be killed by a woman. I asked
whether his famous *djambe le doomb* hadn't made him invulnerable
to her. One elder simply replied that "apparently, at this particular
moment, the *djambe* of this woman had been more powerful." And
he quoted the adage of the *djambe* having "neither father nor
mother, neither brother nor friend." Again, the conclusion is that
the *djambe* made Nkal Selek exceedingly powerful but also extra vulnerable. In the *djambe* world, nothing is certain: Nkal Selek could be
surprised even by a woman.

The Notables and the "Witchcraft of Authority"

The tension between fundamental equality and the emphatic show of personal ambition still marks village politics today. In the present-day context as well, the *djambe* serves as the ultimate explanation of both aspects. In this respect, there is a surprising continuity between Nkal Selek's story and the notables' performance as leaders of the *kaande* (village council) today. Just as in Nkal Selek's case, it is evident to the Maka that the superiority of a great notable can only be explained by the *djambe*. But in this case also, the *djambe* can easily prove to be some sort of an Achilles heel. Both aspects are illustrated by a precarious phase in the career of Mpal, the prominent notable of our village, already introduced above.

During a small palaver that did not seem to be very important, Mpal was suddenly attacked by Moboma, a young man from his own *grande famille*. The palaver was about a complaint by a woman who refused to be married to the brother of her deceased husband. The woman had called Moboma as a witness. Mpal clearly wanted to persuade—or even force—her to accept her new consort. But Moboma did not agree. He took the floor to oppose Mpal. However, his voice broke, and he suddenly stopped talking. Mpal profited from the opportunity to intervene and impose his interpretation of the case. But Moboma tried to start again. And once more, he got completely confused and was not able to continue. He left abruptly.

The next day, Moboma—who regularly did small chores in our house—came to reveal his feelings to us: "Did you see what happened? I could not utter a word. It was as if I was choking. My tongue was swollen and my throat was squeezed. That is the *djambe idjuga* (witchcraft of authority) of old Mpal. It is impossible to contradict him."

During the palaver Mpal had, as usual, displayed his rhetorical talents. Moreover, Moboma always had a tendency to stammer. So I was not that surprised that the latter had been overruled. But to Moboma himself, Mpal's oratory skills were not a sufficient explanation. The very fact that another villager could have such an

ascendancy over him could only have an occult reason—Mpal's
djambe idjuga.

Mpal himself suggested on several occasions that he disposed of
secret forces that raised him above other villagers. During one of his
sessions with me (most of these sessions had a large audience since
he insisted on having everything he said taped), he told me how he
had "eaten the *kaande:*"

If I am now a great *lesje kaande* [speaker in the council], it is because I always served the elders when I was young. Why does everyone listen to me when I begin to speak in the *kaande*? Because
Mpoam, my father [that is, an older brother of his biological fa-
ther] and Fuma [another notable of those days] taught me.
   When they left to hunt in the bush, they told me to come with
them. I was still small. They took a basket, filled it with food, and
put it on my back. I was still very small. On our way, they put
pieces of dry wood in my basket to make a fire. Sometimes I cried
because the basket became so heavy. When we arrived at the *sague*
[hut in the forest], they told me, "We will have a look at our traps.
Go make a fire and our beds, fetch water, and prepare the food."
   I worked until I was exhausted. When they returned, we ate.
Then we went to bed. I slept in Fuma's bed. He deloused my
head, and I scratched his lumps. While I was scratching him he
remained silent. But then, I took some *shu mijuw* [powder from
dried herbs] and rubbed it on his lumps, and he said, "Eem, this
is nice." Then he started to tell me the stories of his ancestors.
   He told me their birth [that is, the genealogy]. He taught me
the stories he used to tell in the *kaande*. Later, when I had grown
up, they gave me the *midu idjuga* [medicine of power]. They gave
me a mixture of herbs and bark. I had to chew it and spit it out.
Those were the wrong words. Then, they gave me another mixture with their saliva. I had to chew and then swallow it. Those
were the right words. This is why everybody has to listen to me
when I start to speak. If someone wants to talk back to me, his
throat will fill itself with dust, and he will be unable to utter a
word.

Mpal suggests here that the old notables showed him the way in the *djambe*. Thus he could "see" what his opponents were plotting. Because of the same force, people felt paralysed when they wanted to oppose him in the *kaande*. But even without such allusions, the villagers would be ready to believe in his *djambe idjuga*. A notable who displayed so much ascendancy during so many years had to be armored against the jealousy of the witches. Clearly, he himself had a well-developed *djambe* that he was able to control and use for strengthening his *idjuga* (authority).

Yet all this show of superiority proved to be balanced, in Mpal's case as well, by the leveling impact of village life. Just as in Nkal Selek's case, Mpal's ascendancy was not definitive. During a subsequent palaver, it became suddenly clear that even this *djambe idjuga* did not automatically guarantee Mpal's supremacy in the *kaande*. This palaver took place only a few weeks after Moboma had been so dramatically humiliated in the *kaande* by Mpal. It was clear that Moboma could not accept this defeat. He kept grumbling about Mpal's arrogance and contempt for people. And indeed, he got his chance when Mpal suddenly ran into difficulties during a subsequent palaver.

This palaver was once more about a conflict within Mpal's *grande famille*. But this time, quite unexpectedly, an accusation against Mpal himself emerged from the usual snowball of accusations. Supposedly, he had contributed to the conflict concerned since he had refused to pay a youngster of the family a certain sum he owed the youth. Apparently, Mpal had not foreseen that he himself would suddenly be the subject of the palaver. He began to defend himself with his usual eloquence, but it was clear that he was ill at ease.

This was Moboma's chance. He came forward and began, at first calmly, but then with more and more emphasis, to expose certain contradictions in what Mpal had said. Then he asked the *kaande* with a dramatic gesture whether a *lesje kaande* like Mpal should be allowed to tell lies in front of everybody. Moboma spoke with such assurance and was so evidently in the right that he received a general applause. And to my great surprise, this time

Mpal was not able to handle the situation. He started to speak again, but he could hardly make himself heard over the general din. Finally, he left abruptly, furiously clearing his way through the crowd with his stick.

Later, I asked Moboma why this time he had been able to resist Mpal's *djambe idjuga:* why hadn't his throat filled with dust? Moboma's reply was of a saintly simplicity: "Of course, he does have the *djambe idjuga,* but this time my indignation was stronger."

Subsequent events demonstrated even more clearly the flip side of this *djambe idjuga.* During the following months several boys died, one after the other, in Mpal's family. Immediately, rumors began to circulate that Mpal's overdeveloped *djambe* was behind these sad events. After all, everybody knows that elders may kill youngsters to prolong their own life and reinforce their energy—that is, their *djambe.* How else could one explain that old Mpal still had so much energy at his age? Didn't he himself boast of his powerful *djambe?* It was striking that these vicious rumors did not directly affect Mpal's prestige as *lesje kaande* (speaker in the council). He continued to dominate the *kaande* as before. And often, people returned from a palaver saying that Mpal had spoken very well.

The parallel with the personal ascendancy of the war heroes of olden days may be clear. Great notables like Mpal owe their superiority to their personal achievements: their rhetorical prowess, their courage, and the self-assurance with which they confront their adversaries.[21] The *djambe idjuga* (the ancestral secret knowledge) is supposed to be an indispensable support for maintaining their personal prestige. But despite this formidable armor, their ascendancy is never guaranteed. Just as a simple woman could kill the fearsome war leader Nkal Selek, because at that particular moment "her *djambe* had been stronger," so did young Moboma succeed in overruling the *djambe idjuga* of Mpal, the old notable, because this time his "indignation was stronger."

One can even say that the *djambe* armor—although strengthening the "big men" in certain respects—makes them more vulnerable in others. In principle, the *djambe idjuga* of a notable like Mpal is certainly a constructive expression of the *djambe.* However, it is linked to the dark core of these representations, the *djambe le njaw* (witch-craft of the house) that would have made Mpal "eat" his little neph-ews. To put it in more general terms: there is a direct link between *djambe* and power. That link inspires great respect, but it makes every leader suspect at the same time.

Conclusion

The *djambe* is like the shadow of politics, always there but difficult to grasp. Nonetheless, this chapter suggests certain general tendencies, even if they are vague.

First, the *djambe* tends to confirm the elders' authority. They have access to the *djambe idjuga* since they are closer to the ancestors, their wisdom, and their secrets. But we saw that even this "construc-tive" use of the *djambe* does not guarantee a definitive supremacy. It would be too simple to see witchcraft as an unequivocal support of gerontocracy.[22] After all, there are specific *djambe* forms in which the young are supposed to surpass their elders.[23] Even more important, this *djambe idjuga* of the elders does not render them immune to the leveling forces in the village. Often these leveling forces manifest themselves as emanations of the very same *djambe*. Mpal, the great notable, could be overruled in the council by a young man whose "indignation"—one could also say his *djambe*—was greater at that particular moment. A notable is never sure of being able to dominate in the *kaande*.

However, even though the old notables remain vulnerable, it is clear that, in general, the *djambe* tends to affirm their ascendancy. Due to their lifelong experience, they are supposed to know their way in the occult world much better than younger villagers. A Maka proverb conveys the occult threat contained in the elders' authority: "A child that bothers the elders will not live for long."

Another general trait, even more important for the present study, is that the close association of power and *djambe* betrays a deep mis-trust of any form of power in these societies. Like the *djambe*, power is always seen as suspect, not to say dangerous. Philippe Laburthe-Tolra (1977) formulates this very well for the neighboring Beti, whose *evu,* as noted above, closely corresponds to the *djambe* of the Maka: "The *evu* [witchcraft] seems to constitute the essence of Power." This implies that "absolute power is evil per se, or at least extremely frightening and mysterious." But it also means that "the *evu* is intimately linked to any exercise of political power" (my translation). Laburthe-Tolra concludes from this that society can hardly function without this dangerous power.[24]

This summarizes well the ambiguity of *djambe* in relation to politics and power. The examples quoted above indicate that the *djambe* offers an ambitious person extra possibilities to enhance his power. This is extremely important in a context, as in the Maka villages, where a leader's ascendancy is never guaranteed but must be proven at every new occasion. Yet, at the same time, the *djambe* indicates the limits to the accumulation of power since it is also an obvious means to curb overly ambitious persons. Within the village, even the best armored person is not immune to the leveling impact of the *djambe.* Even Nkal Selek, the Mpang superman, could be killed by a simple woman.

It remains to be seen whether the *djambe* can also serve to contain the new inequalities introduced by the state and the market.

WITCHCRAFT AND NATIONAL POLITICS:
THE PARADOXES OF THE NEW ELITE

4

The omnipresence of *djambe* (witchcraft) in Maka society derives from the particular context of a constant tension between an egalitarian ideology and highly inegalitarian practices. It follows that the emergence of new inequalities within Maka society since the colonial period constitutes a great problem for its members. It also follows that the Maka tend to understand these changes in terms of discourse on *djambe*.

We saw that in the 1950s and early 1960s new social distinctions emerged among the Maka. Decolonization and the departure of French administrators gave a new, educated elite access to important positions. Through this, unprecedented inequalities arose that undermined the old order. Since then, as elsewhere in Africa, the gap between the income levels of this new elite and those of the peasants has been quite marked.[1] But it is ultimately their political influence, and especially their access to state institutions, that distinguishes this new elite from the villagers. The pronounced authoritarianism of the Cameroonian state reinforces the distance between this elite and the rest of the population.

In the preceding chapter, I underscored the distance between local politics (the palavers of the village council, dominated by the elders) and new institutions of the state, represented by the *sous-préfet* and his gendarmes. At the start of my research, this distance seemed to be absolute: there appeared to be no points of contact between the lively political drama of the village palavers and the constrained authoritarian style of modern politics. There was also vicious political rivalry in the new institutions, but it was determined by "vertical" relations: competition was limited to the elites and hardly involved the villagers; the determining factor was the support of the highest echelon of the single-party. The fundamental logic of the Cameroonian regime was that all decisions were made by the president's entourage (this pertained, most notably, to the distribution of lucrative posts). Plotting among the elites to obtain the backing of those at the top was beyond the villagers, who were not even inclined to get involved. I already referred to their timeless adage: *La politique, c'est l'affaire des Grands* (Politics is the business of the "big men"). This was their excuse for cutting off all my attempts to discuss contemporary politics.

As my stay in the village carried on, I realized that I had to alter my original idea. It appeared that the villagers had their own ways of trying to enter new domains of power, but these were exercised at the margins of formal politics, dominated as it was by the authoritarianism of the postcolonial regime. A common strategy was to strive to establish client relations with members of the elite, especially with people from one's village who had careers in town (as one says in the village: "our sons who live in the city" or simply "our *évolués*"). The latter were assailed by the villagers with all sorts of demands: to intervene at the level of the administration or gendarmerie when a villager had problems, to secure employment for a young villager, and so on.

This clientelist strategy corresponds to the old Maka ethos that kin are the only reliable allies. Indeed, although well settled in the city, the *évolués* are still kin. But this also implies that *djambe* must play its role in these relations. This is, after all, another given in the Maka ethos: *djambe* is not only the dark side of kinship, it is also the discourse most apt to assail inequalities. These basic principles still apply, even to the novel relations between the new elite and villagers. It is not surprising, then, that, for the Maka, *djambe* and modern politics are closely related. Moreover, state authoritarianism reinforces this link by creating an atmosphere of undeclared competition that makes politics and occult forces hard to distinguish.

In his earlier writing on Cameroon, and on the state in Africa more generally, Jean-François Bayart has underscored the importance of "popular modes of political action," which subvert and limit state authoritarianism. In most African countries, the pressure of this authoritarianism is certainly real, and it is not clear that recent movements for democratization will really alleviate it. But Bayart shows that putting emphasis on authoritarianism does not necessarily imply—as many Marxist (or *Marxisant*) analyses of the 1970s suggested—that the popular masses are passive and incapable of initiative. In spite of pressure from above, popular modes of action do influence political developments. Often, they are not easily discernible; they are deployed on the margins of formal politics, in zones where they are not readily detected by the new rulers. Even if these strategies have an apolitical allure, they "weigh" on the state and on the regime's efforts to inscribe its "hegemonic project" in society (Bayart 1979, 1981, and 1989).

Bayart cites witchcraft—next to criminality, prostitution, and derision—as a good example of a popular mode that troubles the new rulers. This makes sense: occult forces are, by definition, hidden, which renders them extra efficacious in an authoritarian context. The intrigue and rumors that surround witchcraft always refer to secrets. Through this, the idiom creates a space, imaginary or not, that is beyond the state's authority.

This view of witchcraft as a popular mode of political action raises many questions, however. First, there is the question of its efficacy. If these popular modes are indeed effective by virtue of their being hidden, are they then practical alternatives to the authoritarian state? Or do they only exercise a diffuse pressure on new relations of domination? But it is especially the term *popular* itself that poses problems. When one labels witchcraft as popular, one is imprecise on two counts: witchcraft is vague by definition, the term *popular* is even more so. Does a force like *djambe* represent something popular for the Maka themselves? If one defines *djambe* as a popular mode of action, one instantly suggests that the elite is not involved.[2] Is this the case?

One might add that, for the villagers, members of the elite from their own community play a specific role in the crystallization of new inequalities. Therefore, speaking of the elite in general terms is erroneous. To be sure, the problem of new inequalities concerns the

politico-administrative elite in general. But a perspective "from below" reveals fundamental differences between the elites from the
village or region ("our sons who are in the city") and the others. In
the case of the Maka, their marginal position relative to the state is
such that the new elite of *originaires* is fairly limited. Nonetheless, a
certain number of *évolués* have been able to obtain important positions with decolonization and the concomitant Africanization of the
state apparatus. After independence, under the Ahidjo regime, the
rigid politics of "regional equilibrium" dictated that every region
(or ethnic group) had the right to a fixed number of positions. This
allowed the Maka elite to consolidate their position at the level of
the state. During the 1970s, almost every Maka village could boast
of one or many *évolués* who had access to the state.

These elites occupied a key position in the relationship between
the villagers and the state. For their former fellow villagers, they were
the obvious intermediaries in their relation to the new authorities.
But they also introduced new inequalities within the village itself.
The Maka, like other Africans, often call the new elites "whites."
This connotes that these people are viewed as the successors to the
whites ("the ones who follow the traces of the whites"); but it also
underlines the general idea that the new elites transgress old catego-
ries. From this perspective, the new elites from one's own village occupy an ambivalent position: they have become "whites" in light of
their new positions, but they remain members of the village community. Meke, my assistant, found a practical solution to this problem. When we spoke of Mr. Fuma, a "native" of his village who had
become a civil servant, he came to the following conclusion: "It's
true, he is a white in the city, in his office, but not when he is with
us." He thus summarized the ambivalent attitude of the villagers vis-
à-vis their own elites.

It is in relation to their own elites that the peasants have become
critically aware of the extent of new inequalities. These *originaires,*
who are the pride of the village, are also the privileged targets of the
villagers in their quest to overcome distances through clientelist relations or other strategies of more threatening tenor.

No wonder that it is again the ambiguity of *djambe* with respect
to power and inequality that is central to an understanding of the

impact of these notions on the role of the new elites. The *djambe* can not only affirm and reinforce power differentials but can also serve to reestablish the idea of a basic equality. The question posed by this chapter is whether the *djambe* is also capable of bridging the new distance between the state elites and the villagers. From the above, we can surmise that the elites who are *originaires* play a key part in this.

The Emergence of the New Maka Elite

The real authorities in the Maka villages are now "absentees": "our sons in the city" (or *nos Grands*)—that is, the eminent members of the urban elite who come from the village (see Geschiere 1982). The villagers always try to learn the elites' opinion in the event of important matters, and they are the only ones who can order people around when they visit the village. This situation is not particular to the Maka region. It is now generally accepted that life in an African village can only be understood in terms of the determining role of city folk.[3] The work of Joseph Gugler on this subject is of particular interest due to its historical depth. In a study of the Ibo of eastern Nigeria during the 1960s (Gugler 1971), he shows how, on the one hand, city-dwellers made considerable efforts to maintain ties with their native village while, on the other hand, the village community employed an array of sanctions to make them respect their obligations to their hometown. At the end of the 1980s, Gugler returned to the same region. In this second study (1991), he noted that despite the fact that a good part of the urban population was now born in the city, the city-dwellers' participation (including the elites) in the life of the village had even increased.

This continuous engagement in the affairs of the home village is a generalized phenomenon in Africa. But there are significant regional variations in the patterns of relations that developed between city-dwellers and their former fellow villagers. Gugler shows how Ibo villages impose penalties on urbanites if the latter neglect their obligations (if, for instance, they do not participate in the annual village festival or fail to construct a house in the village). But such sanctions

seem hardly necessary among the Ibo since most city-dwellers go to
great lengths to make large investments in the village. The situation
is quite different among the Maka, for whom the link between urban
elites and the village is as important, but more ambiguous. Members
of the urban elite often claim that, despite their attachment to the
village, they are obliged to keep their distance. And it is clear that the
villagers, for their part, have no sanctions for the punishment of reti-
cent urbanites.

> In 1991, I returned from a quick visit to "my" Maka village. As
> usual, the car was packed because everyone wanted to take the
> opportunity to go to Yaunde for free. On the road, we passed the
> village of the Maka minister (with the politics of "regional equi-
> librium," the Maka have had one minister in the past successive
> cabinets). One of the passengers pointed out the minister's house
> to me, and a lively discussion ensued. Everyone agreed that it was
> a "miserable" building. A woman said that when the minister re-
> ceived visitors from afar, he was obliged to house them in the
> Catholic mission in the next village. Until then, he had not gone
> to the trouble of building a suitable house in the village. She con-
> cluded loudly, and with applause from the other passengers, "Ah,
> the Maka big men don't do anything for their village. They don't
> invest a thing. They are so rich, but they spend their money on
> drink and women; and nothing for the village. So, how can we
> have development here?"

For the Maka, especially the youth, complaining about the indiffer-
ence of the Maka elites has become commonplace. They contrast
their elites with the elites of other communities (with special mention
of the Bamileke of the West), who are said to take better care of their
native regions.

Unfortunately, we still lack comparative material on different patterns in the relations between urbanites and villagers. Variations in
these relations have important implications, for instance, for understanding regional differences in the nature and coherence of ethnic
networks or in new modes of accumulation of wealth and power.
These personal links between the urban elites and native villagers

have played a crucial role in the construction of ethnic networks that parallel the increase of scale in political and economic relations. But the examples of the Maka and the Ibo indicate that there are considerable differences in the content of these exchanges. Such variations must have significant consequences for "ethnicity" or new modes of accumulation. Moreover, these differences must have deepened over the last decade with the degradation of the state and the increased preoccupation with private entrepreneurs by the development establishment.

The variable relations between the urban elites and villagers may also shed light on different possible articulations between discourses on witchcraft and contemporary politico-economic changes. Among the Maka, and surely not only them, the *évolués* dominate villagers' speculations about the impact of *djambe* on modern politics and the accumulation of wealth. At the same time, they play an important part in "modernizing" *djambe*. There is good reason, therefore, to further explore the particular characteristics of the new Maka elite.

Who are these Maka *Grands,* and why are the villagers so unhappy with them? During the 1970s, the contours of this elite were still quite clear. They were a small and well-defined group of people who, in the years following independence and with the help of diplomas, had shining careers in the civil service (in the territorial administration or in the ministries at Yaunde, in education or public health). Often they combined these positions with important posts in the "unified party." The distinguishing mark of this new elite was that they were all functionaries. Apparently, the chances for success as private entrepreneurs were quite limited for the Maka.[4]

Common to the careers of all these Maka *Grands* was that they were built on school diplomas. Having a diploma was essential to becoming a functionary. In the Maka region, access to education increased dramatically after World War II. For the first-generation elites, who were born in the 1920s and 1930s, the simple fact of having attended school was still exceptional, being the result of particular circumstances: for instance, because the parents sought to avoid forced labor by taking refuge at the mission, where children were obligated to go to school. In those days, the French still had to coerce parents into sending children to school. The Cameroonian author Mongo Beti illustrates this sorry situation: "Do you remember the era? Fathers took their children to school like one pushes cattle toward the slaughterhouse . . . these pitiful young children! Helped by distant kin, or their fathers' vague relations, undernourished, famished, thrashed all day long by ignorant monitors, dazed by books that presented a universe with no resemblance to their own [. . .] that was us, do you remember?" (Beti 1957, 231; my translation).

There is good reason for this last question, "Do you remember?" At the time when Mongo Beti was penning these lines, these pitiful youngsters, who finally had obtained their diplomas, were well on the road to dazzling careers. With decolonization, the Africanization of the public service sector, and independence, scores of positions became vacant while there were few educated candidates to fill them. During this time, a career like that of Ahmadou Ahidjo, a postal worker who became president, was perfectly conceivable.

The Maka elites all climbed rapidly in their careers during this period. In this region, where education was a relatively late development, fairly modest qualifications sufficed for impressive positions. People always said that Raymond Malouma—the big Maka politician who monopolized the position of Member of Parliament for the region during the 1960s and 1970s and who even sat on the national political bureau of the single-party—had never finished primary school. Clearly, the advent of the first generation of Maka elites was marked by remarkable social mobility. But it was also tainted with great uncertainty. The biographies of the Maka *Grands* reveal that their careers were full of surprises. Several of them were still astonished that the young men who opted for the territorial administration had made such spectacular careers. During the 1950s, at least according to my informants, this entrance examination was much less esteemed than those for the teaching or health professions. In these latter domains, even young Cameroonians could take on serious responsibilities whereas, in the administration, they would always remain subordinates. "And now, they are the ones who command us," lamented several of my interlocutors (all of whom worked, evidently, in other sectors).[5]

The villagers of the same generation are still somewhat astonished by their former classmates, who have had such fast-paced careers. In the past, school was said to be a place "where the instructor had to hit the fingers of the children so as to make them more flexible for writing." Only later, when young graduates had monopolized enviable jobs, did people understand that "school was progress." Indeed, the unexpected success of these first pupils inspired a radical reevaluation of teaching. Since the 1950s, school has become sacrosanct for the Maka. The villages compete fiercely to have their own schools, and almost all children attend school for at least a few years. In 1970, education rates in all the villages of the Maka district where I lived were already above 70 percent (and for most villages, even above 90 percent).[6] The consequence was the much discussed devaluation of diplomas. Today, the criteria for starting a profession become ever higher. Even those with university diplomas, which are still rare in this region, have great difficulty finding employment.

At the same time, social stratification has become more complex. The gap between the elites and the villagers, which was so marked at the beginning of the 1970s, has been mitigated by the emergence of a subelite since a considerable number of younger persons have managed to obtain positions in the civil service (most notably in the army and police force, which until recently were considered less prestigious). Thus, relations between the villagers and the urban elites have become more graduated. Nevertheless, the special status of the "true big people"—school directors, doctors, and, especially, politicians or civil servants who have *postes de commandement*—still translates into clear distinctions in modes of consumption, even when they visit the village. The houses the elites build are in another class than the rest (even though villagers laugh at their avarice). Many have installed electric generators (reserved for their own use) or have cars. Most of all, though, their lifestyles are different or, as the villagers say, "more civilized," including such luxury items as tableware and expensive clothing.

The main characteristic of relations between the villagers and the elites is their ambivalence. Obviously, the villagers are proud of the success of "their" elites. After all, they do call them "our sons in the city." But, as we have seen, they immediately add that their "sons" neglect the village. The elites, for their part, brag about their village, but they also complain about the "impossible village mentality." And both the villagers and the *évolués* cite the Bamileke as the prime example of a community where relationships are better organized. The villagers say that, among the Bamileke, the elites really take care of the village, while the Maka elites lament that, elsewhere, people show "more respect."

What are the causes of this disquiet? From a politico-economic point of view, relations between the Maka villagers and their elites seem, indeed, not well balanced. It is quite clear why the villagers have every reason to maintain these relations. As one might expect, they try, in all sorts of ways, to profit from the wealth (immense, in their eyes) of the new elites. But more important still is the access the elites can give them to public services. This is, above all, what gives the elites a monopoly position vis-à-vis the villagers. Under the one-party state—or, to use the now defunct official Cameroonian idiom, the "unified party"—political institutions offered the villagers little possibility of expressing their interests and wishes. This is why the villagers try to push their sons in the city, in keeping with the Maka principle that kin is the basis of alliance, into some sort of role as "brokers." They expect their elites to defend the interests of the village at the level of the state; for instance, these elites should procure a school or clinic for the village, assist the villagers in case of problems with gendarmes, find work for them in the city, help them obtain scholarships, and so forth.

The Maka elites bemoan these demands and supplications, always maintaining that, after all, their own true interests are not in the village. And indeed, the economic advantage of their links with the village is not quite apparent. There is still no regular practice of wage labor in the Maka villages. For the villagers, it goes without saying that a young man would always prefer to have his own plantations, which is possible to the extent that there is available land.[7] Moreover, relationships in the village are so heavily dominated by the notion of kinship that it is almost impossible to hire outside labor for long periods of time. In the end, this always brings problems, such as brawls and witchcraft accusations. One consequence is that the few Maka elites who have tried to profit from their access to village land by creating larger plantations are always confronted with a serious labor problem, like the French colonists before them.[8] In the 1970s, people recounted, as some sort of a joke, the story of a former secretary of state who wanted to create cocoa plantations on a very large scale. In the end, he was forced to recruit Pygmies, who "belonged" to his village, as workers. For the Maka, it was self-evident that Pygmies, being born hunters, would not work for long on the plantations. Sooner or later they would disappear into the forest. And indeed, the plantations of this *évolué* were a great disaster. The mere fact that the secretary of state had to use Pygmies as laborers is an indication of how difficult it is for the Maka elite to invest their earnings in the cash-crop economy of the village. Under such circumstances, the general opinion that investments in the city (such as building houses or running taxis) are more profitable may very well be justified.

It is also clear that, from a political point of view—at least until the elections of the 1990s—the support of the villagers mattered little, even for those who had serious political ambitions. Under the one-party state, villagers could only confirm the list of candidates decided by the national party bureau. Elections were completely ritualized as symbolic expressions of popular support. There were only "yes" bulletins, and usually there was no secret ballot for lack of polling booths. Those who refused to vote did not receive a stamp on their party card. This meant that they were exposed to constant harassment by gendarmes during the frequent controls. This was the time when villages could boast of having voted "103.60 percent yes" (counting the votes of the unregistered) because it was well understood that the villages with the highest percentages would be well treated by the *sous-préfet*. Politicians were even dissuaded from cultivating popular support in the villages. They were warned explicitly that such efforts would only serve to create division, whereas the party insisted, above all, on unity. National ideology reiterated, over and over, that the entire population was to be united behind the president. There was no place for personal political machines—politicians were reminded time and again that they owed their investiture to the party and not to their popularity. Consequently, the fierce competition among elites for desirable positions unfurled above the heads of the villagers. Politicians were obliged to turn their back on the villagers insofar as the decisive factor of their success was at the summit of the party. In such a political configuration, the villagers' support was indeed of little importance to the *évolués* who harbored political ambitions.

Why, then, do the elites maintain such an interest in the home village? Apparently, emotions play an important role. But there as well, ambiguity reigns. Members of the elite always insist that, for them, links to the village have no direct interest, that they only perpetuate them out of respect for their kin. Even if the villagers drive them to despair, how could they abandon their kin? Yet this emotional bind does have a concrete basis. Most elites profess that they will one day return to the village to retire, but it is not certain that they will do so. Most of them also say that life in the village has become too rough for them; during their vacations in the village, they complain of everything—noise, lack of comfort, the food—and often return to the city after just a few days. In the East, a few *évolués* did return recently to the region to retire, but they chose to establish themselves in small towns, not the villages.[9]

This aversion to village life has deeper reasons than mere physical discomfort. Certain *Grands* admitted to me that they were afraid of the village. Several used the same phrase: "You have to keep your distance because, otherwise, you risk being *eaten* by the villagers." As we have seen, the word *eat* is full of meaning. This fear of being "eaten" could mean that the elites fear being plundered by the villagers and their constant demands. But there is also the reference to the world of *djambe* and the *minjindjamb* (witches), which are motivated primarily by the desire to "eat" people. It is again this backdrop of *djambe,* which seems to be omnipresent in the village, that makes the elites prudent in their relations with the villagers.

However, it would be overly simplistic to assume that threats of *djambe* only come from the villagers, despite the elites' pretensions. *Djambe* introduces its inherent ambiguity also into the rapport between the urban elites and the villagers. Here also, again, *djambe* is not merely a weapon of the weak against the strong but also a weapon of the powerful themselves. Indeed, it is through the *djambe* that one can capture the complexity of these relations.

The *Djambe:* A Popular Mode of Political Action?

The distance between the villagers and the elite is a reflection of the gap between local and national politics. The villagers have their own ways of suggesting that their contribution to high-level politics is minimal, and that there is still a great distance between them and the new "whites," such as the current comment: "We are like women here; anytime somebody from the town comes to order us around, all we can say is "yes." Such notions of distance and submission influence even their interactions with the elites of their own village, who have an exceptional degree of authority over their former fellow villagers: unlike the village chiefs or the elders, when the elites give orders to villagers, they are obeyed. That is only logical; the villagers know that they depend, in myriad ways, on their elites, especially on their capacity to intervene with the authorities.

However, there are other sides to this relationship. The villagers also recount how they are exploited by their own elites: they claim that they have worked in the plantations of the elites without compensation, or that the *évolués* promised them lodging while they were in the city but used them as unpaid domestics. The moral of these stories is always the same: a villager has no sway over the *évolués*.

Obviously, the actual situation cannot be reduced to this facile image of radical distance between the village world and that of the urban elites. The villagers have their own strategies for accessing state institutions, and these target the *évolués*. As noted previously, the people of the village mobilize discourse on kin to oblige their successful family members ("our sons who work in the city") to serve as intermediaries. And it is through these intermediaries that kin and *djambe,* as basic elements of local political life, enter into national politics.

It took me a certain amount of time to understand that the interaction between village politics and state politics was much more complex than the simple opposition between authority and obedience put forth by both elites and villagers. I had a sort of revelation when friends from the village told me the "truth" about the mysterious illness and healing of Mr. Fuma, one of the elites of our village:

During the 1970s, "Monsieur Fuma" enjoyed great prestige in the village due to his important political contacts. In the early 1950s, he was one of the first Maka people to earn a secondary school certificate. Afterward, he became a public servant; first he was a school instructor, then a school inspector. More importantly, after independence, he obtained a series of important positions in the regional section of the "unified party," the UC, later renamed the UNC. Because of his political weight, people deemed Fuma a *grand patron*. Fuma returned to the village regularly, especially during holidays. In 1971, when I interviewed him, he was a quadragenarian; he was very formal and often very tense. Even in the village, among his own people, he never seemed to relax. Other elites rejoiced at the villagers' conspicuous signs of respect. Fuma always kept his distance.

In the village, everyone knew why he had this reserved manner. During the 1960s, Fuma retired temporarily to the village because of certain political problems in the city. Some months later, he fell victim to an undetermined but persistent illness. In his conversations with me, Fuma would never speak about his illness, but he implied that witchcraft had played a role. First, he consulted Western doctors, but he quickly understood that Western medicine was powerless against such an illness. Then, he visited several *onkong* (healers). Finally, a *nkong* who lived among the Djem (forty miles away) cured him. Fuma then left the village to live again in the city.

Fuma did not want to explain to me what sort of witchcraft and which sort of witches had attacked him, but the villagers liked to gossip about the affair. According to them, the witches had prepared *kulekwak* (a mix of herbs and saliva) and put it on the path behind Fuma's house. A few days later, Fuma walked on it, and the *kulekwak* entered his body. Evidently, Fuma had his own defenses in the world of the *djambe*. His wife claimed in public that, when thieves came to rob their house, they did not find anything because Fuma's *bufe* (amulets) had blinded them. Apparently, this protection was not sufficient against the *kulekwak*. Witches had "broken" the force of his amulets and would have surely killed him if the Djem *nkong* had not, in his turn, broken their powers.

The villagers added that the protection of Fuma's *bufe* could only have been broken by attackers from within his own household. For them, Fuma's illness was, once more, proof of the terrible force of *djambe le njaw* (witchcraft of the house). As always in witchcraft affairs among the Maka, it was almost impossible to deduce from the flow of rumors who the true instigators of the attack might have been. But there were a few direct allusions to Fuma's cousins, who wasted their meager income from their cocoa plantations on great quantities of palm wine. Their motive was said to have been jealousy, as is almost always the case. When the *sous-préfet* visited the village, Fuma offered him a grand banquet, but he refused to let his drunk cousins attend. For them, this meant that Fuma's relationship with the *sous-préfet* was more important than his relationship with his own kin. This is why they delivered him to the *minjindjamb* (witches).

I discussed at length this case, as well as others, with the villagers and members of the elite. As one might suspect, they offered greatly divergent interpretations. For several villagers, such stories were examples of how *djambe* could serve as a weapon against the new elites. According to them, the moral of these stories was that the elites had better share their new riches; otherwise, the jealousy of their kin could prove fatal. This implies that the *djambe* is indeed a sort of "popular mode of political action," to repeat Bayart's expression. However, the problem remains that this mode of action is often so diffuse as to make it impossible to know whether something "really" happened. It is already impossible to discern concrete actors, let alone to know if they "really" acted against their supposed victim. In the case of Fuma's illness, for instance, the belief that his cousins were the guilty parties was only one of numerous hypotheses put forth by my informants.

This is typical with regard to *djambe,* especially when novel power relations are at stake. I made reference, above, to the functionaries' diatribes against the villagers who supposedly ruin everything with their witchcraft. Here again, it is often impossible to verify whether someone really acted against the government and its projects. One often has the impression that it is only because the new elites insist on the "subversive" nature of *djambe* that it takes on such characteristics. As indicated earlier, *djambe* is extremely malleable, lending itself to all sorts of uses and interpretations. It is not clear that *djambe*, in itself, stands in opposition to relations of domination, be they old or new. But the functionaries' discourse establishes an image of the *djambe* as a force of contestation against the State and new inequalities. The very invisibility that prevents one from knowing if *djambe* is, indeed, a "popular mode of action" directed against the new elites also explains why the elites feel so threatened by these occult forces.

Jean-François Bayart (1981, 1990) suggests that, under authoritarian regimes, popular modes of political action are expressed most often in the margins of the formal political domain, since this is controlled, and even defined, by those who dominate. Popular modes of action are all the more effective when expressed in elusive, intangible, or even invisible forms. This is certainly the case for *djambe*, as for witchcraft more generally. All the examples related herein show how difficult it is to locate, and hence capture, actors in the domain of the occult. The impressive disciplinary apparatuses used by the state and the elite for protection are powerless in this context. Fuma, for example, did not even try to take action against his cousins. His *nkong* was supposed to have evened the score in nocturnal confrontations between witches without there necessarily being notable effects in the daytime world. It is through this invisibility that *djambe* escapes state authoritarianism and profoundly marks the formation of new relations of power. For the elites, *djambe* is an omnipresent but diffuse force emanating from the village and menacing their new positions.

But even if the *djambe*, as a popular mode of action, has real effects in the daytime world, it often works in ways contrary to the villagers' intentions. The pressure of occult forces hardly seems to reinforce links with the elites. On the contrary, it tends to keep them at a distance. When I spoke to members of the elite about cases like Fuma's illness, they gave explanations that differed strongly from those offered by the villagers (to whom the whole affair confirmed that the elites should respect their obligations to share with kin). But to Fuma's colleagues, the moral was, rather, that one should keep a distance from the village in order to avoid being a victim of these leveling forces. From their viewpoint, it was Fuma's own fault for having returned to the village. If one ventures too far in the intimate sphere of the village, one becomes exposed to the terrible danger of *djambe le njaw* (witchcraft of the house). This is the deep significance of the elites' expression that they feared being "eaten" by the villagers.

What is new is that the urban elites can actually maintain such a distance. The old war heros or the old *lesje kaande* (notables) had to live among their brothers; even if they were heavily armored (*blindés*), they were still vulnerable to the egalitarian force of *djambe*. This is not the case for the new elites. Being based in the city, they are relatively protected from the occult forces of the village. The very idea that *djambe*, as an egalitarian force, impacts upon new inequalities increases their reticence. Doubtless, this is one reason why the Maka villagers complain that their elites do so little for the village.

The efficacy of *djambe* as a popular mode of action seems, then, quite limited. While these notions clearly have a certain leveling effect, their impact on new inequalities is limited. The *djambe* does not seem to offer an alternative model for action. Perhaps there is a basic paradox to such modes of political action. Effective because they are invisible, these modes are hardly capable (precisely because they are so diffuse) of being vehicles for a "counterproject" (Bayart 1981).

One might also wonder whether *djambe* can even be characterized as a *popular* mode of action? The examples cited show that it is not a force reserved for the villagers. The elites make use of it also, and often with more success. Fuma's wife bragged, for example, about the exceptional force of his *bufe* (amulets) that supposedly blinded thieves. And the story of Fuma's illness shows that, while his kin could threaten him, he found an ally in the *djambe*, who eclipsed the forces of the villagers. The Djem *nkong* who broke the spell was generally considered to be a sort of "super" *nkong* against whom the powers of a simple villager were of no avail.

The new power relations that engendered the new elites also transformed notions of witchcraft and its practices. For the Maka, the most formidable occult weapons are now the "lightning" of the Hausa (a Muslim group in the North) and techniques borrowed from the West.[10] And people who live in the city are said to have access to these new arms. This urban witchcraft culture is, moreover, increasingly commercialized or, better yet, "commodified." The *bufe* (fetishes) are sold on the market, and witch doctors sell their services to the highest bidder.[11] Obviously, members of the new elite have much more money than villagers. And indeed one can hear them bragging to the villagers about how they have become invulnerable to village *djambe* because they are able to procure the services of the best *onkong*. The villagers, for their part, affirm that they are in fact powerless against such strong occult forces. Cases like that of Fuma, who exposed himself to occult forces in the village because he got too close to his kin, are considered exceptional.

Thus the leveling side of the *djambe* certainly affects new relations of domination; it gives these reports their dangerous hue. This is why the new elites admit to being afraid of the villagers; it is why the *sous-préfet* thinks it is necessary to always be vigilant in the face of the villagers' tendency toward "subversion" and their use of the occult to sabotage government projects. But the other side of the *djambe,* its "accumulative" side, is also very present in relations between the new elites and villagers. Modern transformations of *djambe* discourse express quite clearly the idea that the elites' power is of an unprecedented scale, that it exceeds past limits. Being based in the city, the new elites can avoid the leveling pressures of *djambe.* Moreover, their wealth gives them access to occult forces that largely surpass the village *djambe.* In relations between the villagers and the new elites, *djambe* is certainly not only a popular mode of political action. It seems, instead, that this discourse serves to affirm the new distance separating villagers from their "sons in the city."

The New Elite and the "Modernity" of Witchcraft

Witchcraft not only dominates relations between the new elite and villagers, it also marks elite behavior and their struggles in the arena of modern politics. This may seem surprising, insofar as political competition in modern settings differs radically from local political processes. Nonetheless, witchcraft remains, for both elites and villagers, the preferred discourse when it comes to interpreting the vicissitudes of modern politics. The question is the extent to which these longstanding concepts have undergone specific transformations by accommodating new forms of power and politics.

As in most African countries, national politics has practically no forebears in Cameroon. The colonial government imposed a narrowly defined bureaucratic regime that gave no place to formal politics, and certainly not for Cameroonians. Only at the very end of the colonial period did the government allow for some semblance of national political life: representative assemblies were created and elections organized, which immediately gave rise to vigorous political competition. But in Cameroon, as elsewhere on the continent, this was nipped in the bud by the creation of a one-party system during the first years of independence. At the time of the proclamation of independence (1960), parties proliferated.[12] By 1962, there remained only one, the *Union Camerounaise* (UC; later renamed the *Union Nationale Camerounaise* or UNC) of the first president, Ahmadou Ahidjo. Through a skillful management of coercion and coaptation, the other parties were quickly swallowed by the prevailing UC.

Certain particularities of the political climate established by Ahidjo's regime can be understood only with reference to the historical circumstances of independence. At the end of the 1940s, the French confronted a radical opposition movement, the *Union des Populations du Cameroun* (UPC) led by Um Nyobe. In 1955, this movement pursued, with some success, a guerilla operation first in southern and then western Cameroon. After some maneuvering, the French promoted Ahidjo, one of the better educated representatives of the North, as prime minister; they hoped that he would be a more "cooperative" leader. Apparently, the French viewed Ahidjo as a figure of transition who, once the UPC resistance was quashed, would give way to a leader from the South, the more developed part of the colony. However, once in power, Ahidjo demonstrated unexpected tactical prowess and consolidated his position in power. The French finally transmitted the helm of the state of Cameroon to him in 1960. In the following years, Ahidjo was able, with the active support of the French, to suppress the UPC resistance, along with all other forms of opposition.

But the specter of the UPC continued to haunt Cameroonian political life. Up until the 1980s, Ahidjo constantly evoked the bloody consequences of this divisive moment so as to incite the population to unite behind the president, the "Father of the nation." National ideology, repeated endlessly during party meetings, preached "unity" and the "duty for continuous vigilance" against "subversion" that loomed everywhere. The effects of this bleak but persistent propaganda should not be underestimated. The Manichean logics of this ideology ("unity" versus "subversion," hyphenated by "vigilance") informed the emergent political culture. One of the key terms used by the regime was the necessity to better *encadrer* (organize in a military sense) the population. All forms of association that escaped the confines of the single-party were strictly forbidden: they unsettled the idea of unity. Even the founding of a checkers club by a few boys in the village where I lived in the early 1970s was interpreted as an act of subversion and provoked an energetic intervention by the gendarmes. The population was supposed to *militer* (militate) only under the aegis of the UNC.[13]

In the party itself, there was no delegation of power, and this was justified, again, by the call for unity behind the president. The latter was presumed to represent the "healthy and legitimate ambitions" of the nation, and so it was hardly necessary to consult the population.[14] In keeping with this postulate, all decisions were made at the top; even for lower positions in the politico-administrative hierarchy, candidates were designated by the party leadership without any popular consultation. The responsibility for the execution of directives from on high lay with the territorial administration, the backbone of the regime.

This heavy emphasis on the administration and the lack of input from below meant that the party organization, which formed an impressive structure on paper, had no specific function to perform. At the different levels of the hierarchy, party leaders were supposed to uphold the actions of the administrative authorities (governors, *préfets,* and *sous-préfets*), which was a most unrewarding job. In general, these delegates remained in the shadows while the bureaucrats were, in the eyes of the population, the real representatives of state power. In practice, the only real function of the party organization was that of an intelligence service: at all levels, members were held to be "vigilant." Otherwise, it functioned as a network for political mobility. Under President Ahidjo and, more recently, Biya, the party was the only path for ambitious individuals who aspired to a political career. Since all political activity outside the party was strictly prohibited, intense competition between aspiring politicians took place within the party.

Ahidjo, at the summit of the party, sought to control this competition in all sorts of ways. One of the secrets of his success was his political program of *équilibre régional* (regional equilibrium). The history of his own party, the UNC, is characteristic in this respect. Ahidjo founded the party as the UC in 1958, after being designated prime minister by the French. It was only through this position that he was able to integrate most of the northern politicians into the party. But he also tried, from the beginning, to give it national scope by coopting elites from other regions. Through this, he was able to carry the crucial elections of 1960. From then on, Ahidjo maintained the principle of a more or less equal partition of party and government positions between the different regions of the country. Certain key posts were reserved for "his" Fulbe coethnics from the North, but the regime offered ambitious politicians from all other regions the possibility for mobility within the hierarchy.

Cooptation of the elites gave the party a wide base. But one of the disadvantages of this system of cooptation was that quarrels, often longstanding and tenacious, between established regional leaders became an essential part of the party as well. In the Maka region, for example, the regional committees of the party seemed to break apart quite regularly due to personal disputes that sometimes dated back to the colonial era. The party leadership always tried to appease these conflicts by insisting on the duties of all politicians to unite behind the "Father of the nation." For the villagers, these conflicts were shrouded in mystery: rumors circulated in the villages about violent confrontations between politicians; then, a black Mercedes would drive through—the status symbol of the Maka MP who, during the 1970s, also sat on the party's national political bureau; and people said that the troublemakers would have to pipe down. That was the extent of it for the villagers; only the very curious among them continued to speculate about what really happened.

The regional politicians were repeatedly reminded by their superiors that the continuity of their positions depended on the good will of the summit. The national political bureau (in essence, the president's confidants) selected candidates for all levels. As noted above, elections were organized in such a manner that voters could only approve of the party's choice. Popular support was not really important for a candidate. It was even risky for a politician to try to mobilize voters behind his name. His colleagues from the same region, who usually coveted his position, could alert his superiors to his *abus de fonction de façon politique* (political abuse of his function)—that is, his attempt to create a personal clientele, which was seen as an act of subversion since it "perturbed the unity of the population behind the president." [15]

All these factors complicated political competition at the regional level. Motives for dissension were not lacking—old quarrels intertwined with competition for new posts—but these conflicts were fought out behind closed doors. The party summit insisted, above all, that these disputes remain hidden so as not to tarnish the image of the "unified party." Therefore, the protagonists were certainly not encouraged to seek support within the populace. Conflicts were to be resolved *"en petit comité,"* and politicians were never to forget that their futures depended entirely on the favors of the summit.

A particular consequence of the logics of regional equilibrium was that politicians had to fear potential competition from within their entourage much more than from their colleagues from other regions. Each region (in practice, each ethnicity) had the right to a fixed number of high-level positions; thus a politician or high civil servant could normally be replaced only by someone from his own group. Competition did not ensue between elites from different ethnic groups, then, but rather among those of each group.

Furthermore, decisions were made at the top in an abrupt and unpredictable, if not capricious, manner. They still are. Often, functionaries or politicians learn about their promotions or disfavor on the radio. This is why, everywhere in Cameroon, civil servants are riveted to their radio for the news at one o'clock. This manner of communicating elicits the omnipotence of the summit of the regime—the president's direct entourage—and aggravates the insecurity of those who depend on the state.

All this creates, indeed, a striking parallel between the political climate engendered by the Ahidjo regime and the occult world of
witchcraft: both are worlds of uncertainty and violent but secret confrontations. Most of all, one fears primarily the treason that comes
from within.

In the Maka region, the most spectacular example of the uncertainties of modern politics is the brutal fall of Jean Mabaya in
1962. Mabaya had been the uncontested leader of the East and
could boast of an impressive career. But he was pushed aside by a
simple decision made by President Ahidjo.

Previously, Mabaya was introduced in a fairly strange context:
Mendouga, the healer, recounted how she had been initiated by
her "professor." The climax of the story was the moment when
her professor sent her to the *mindjim* (the dead, but also the spirits of witches). There, she met Mabaya! She always laughed at this
memory, and especially at the image of his perplexed face when
she said to him that she suddenly understood why he told the
people that the phantoms in the forest would vote for him (this
was a famous expression that the villagers always attributed to Mabaya when they spoke of his electoral victories). Indeed, Mabaya
won a long series of elections in the 1950s and early 1960s. For
the villagers, it was clear that this success resulted from the support
of the occult.

Jean Mabaya was the son of the district chief of Motchebum.
His political career began in 1952 when he won a big victory in
the elections for the ARCAM (*Assemblée régionale du Cameroun*,
established by the French in 1946). In this victory, Mabaya brushed
aside the old deputy, Effoudou, one of the two paramount chiefs
of the Maka. This changing of the guard was significant. Effoudou
was an old-style chief; he got on well with the French (in a colonial
report he is described as "very flexible, in hand, he follows our
orders to the letter"[16]). And the support of the colonial government was the main cause of his being elected deputy in the first
elections in 1948. Mabaya was also a chief (he had succeeded his
father), but of another caliber. In the 1930s, he was the first son
of the East to earn a primary school diploma. After this, he worked
in many parts of Cameroon as a catechist and instructor. He was

fiercely opposed to the French, perhaps as a result of his experiences in other parts of the colony. The mere fact that he was
elected in 1952 was a defeat for colonial interests and a sign that
even in the East Province—often thought of as isolated and backward—things were changing.

As a deputy in Maka country, the most populated part of the
East Province, Mabaya played a crucial role in the formation of
political parties during the 1950s. He followed a simple strategy
of associating himself with the party that was in power in Yaunde:
first Mbida's Democrats; then, after Mbida's demise in 1958, the
Action nationale of Assalé, who represented the South in the government.[17] But even before the decisive 1960 elections, he rallied
with the UC of Ahidjo, who was then consolidating his control
over the state. During this time, Mabaya played a central role in
the expansion of the UC (until then, essentially a northern party)
in the East Province. My informants still remembered the way in
which he had traveled the entire region to found cells and committees for the party.

This simple strategy had its rewards. Under Ahidjo's regime,
Mabaya was compensated for his support with important positions. At independence in 1960, he was named president of the
new National Assembly. In the discussions I had with him in the
early 1970s, he always bragged that, at this time, he was the second person in Cameroon, after the president. He even told me
about how, when he was on an official visit in Europe, the Germans gave his name to a large warboat. Later, he became minister
of war and then agriculture.

In 1962, a dramatic turnaround came to pass. Mabaya was relieved of all his functions and put in prison. After several months,
he was released, but this was the end of his political career: he was
forced to retire to his native village. For the villagers, the occult
forces of his Baka ("Pygmy") wife were the sole cause of his fairly
speedy liberation. Other politicians who had fallen from grace
were not as lucky.

The role of this Baka woman constituted one link between Mabaya and the occult. For the villagers, it was obvious that this
woman, like all Pygmies, was disposed of special forces. She was

often mentioned in commentary on Mabaya's success. Such associations were not made by only the villagers—Mabaya himself contributed to them. Like other chiefs, he was a great polygamist, with dozens of wives, but it was nonetheless remarkable that he had included this Baka woman among his wives. At the time, it was still very rare for a Maka man to formalize relations with a Pygmy woman.[18] The very fact that Mabaya gave publicity to this liaison—this woman was often seen in his retinue—indicated that he judged it useful for his renown.

Another characteristic of Mabaya's fall from power was that it was completely unexpected. The villagers, like members of the regional elite, were never certain about the real cause. Some thought that Mabaya, as minister of war, had tried to create a personal clientele and was suspected of preparing a *coup d'état*. Others said that he had called the Bamileke people *maquisards* (because of their role in the UPC guerillas) and was never forgiven by them. Still others claimed that he had always tried to sabotage the careers of the other eastern *évolués:* for example, he refused to grant scholarships for study in France to young university students from the region. These people argued that his own jealousy with respect to close colleagues had proved fatal.

It was clear, and here everyone agreed, that his close collaborator, Raymond Malouma, was the one who profited most from Mabaya's demise. My spokesmen insisted that, initially, Malouma had been strongly supported by Mabaya. Malouma's political career took off only when he obtained a position in the secretariat of the National Assembly at the time of independence, when Mabaya was president of that body. Some added that this was a kind of life-saving operation since Malouma had just been dismissed from the administration due to accusations of malversation. But after Mabaya's fall, in 1962, his old client, Malouma, assumed all his duties. Malouma remained MP of the region until the 1980s and was able to monopolize other key positions in the party hierarchy for the East Province.

The end of this story recalls the betrayal of Evina, the old Yebekolo chief, by Nkal Selek, the general of the Mpang (the arch-theme of the oral tradition of the region, recounted above). The

obvious difference is that, this time, it was the party summit, and
not the old witch with her basket of medicine, that decided the
outcome of the affair. But many of my informants were conscious
of the continuity between these matters. Their commentary on
Mabaya's demise was that, in politics, things happen as they do in
witchcraft: the most dangerous attacks come from within.

The sudden fall of Mabaya and the equally sudden rise of Malouma
were dramatic events. But they are certainly not exceptional; at the
lower levels of the party hierarchy, such abrupt reshufflings were, and
are, quite common. It is typical that these changes were ordained in
such an abrupt manner by the party summit. The villagers were not
the only ones who were ignorant about the reasons for what was
happening. Members of the elite also became lost in speculation
about the causes of these sudden shifts. The world of the regional
elite was, and still is, full of uncertainty and suspicion. All had their
eyes fixed on the summit, but the reasons for unexpected changes in
the preferences of those at the very top were difficult to surmise. In
this situation, the association with witchcraft becomes almost inevitable. The opacity of modern political relations reinforces the capacity of witchcraft to conceal political actors and their actions. It is almost impossible to discern concrete actions from the rumors that
accompanied the rise and sudden fall of Mabaya or the swift advent
of Malouma. The machinations of these politicians in their relation
to national leaders are as difficult to unravel as it is to discern the
exact role of Mabaya's "Pygmy" wife or of Mabaya's pronounce-
ments about the *mindjim* "who would vote for him." But it is clear
that these supposed acts, real or not, play an important role in political processes. Other actors do take them into account in devising
their strategies. Clearly, even imaginary actions can induce concrete
reactions. The following is a good example of the reality of witchcraft
in political struggles amongst the elite:

> In the early 1970s, an old dispute between Pierre Mimbang and
> André Bekobe, two eminent politicians from the East Province,
> took an unexpected turn. Their conflict goes back to the 1950s,
> when they were competing fiercely for the position of *chef de can-*

ton. One day, Mimbang, who had just become chief, physically attacked Bekobe in front of the French administrator. The latter dismissed Mimbang from his new post and put Bekobe in his place. Since that incident, hostilities between the two had only intensified.

Mimbang, who had a better education than Bekobe, was more successful when political parties were established at the time of independence. He became mayor of the commune and filled many important posts in the party subsection. Bekobe remained canton chief and received only more modest positions in the party hierarchy. There were constant rumors about new confrontations between the two adversaries and other politicians of the department. But these intrigues always took place in secret. The villagers reiterated these rumors, but they became lost in conjecture about what really happened. As said, when Malouma's famous black Mercedes (he was then MP) was seen driving down the trail, they would comment, "Ah, he's going to put them in order; now they'll have some heat!"

In 1973, a dramatic development transpired: Mimbang had a fatal car accident. On return from a visit with his *nkong*, his driver lost control of the Land Rover, and the car sped off into the bush; Mimbang was mortally wounded. In itself, the accident was not bizarre: they had arrived at a point on the trail that was notoriously difficult; it had just rained, and the driver had a reputation for being "too energetic." But in the villages, rumors immediately sprang up. People said that the road had been armored (*blindé*) so that the car entered the forest. These rumors were reinforced when it was found that certain sworn enemies of Mimbang had taken refuge with their own *onkong*. These refugees were none other than Bekobe and François Mimbang, another politician who had his own reasons for being in conflict with the victim, Pierre Mimbang.[19]

An informant who had links to the entourage of the deceased gave me his interpretations of the incident. He "knew" that André Bekobe and François Mimbang had prepared the death of Pierre Mimbang. To do so, they had obtained the consent of Pierre Menkambe, a renowned witch of the Bekobe family. Hadn't this

Menkambe been seen creeping into Mimbang's courtyard during the night? In the dark, there had been a confrontation between Menkambe and the witches who guarded Mimbang's house. Apparently, Menkambe was stronger and decided, in keeping with the demands of Bekobe and François Mimbang, that, in the next month, Pierre Mimbang would no longer be living. The next day, Mimbang felt ill. Warned by his entourage of the sinister plans of Menkambe, he went quickly to the village of his *nkong* to be cured. After a few days, he felt better and decided to return home to participate in an official meeting. His *nkong* warned him not to go because his enemies had put formidable barriers on the road. But Mimbang left anyway. Six miles from the *nkong*'s village, the car left the road, and Mimbang died instantly.

This was only one of the interpretations that circulated in the village (probably the version put forth by those close to Pierre Mimbang). Other villagers affirmed that André Bekobe, François Mimbang, and Pierre Menkambe had taken refuge with their *on-kong*, which proved that they were involved. Apparently, they feared the vengeance of Mimbang's kin. It was said that the first wife of Mimbang had already visited a very famous *nkong*. Bekobe and his men might indeed need the protection of their *onkong*.

From the villagers' perspective, it was only logical to interpret these intrigues and confrontations in terms of *djambe*. It was their way of explaining the vicissitudes of high-level politics. This can be viewed as a manner of rendering such events comprehensible or even as an effort to appropriate them. In this context, *djambe* discourse also expresses the gap that separates villagers from the elite world. In the *djambe* version, as in the official version, of these events, the villagers play no part: confrontations between the politicians seem to unfurl above their heads. Only a few "super-witches"—the *onkong* reputed for their extraordinary forces—have a significant role. The outcome of this story confirms this general pattern. Conflict among the elites takes place behind closed doors; the population remains uninformed. But this bolsters the villagers' tendency to interpret these incidents in the language of *djambe*.

This and other similar examples indicate, moreover, that the elites themselves also tend to interpret these events in terms of witchcraft. We saw that the protagonists in the Mimbang affair did seek the protection of a *nkong*, which is certainly not unusual. The new elites express themselves less overtly than the villagers on witchcraft matters, but despite their modern education, they still feel profoundly involved in *djambe*. They find all sorts of special protection indispensable; they covet their *bufè* (amulets) and seek out the very best *onkong*. By alluding to their special forms of protection, they underscore their distance from the villagers, who do not have recourse to such special services. But those allusions are even more meant for other elites since they are the most dangerous rivals in the fierce competition of the new political arenas.

Hence the *nkong* has an essential role to play for the elites. Several *onkong* who boasted about having *évolués* among their clients described to me the services they rendered to these eminent clients. They had to protect the elites against sneak attacks; they were, above all, supposed to "see" what their clients' adversaries were preparing so that their plans could be anticipated, neutralized, or sidetracked. All the familiar themes of *djambe* are reiterated in this new setting: the client is to be made invulnerable and is to receive a second pair of eyes to see what happens in the night. The old adage that the *djambe* and power are indivisible is accepted by the new elites to the point where they do not distinguish between the two. The lack of transparence in political competition within the party, uncertainty about the party summit's favor, and the ever-present possibility of an abrupt fall from grace all strengthen this association between *djambe* and power.

It might seem surprising that the *djambe* retains its force in this context since modern political competition is of an entirely novel character: politicians acquire as many positions as possible (which was and is still reprehended in the village); they are completely dependent upon the party summit and must respect the hierarchy at all costs (which goes against the grain of the egalitarian Maka ethos). But, as we have seen, there is also continuity. The new elites demand the same services of their *onkong* as did the old war hero, Nkal Selek. Stories about the intrigues that consume the new elites reveal the same old ambivalence: the *djambe* can protect, but it also exposes a *djambe* person to unprecedented danger. On the way back from his *nkong*, Pierre Mimbang was killed by the very *djambe* forces that he had attempted to mobilize in his favor. This mimics, again, the fate of Evina, the old Yebekolo chief who was deceived by Nkal Selek with the help of the same *djambe* that should have rendered him invulnerable. Another old adage, which says that the *djambe* attacks from within, remains equally relevant: one fears, most of all, deception by kin, close collaborators, or other intimates.

The question is whether one can discern, underneath this apparent continuity, certain transformations in witchcraft conceptions, especially in the way they affect everyday relations. One may wonder, for example, whether the long-standing link between witchcraft and kin is applicable in contexts where sociopolitical relations are reproduced on once unfathomable scales. The introduction, for instance, of new techniques from Europe seems to countervail against the association between witchcraft and domestic relationships. In Duala, people speak of gangs of witches that have international liaisons with the mafia. Nonetheless, the link to kin, or at least intimacy, remains strong. In the case cited above, it was said that even a formidable witch like Pierre Menkambe could strike Pierre Mimbang only because he had collaborators in the victim's own household.

The role of witchcraft in modern politics is a theme that is riddled with contradictions. This is an unavoidable result of the transposition of a discourse narrowly associated with the private, domestic world on a regional, and even national, plan. The political struggles that take place on these higher levels are integrated into local discourses on witchcraft and are thus linked to the world of kinship and the family. We see below that this extension of local discourses, a sort of precarious fusion of witchcraft and state authoritarianism, can have dangerous consequences.

In modern contexts, the *djambe* discourse seems to have become more hierarchical. We saw already that the *djambe* can no longer bridge the distance between villagers and the modern elites. The villagers and their occult forces seem no longer able to pierce the "super armor" of the new elites. One might add that the modern avatars of the *djambe* seem to have given hierarchy to relationships among the elites themselves. It stands to reason that the most eminent among them, thanks to their wealth and political weight, have access to the best *midu* (medicine). In the 1970s, several informants explained to me why Raymond Malouma was reinstated by the party summit at every election and why it was impossible to beat him. Their reasoning, briefly mentioned above, was simple: Malouma had secured the support of the best *nkong* in the region—someone from the Djem area, in the deep forest toward the South. His competitors had all tried to buy the services of this *nkong,* but Malouma could pay the highest price due to his many political positions. Therefore, he was unbeatable.

In these explanations, the leveling side of *djambe* is relegated to the background. Modern transformations of the *djambe* discourse confirm that accumulation has acquired an accelerated pace in Cameroon today.

In these new contexts, there flourishes the remarkable capacity for witchcraft discourse to give a central place to human actors while, at the same, hiding them from view. In chapter 1, I evoked the problematic relationship between these discourses and "methodological individualism," which has had such a profound influence in Western social science. On the one hand, witchcraft emphasizes human action and the role of individual agents as the ultimate explanatory factor. But, on the other hand, it practically precludes discerning these actors as well as distinguishing between imaginary and concrete action. In this sense, it seems to work against the very act of interpretation. For the Maka, this is not problematic: the reality of witches and their invisible actions are not in doubt. This is related to a specific conception of "personhood" and human action; every person has a double and can learn to double himself or herself.

This conception is no doubt divergent from Western notions that found scientific discourse. However, these differences must not be exaggerated. As I noted earlier, despite efforts to reduce the vicissitudes of politics (or other realms) to well-defined human action, Westerners also often wonder what "really" happened. The true circumstances behind important events like the murder of John F. Kennedy or, to cite a less dramatic example, the brutal fall of Margaret Thatcher remain as uncertain as the unexpected detours in the career of Jean Mabaya. Even though, or perhaps because, such events receive extensive media coverage, they remain subject to speculation and incessant reinterpretation. Yet, in the West as in Cameroon, people feel free to formulate political analyses despite considerable uncertainty about what really happened. Just as for witchcraft, the problem is one of taking into account the effects of actions that cannot be verified in reality.

Thus the study of witchcraft and its diffuse political effects raises more general problems. It may help to relativize the self-evident quality of terms like *action, effect,* or even *rationality.* It is precisely in this field, where one refers constantly to human agency—a basic tendency of witchcraft discourse—that one must realize that human action is pervaded by double meanings. Might this be the ultimate moral of witchcraft?

Epilogue: A Sudden Change in the Role of the Maka Elites

The first version of this chapter was written in the early 1990s. When I returned to Makaland in 1994, I found, however, that there had been some striking changes in the relation between elites and their villages, and not in the direction I had expected. Suddenly, the urban elites were more noticeably present in the countryside. I met several eminent civil servants from Yaunde and Duala who were visiting their former fellow villagers and who apparently returned to the area regularly. Most importantly, the elites were now building in their villages on a truly grand scale. I visited a whole series of building sites in the various villages where impressive mansions were being erected. Clearly, the outburst of one of our passengers during my 1991 visit— who exclaimed that Maka elites were too stingy to build a proper house in the village—was no longer appropriate. One could see that the new elite houses, though still under construction, were to be impressive mansions. The president of the new Association des Elites Maka Mboans was even building a kind of Islamic mansion, complete with pillars and arches; it looked like an imitation of a *lamido* (chief's) palace from northern Cameroon.

The background of this sudden change seems to be that the government is now attributing a new political role to the elite associations. Throughout the period of one-party rule, such associations were certainly not stimulated by the regime. As mentioned before, all forms of organization outside the one-party were formally forbidden, and regional elites were definitely not encouraged to form autonomous associations.[20] However, all this changed abruptly in the early 1990s with the imposition of a multiparty system. Several authors emphasize that there are clear signs that the regime now sees elite associations, as opposed to the party structures, as a much safer way to *encadrer les masses populaires* (see especially Nyamnjoh and Rowlands in press). The reasons are clear. Because of the imposition of a multiparty system, the regime's control over political life is threatened: even in a solid RDPC (the ruling party) fief like Makaland, other parties are now active. Ambitious politicians and especially the voters can therefore always switch sides. However, the elites from the area are nearly all in public service, so the regime has direct control over them. Moreover, because of their reports to their respective regions of origin, they are the obvious persons to try to win votes for the incumbent government.

For Makaland, the turning point seems to have been the presidential elections of 1992, when President Paul Biya's reelection was far from guaranteed.[21] Many civil servants were sent to their home area to campaign for Biya, and the elite associations—which until then had manifested themselves, at most, informally and in the urban context—were suddenly actively encouraged by the regime.[22] Since then, these associations have become an important factor in the region, even from the perspective of the villagers.

For me, this sudden engagement of the Maka elites in the region came as a surprise. Indeed, I strongly emphasized above the problems involved in the relations between the elites and their home areas. It seems typical that the change was triggered by an outside intervention—that is, the regime's sudden encouragement of elite associations as a way to deal with the threat of a multiparty system. This illustrates, once more, how important national politics are in the emergence of such ethnic movements.

However, the internal problems mentioned above still do affect the functioning of the new associations. For one, the old segmentary idiom manifests itself in this context as well. During the few years of their existence, the associations have tended to split up continuously: from region to *département,* to *arrondissement,* to *piste* (road), and so on—all this because one of the constitutive segments at each level invariably feels neglected. And of more direct importance for our topic, the old obsession with witchcraft in the relations between elites and villagers persists. In 1995, when I visited Yaunde again, one of the Maka elite associatons in the city invited me to come talk about my research. Inevitably, one of the most pressing issues during this exciting meeting turned out to be witchcraft. Most interestingly, the elites present did show themselves to be conscious of a certain ambivalence: while the occult remains very important to the elite as well, one way or another, these forces have to be contained if they are to bring *développement* to the village. The relation between the elites and the village is still beset by the fear of the occult. But the recent revival of the elite associations shows that this makes this relation far from static. All sorts of surprising turns are possible (see Geschiere 1996).

COMPARATIVE INTERSTICE 2:
THE TEMPTATIONS OF POWER

Maka discourse on *djambe* expresses a fascination with power as much as a distrust of it. In the village, this ambiguity is represented by an omnipresent tension between images of *djambe* as a leveling force, on the one hand, and as a means of accumulation, on the other. In relations with the new power holders outside the village, the same ambivalence persists, but the leveling impact of *djambe* is less evident. It is hard to know if the *djambe* is used effectively as a popular mode of political action in the struggle against new inequalities. It seems, instead, that the elite give the *djambe* its subversive punch by insisting that it undermines new relations of domination. But it is evident that *djambe* can encourage novel modes of accumulating power—now practiced by modern politicians—and affirm new inequalities. Yet even in this modern context, the *djambe* is still marked by the old ambivalence. Support in the world of *djambe* is indispensable for politicians who seek to aggrandize power. However, the same *djambe* constitutes a great danger as well; by entering into the world of occult forces, these leaders expose themselves to new and terrible dangers.

The Maka politicians' obsessions with occult forces is not unusual. In other parts of Cameroon, new political leaders are associated with *la sorcellerie* as well. There too, interpretations of events in terms of occult forces manifest the same combination of fascination and distrust. Nonetheless, one can discern distinct regional trajectories that have varying implications for everyday relations.

In the forest societies of the South and Center Provinces of Cameroon, the rapport between witchcraft and power corresponds more or less to that of the Maka. Philippe Laburthe-Tolra (1977) shows, with respect to the Beti people, how representations of *evu* express similar ideas about power. We noted, above, the paradoxes around which this anthropologist turned: *evu* is surely evil, but it is also indispensable for all forms of power. Laburthe-Tolra even asserts that discourse on *evu* expresses the idea that power is "original sin" for the Beti (p. 1080); but his informants also indicate that without power, and hence without *evu,* the community cannot function. The author gives striking examples of the ways in which some Beti strive to prove their worth, exhibiting a true obsession with power.[1] He concludes that discourse on *evu* offers a condensed expression of the tension between an egalitarian ideology and a resolute practice of inequality.

The same tension is expressed in even more dramatic terms by Élisabeth Copet-Rougier for the Kako (or Kaka), who live to the northeast of the Maka. Their discourse on *lembo* (the equivalent of *evu* or *djambe*) manifests the same obsession. *Lembo* is the expression of jealousy by close kin and is thus a deadly threat to ambitious people. But it is also indispensable to all "strong men" who wish to protect themselves from this jealousy and outdo rivals. Copet-Rougier (1986a, 85) describes *lembo* as "anti-power" and "anti-social," but she adds that it is indissociable from power. Great warriors of the past were obliged to secure support in the invisible world in order to sustain their force in the everyday world: *dume* (force) is fed by *lembo*.[2] Copet-Rougier (1986b, 66) even concludes that, for the Kako, all "strong men" are "necessarily criminal" or even "absolute transgressors"; apparently this is true for warriors of the past as much as for modern politicians. Indeed, such expressions indicate a strong distrust of power as intrinsically linked to the dark forces of witchcraft.

As one might expect, there is a clear contrast here with the societies of the Grassfields of western Cameroon. In this region, the question of power is inevitably linked to the position of the chief, who is the pivot of society. In the literature on this region, there is a certain ambiguity concerning the relationship of the chief and his court to the "dark side" of power. Some authors insist that the chief is strictly separated from witchcraft. Others seem to have a broader vision of these occult forces; they see a direct link between these forces and the power of the chief.[3] It is clear, however, that in these societies, there is a real effort to dissociate the chief from negative manifestations of the occult. For the Nso of the Northwest, Miriam Goheen (1996) points out that the chief is closely associated with *sem* (the occult force) either in his person or through the notables who surround him; but this *sem* must be distinguished at all costs from *sem arim*—the *sem* of the man-eaters, or witches.

Discourse on *evu* or *djambe,* on the one hand, and that on *sem* or similar notions put forth by the Grassfields societies, on the other hand, express different ways of conceptualizing power and inequality. In the forest societies, emphasis is put on the tension between an egalitarian ideology and the practice of inequality. Witchcraft discourse discloses profound distrust of power as such, but it also reveals an obsession with personal ambition and valor in all its forms. *La sorcellerie* becomes a vicious circle because it confirms equality but encourages ambition and inequality at the same time. For the Grassfields societies, a similar discourse refers, instead, to the need to separate the "legitimate" power of the chief from this ambiguous domain. Here, witchcraft notions seem more compartmentalized. Because attempts are made to dissociate the chief from these dark forces, the circularity of discourse on witchcraft can be ruptured. The chief has the moral authority to legitimate the personal ambitions of his subjects and set them apart from egotistical, and hence dangerous, expressions of the occult. In this way, he can contain the latter. But can this separation between the chief and the occult always be maintained? As discussed below, even in these societies, this separation becomes ever more difficult under the impact of new forms of inequality and authority. Nonetheless, the circularity of discourses on witchcraft seems less inevitable here than in the forest societies.

Clearly, in both scenarios modern power relations and new possibilities for accumulation pose problems. Discourses on witchcraft in the Grassfields societies translate, as much as in the forest societies, profound distrust of power: they are subtended by the firm belief that all forms of power can easily degenerate. This fear is reinforced by the emergence of new forms of power and wealth that seem to be beyond the reach of local communities. This is the wider background against which the common association of the vicissitudes of modern politics with the occult must be understood. This association is more than an exotic particularity or a pathetic effort to contain new relations within the bounds of traditional concepts. Rather, at issue are universal problems of power and inequality—how a practice of inequality can be reconciled with the notion of a fundamental equality.[4] One may wonder whether other cultural logics work better in mastering such problems.

The problem of power has reached unprecedented dimensions in Africa today. This is one reason why notions like *evu, djambe,* or *sem* are essential for understanding modern conditions. Recent scholarship reflects concern about this, using strong words to convey the terrifying nature of contemporary state power. Achille Mbembe (1992) refers, with regard to postcolonial Africa, to "the obscenity of power" in his "Provisional Notes on the Postcolony." I noted previously the heavily charged subtitle of Jean-François Bayart's *The State in Africa: The politics of the belly (L'État en Afrique: La politique du ventre)*. For Bayart, this voracious style of governing is not particularly African, but it is reproduced particularly well on this continent. He emphasizes that this is a historical mode of action; its specificity is established in its historicity. In Africa, this specificity is linked to particular politico-economic relations—most notably, the "strategies of extraversion" deployed by African elites who maintain themselves more through external "rents" (such as development aid) than by exploiting national resources. But Bayart especially conjoins the strength of this politics of the belly to a specific imaginary (*imaginaire*) that makes a direct connection between "eating" and power. One might add that this same imaginary links eating and power directly to occult forces and witchcraft. We have seen striking examples of the strength of this association in people's thoughts. It is also by way of this association that witchcraft enters into the modern political arena and serves to explain the troubling aspects of power in its new forms.[5]

Johannes Fabian has constructed an entire book, *Power and Performance* (1990), around a brief but pithy Shaba (Zaire) proverb: "Power is eaten whole." A simple question he posed about this proverb inspired a theater group in Lubumbashi to turn it into a play. The actors seemed intrigued by the articulation between notions of eating, power, and totality—probably because they live in a situation where accumulation and the arbitrary nature of power have taken on disconcerting forms. Here, again, the association between power and eating (and hence witchcraft) expresses profound anxiety as well as a true obsession with new forms of power.

In Africa, people often feel that power has lost all sense of proportion. The colonial conquerors' display of power shocked local populations, especially during the first decades of the colonial administration.[6] In this respect, the examples from the Maka cited above—forced labor, forced resettlement of whole villages, deportations, and all other coercive measures to make the population work harder—were certainly not exceptional. After independence, postcolonial power hardly lost its arbitrary nature. To the contrary, it seemed more capricious than ever. And the regimes' access to development aid only reinforced the concentration of power at the national level. Thus it remained largely concealed from the populace. To understand or even appropriate new forms of power, people use the old, local representations. But through this, the scale of such representations is expanded, although they remain rooted in the sphere of kinship and the home.

Discourse on *la sorcellerie* in modern contexts reveals the extent to which power relations are problematic for African societies today. At the level of the village, today, as in the past, witchcraft establishes the limits of power. One hesitates in following anthropologists like Max Gluckman (1955), who characterized such beliefs as "eufunctional" since they exhort people to respect order. Yet it is clear that in societies like those of the Maka or the Beti, witchcraft expresses a deep distrust of power and thus indicates the means of containing it. Hence it surely reminds people of certain limits that should not be transgressed. But in the case of the new power holders, these limits seem to evaporate, and witchcraft serves, instead, to explain the accumulation of power. It seems, then, that modern transformations have tended to corrupt notions on witchcraft, so that it risks degenerating into a discourse on power and especially on disempowerment.

There are, however, important regional variations. The variable tones of notions on occult forces in the Grassfields and the forest societies of Cameroon, which I compared in brief, also have an impact on new inequalities. In the mountains, the chief can legitimate—Goheen (1996) says "socialize"—the more or less suspect wealth and power of the new elites. By allowing them to buy titles (often neotraditional ones) in the courtly associations, the chief reinforces his own position; he also gains authority over new forms of accumulation. Evidently, one must avoid making a radical opposition between these societies and those of the forest. We see below, for example, that it is not clear that the Grassfields chiefs will indeed succeed in domesticating new inequalities in the future. But there are clear differences here with the forest societies, where the wealth of the new elites still seems to constitute an unresolved problem. It is no accident that in these forest societies the fear of new witchcraft threats has led to a panicky search for new sanctions. We see below that this search has had dramatic consequences.

WITCHCRAFT AND THE ART OF GETTING RICH: REGIONAL VARIATIONS

5

New consumption goods—no longer only of Western provenance but increasingly made in Japan or Korea—play a crucial
role in people's images of modernity in Cameroon as much as in
other African countries. No wonder that these goods have become
the focus of varying but very vehement witchcraft rumors. Such rumors about the dark side of the new objects of wealth offer a good
starting point for exploring the conceptual link between witchcraft
and people's images of a modern way of life. Apparently this link is
obvious to many in Africa today, as elsewhere.[1] It is also clear that
this directly affects the way people perceive new forms of enrichment
and entrepreneurship. But as generalized as these representations
may be, there are striking regional variations in the ways in which
such dark rumors affect relations in the daylight world. This chapter
starts with such rumors on a new witchcraft of riches and explores
regional variations in its effects in different parts of southern and
western Cameroon.

Cameroon is no exception on the African continent—or in the new
global *oekumene* altogether[2]—as far as a general obsession with new
consumption goods is concerned. In his fascinating book *L'esprit
d'entreprise au Cameroun*, Jean-Pierre Warnier writes, "The taste of
Cameroonians for everything that is imported rather than produced
locally is proverbial."[3] To many Cameroonians, imported goods
have become crucial in the definition and expression of their identity.
But people use these goods in their own ways to mark their place in

a "material civilization of success": these goods "embody the image of what one desires to be" (Warnier 1993, 169). Although many Western observers tend to view this obsession with modern forms of consumerism with some irony, one must say that most Cameroonians are at least still self-conscious about this new phenomenon. *Radio Trottoir* is full of jokes on the Cameroonian obsession with modern things: on the fact that, until recently, Cameroon was one of the main importers of French champagne (and it is true that the *préfet* [senior district officer] of Abong-Mbang, deep in the "backward" East Province, used to celebrate his young daughter's birthday with two crates of vintage champagne); on the elite who drink only the best Scotch whiskey; or on the *filles libres* of Yaunde with their war cry: "Get lost poor sot, you don't even have a Pajero." [4]

However, this obsession with modern goods has its flip side in a deep mistrust of the sources of these goods. *Radio Trottoir* is also full of stories on the theme of how arrogance is punished. In some parts of the East, people say that a man who plants a cocoa tree will not live to reap its fruits. And during my long, long trips in a *taxi-brousse*, my fellow travelers have often explained to me why there is a grave before each modern house alongside the road: these are the last resting places of people who had demonstrated too much ambition by constructing such impressive houses. As one might expect, such a mixture of fascination and rejection proves to be a fertile breeding ground for novel uses and experiments with the ancient themes of witchcraft and sorcery.

These themes seem to be all the more applicable since, in this context again, witchcraft discourses are highly ambiguous in their implications. These discourses can serve to express distrust with respect to new forms of wealth through rumors about new, and therefore particularly dangerous, occult threats. Such rumors seem to confirm the stereotype quoted above; that is, of witchcraft as a traditional barrier against development and innovation. But again, this aspect should not mask efforts, expressed by the same discourses, to appropriate the new riches. It is true that people tend to associate the nouveaux riches with such occult forces in order to make them suspect. But it is also true that the rich may encourage such associations in order to protect themselves against the jealousy and hidden aggression of

their close kin. It is precisely because of this ambiguity that such notions can become a kind of *passe-partout,* a panacea that can explain
anything, even baffling modern changes. Indeed, this ambiguity is
not particular to sorcery discourses or to the African context. As Johannes Fabian remarks, referring to Michel Foucault: "It is precisely
their dispersal in many kinds of expression that makes tenets of a discourse 'central,' in the sense of being ideologically and practically
effective" (Fabian 1990, 39). It is because of this fluidity, which allows for all sorts of interpretations, that these discourses become so
all-pervasive, even in modern contexts.

In Cameroon, such reflections on new forms of wealth find expression in beliefs in a new form of witchcraft that bears various
names: *ekong, famla, kupe, nyongo.* They have, however, a basic idea
in common: a new type of witches who no longer eat their victims,
but who transform them into a kind of zombie and put them to work
on "invisible plantations." The nouveaux riches supposedly owe
their success to the exploitation of these zombies' labor. People insist on the novelty of this form of witchcraft and often relate it to
the arrival of the Europeans and the introduction of new luxury
items. Since colonial times, especially after independence, these representations spread rapidly throughout southern and western Cameroon. Because they involve a new form of witchcraft, they created
general fear and uncertainty in these regions. However, it seems
that people attempt to deal with this new threat in different ways.
Apparently, some societies are more unsure than others on how to
contain it.

Such variations seem to be closely related to the ways in which the
new forms of wealth have been incorporated, or not, into these societies. In this context, the contrast noted previously between the
societies of the western Grassfields and those of the southern forest
areas comes up again. In the Grassfields societies, which are marked
by the emergence of a group of highly successful new entrepreneurs,
people seem to believe that these new forms of witchcraft can still be
domesticated. In the forest societies, on the contrary, these new
forms of wealth seem to pose still unresolved problems; here the uncertainty of how to deal with new forms of witchcraft seems to be
much greater. These variations find expression in the ethnic propa-

ganda that, as we have seen, threatens to overrun the newly created space for political debate in the country. In pamphlets supporting President Biya, *famla* is regularly referred to as the real explanation for the economic success of the Bamileke entrepreneurs from the West. The aim is clearly to rouse the widespread fear that this group will succeed in dominating the national economy. Anti-Biya pamphlets often contain allusions to the "familialism" of the Beti and their fear of the *evu* that comes from "within the house" and that is supposedly the true cause of unbridled corruption among politicians from this group. In view of such an "ethnicization" of witchcraft, it seems to be a matter of some urgency to understand the historical factors influencing different regional trajectories in the interaction between discourses on the occult forces and new opportunities for enrichment.

This chapter therefore compares various interpretations of new modes of accumulation in terms of sorcery and witchcraft. Among the Maka of the East Province, who had a central place in the preceding chapters, new ideas on *ekong* and *famla* have not yet taken root. Instead, the Maka still explain the new forms of wealth, at least within the villages, in terms of the old *djambe* discourse, albeit with certain transformations. In later sections of this chapter, this view is compared with new notions on witchcraft, wealth, and zombies in the southern and western parts of the country. Despite the mixing of different cultural elements in urban contexts, it is still possible to distinguish varying regional trajectories in the linking of wealth and witchcraft. These representations all express a true obsession with new objects of wealth that constitute the most concrete, but also the most shocking, expression of new inequalities. But, at the same time, they seem to express different ways of confronting these inequalities.

The Maka and the "Witchcraft of the Whites"

In 1971, when I first came to the Maka region, new forms of wealth were the objects of lively debate. My informants made me understand, in a somewhat secretive way, that "not long ago" people had been afraid to plant cocoa trees. The proverb quoted above indicates why: people who dared to do so would not live to reap the fruits from their labor because of the jealousy of their fellow villagers. Furthermore, I was told that, in those days, the people who had constructed the "modern" houses with tin roofs did not dare to sleep in them.

It was no accident that cocoa trees and houses with tin roofs were the objects of such fears: they were seen as the most obvious symbols of new riches in the villages. In this region, the cultivation of cocoa spread only quite recently. As noted above, villagers began to create their own farms only after 1945, and only later money began to circulate in significant quantities in the villages. However, not all villagers profited to the same degree from these new opportunities to enrich oneself. In 1971, a small group of *grands planteurs* distinguished themselves from their fellow villagers on the basis of their annual revenues from their relatively large cocoa farms. The cultivation of cocoa, and later coffee, introduced new inequalities within village society.[5]

The new wealth was invested most notably in the construction of a new type of house with roofs of corrugated iron and mud-brick walls.[6] This was encouraged in no uncertain terms by the government. During his annual tour through the villages, the *sous-préfet* (district officer) used to reproach every man who had not yet constructed *en tôle* (that is, with an iron roof) and warn him that he had better do so before next year's tour. All this was clearly related to the fact that ALEUCAM—at the time, by far the most important industry in Cameroon—produced corrugated iron.[7] The government efforts were supported by a Dutch development project that offered technical assistance to villagers who wanted to construct modern houses. The project incited great enthusiasm among the people since each *grand planteur* wanted to prove his worth by building such a house. However, they interpreted the project in their own ways. The Dutch strongly advocated installing concrete floors in these houses for hygienic reasons, but very few people did so. Instead, they preferred to make the house as large as possible. One villager, for instance, boasted at every occasion that his house was by far the biggest in the village. It was indeed a gigantic construction of sixteen rooms. On my arrival, the chief and his notables immediately decided that I had to live there since it was the most "modern" house in the village.

I did not dare turn down this generous offer right away, but it seemed to me a haunted place with all these empty rooms; it took a lot of diplomacy to settle for more modest quarters. Among the Maka, as elsewhere in Africa, houses with tin roofs have become the principal status symbol. Making your house as big as possible is one of the new manifestations of individual ambition and social superiority in this society.

In the beginning, allusions to the dangers of sleeping in such a modern house or of planting a cocoa tree made little sense to me. Only later did I understand that here, as well, the *djambe* was involved. The idea was that people who slept in such houses or planted these trees would not live to enjoy their riches since they displayed their wealth too ostentatiously and therefore attracted the jealousy of their own people. As discussed previously, the Maka firmly believe that jealousy within the family is a mortal threat because of the *djambe le njaw* (witchcraft of the house).

In 1971, however, everybody agreed that the Maka had overcome these old fears: people slept in their modern houses, and many had created cocoa plantations. When I asked the villagers how they had overcome the witchcraft ban on these new forms of wealth, their reply was simple: things had changed "by themselves." Enterprising villagers had had the courage to plant cocoa trees despite all warnings and had not died; on the contrary, they had become *grands planteurs*. Similarly, a few diehards showed that they could build a modern house and live, or even sleep, in it. However, during my first stay with the Maka, a current joke was still to ask somebody why he had not slept in his house last night, whereupon the addressed would say something like "f—— off" and insist that, of course, he had slept under his own roof. But behind his back, people would say that only a few years ago he still slept in a miserable kitchen behind his new house since he was "too superstitious."

When I made a short trip further into the interior, to Yokaduma, close to the border with the Central African Republic, I noted that similar fears were still prominent here. In this more isolated region, the spread of cocoa cultivation had just started, and one of the reasons the villagers gave for this delay was the old adage of a man not living to reap the fruits from a tree he had planted. The anthropologist Edwin Ardener described similar fears among the Bakweri, near the coast of southwest Cameroon (Ardener 1970). However, in this area, such fears would have been overcome in the 1950s.

A comparison of the Bakweri, Maka, and Yokaduma examples seems, at first sight, a striking confirmation of the stereotype of witchcraft as a "traditional" barrier that has to be overcome, in one region after another, before "development" can take off. Among the Bakweri, near the coast, this threshold had been crossed already in the 1950s; among the Maka, further into the interior, this occurred later; and in Yokaduma, this transition had not yet taken place in 1971. The greater the distance from the coast, the longer the witchcraft ban on the new riches seems to persist.[8] But, of course, on closer inspection, such a linear vision turns out to be too simplistic. Instead, it seems that the logics of the local discourses on witchcraft and inequality impose their own dynamics on the developments in each of these regions. I return to the Bakweri example below. In the Maka case, it is clear that the incorporation of new forms of riches within village society did not force a breakthrough in the witchcraft beliefs: instead, they were transformed by it.

When I continued my research, I was struck by incidental remarks indicating that people tended to link the *grands planteurs* to the *djambe*. I tried to discuss this but got only vague answers, as one might expect. However, one day my neighbor, clearly somewhat irritated by my continuous probing, replied with a question that to him was clearly rhetorical: "Of course these people know their way in the *djambe*. How else would they have dared to defy the witches' jealousy?" I was to hear many more answers with a similar tenor. Clearly, people still believed that planting a cocoa tree or building a modern house was quite dangerous since such possessions would inevitably evoke jealousy. Therefore, those who dared to do so must themselves be armored (*blindés*) by the occult forces.

My informants linked the success of the *grands planteurs* to a new form of *djambe,* the "sorcery of success," which they also called the *djambe le mintang.* The last name somewhat surprised me since it means "the witchcraft of the whites." To the villagers, however, it was self-evident: "You white people have your own kind of sorcery, but you use it to construct things and to get rich. That is exactly what the *grands planteurs* have done. Therefore they must have your witchcraft."[9]

But this more positive side of the *djambe* is difficult to separate from its more suspect manifestations. In this respect there is a clear parallel with the old notables and the *djambe idjuga* (witchcraft of authority) they display, as noted above, in the *kaande* (village council).

The example of Mbon, who was by far the richest farmer in the village where I lived in 1971, illustrates the ambiguity and the circularity of the *djambe* discourse in relation to new riches. Mbon had considerable prestige in the village. He owed his riches to his hard work, but also to the sensible way in which he had used his money. In the 1950s, he worked for some time as a carpenter in town. After his return to the village, he used his earnings from town to hire working groups. In this way, he immediately created quite large farms.[10] After this, he paid bridewealth for two wives who were considered to be hard workers, too; thus, he had enough labor at his disposal to maintain his vast cocoa plantations.

I considered Mbon to be one of the most enterprising figures in the village. He was still quite young (in 1971, he was about forty years old). He lived in an impressive modern house, which was exceptionally well built. When I left, after my second stay, he was very keen to buy my motorbike, and after only two lessons he paraded up and down the village on it. The villagers also often quoted Mbon as "the most dynamic" farmer of the village. However, to them, his success had hidden causes.

Mbon was the first farmer to create cocoa farms on a large scale. For my informants, this could only mean that he knew his way in the world of the *djambe*. How else could he have resisted the attacks of the jealous witches? Apparently, this did not directly imply that my spokesmen believed Mbon left his body at night like a true *njindjamb* (possessor of the *djambe*) to fly off to the *shumbu* (nightly encounter). Rather, they wanted to indicate that Mbon apparently knew how to defend himself in this dark world. However, when several of his close relatives fell ill, the neighbors began to whisper about his all too powerful *djambe*. As in the case of Mpal, the old notable respected for his *djambe idjuga,* people did not hesitate to associate Mbon with nightly escapades as soon as suspect things were happening in his immediate environment. After all, the *djambe* can be used for highly different aims—to construct but also to destroy; to enrich oneself but also to kill one's relatives. One can never be sure how a person will use his *djambe*.

Mbon's tragic death in 1991 encouraged further rumors. One night, when he stayed in his hut in the bush, near his plantations, Mbon fell into the fire. The next morning he was found dead from his burns. My assistant explained to me that Mbon had suffered for some time from epileptic attacks; doubtless he had fallen into the fire during one of these attacks. But other villagers made me understand that there was a more sinister explanation. According to them, Mbon must have been busy preparing his "medicine" that night. This was why he stayed in the bush and why he had made such a big fire. But, as is usual among the witches, his own sorcery had been his undoing.

Not all villagers accepted this explanation; some still mentioned Mbon as the best example of a *planteur dynamique*. However, it is characteristic that the quick association of the economic success of the *grands planteurs* with the *djambe* could degenerate into tenacious rumors that they behaved, after all, as true *minjindjamb*. There is, indeed, a close parallel here with the old village notables and the ways in which they became enmeshed in the *djambe* (see chapter 3).

All this hardly corresponds to the image, suggested above, of witchcraft as a kind of barrier to cash cropping, which was successfully overcome in successive stages in different parts of Cameroon. On the contrary, it is clear that the spread of cash crops and new forms of wealth did not break out of the *djambe* framework. The Maka examples, rather, highlight the strong circularity of these representations. The new opportunities for enrichment do not seem to undermine the validity of the *djambe* discourse; on the contrary, they are trapped in its vicious circles. Maka representations of the *djambe* of success with respect to the richer farmers offer a perfect example of a catch-22: if a farmer dares to defy the witches' jealousy, he must have his own supports in the world of the *djambe*. This makes one wonder if there is ever an escape from the vicious circles of this *djambe.* Elsewhere as well, new forms of wealth and witchcraft seemed to be inextricably intertwined. But in other regions, different trajectories were followed.

Obasinjom and the "Banana Boom" among the Bakweri

The example of the Bakweri in the Southwest Province offers an interesting comparison. Here, as well, people had severe doubts about new riches, which were again focused on modern houses with tin roofs. But the solution they found was very different. I referred previously to Edwin Ardener, the well-known English anthropologist who, in the 1950s, witnessed a dramatic reversal in Bakweri fears of new riches and the forms of witchcraft associated with them. Later (1970), he wrote a pioneering article about the complex interactions between economic changes and the dynamics of conceptions on witchcraft, which was based on his experience of the 1950s.

The Bakweri are a small group (now totaling about sixteen thousand persons) living on the steep but fertile slopes of Mt. Cameroon, near the coast in southwest Cameroon. Prior to the colonial conquest of 1894, they formed a highly segmentary society dominated by an egalitarian ideology. Ardener emphasizes that there were nonetheless strong tendencies toward accumulation, notably of goats, pigs, and dwarf cattle. But such tendencies were restricted by the belief in *liemba* (witchcraft), which was, and still is, closely linked to jealousy. To protect oneself against this threat, the wealth that a family head had accumulated was to be regularly destroyed in big *potlatch*-like ceremonies. It was especially through such ostentatious destruction that a man reinforced his prestige among his fellow villagers.

The Germans, the first colonizers of Cameroon, initially showed a certain respect for the Bakweri, whom they saw as wild mountaineers, highly *unbossmässig* (not ready to obey). This reputation, which was more or less similar to that of the Maka, was reinforced when the Bakweri also killed "their" German. In 1891, Buea, the main village on the mountain, succeeded in beating off a German expedition and killing its commander. As among the Maka, this event was to become a major theme in the oral tradition. It was only in 1894 that this part of Bakweriland was definitively "pacified." Later on, a completely different stereotype of the Bakweri as "lazy" and "apathetic" emerged, and this sticks with them even today.

This second stereotype was linked to specific aspects of the colonial exploitation of the area. The Germans quickly discovered that the volcanic soil around Mt. Cameroon was very fertile. In the 1880s, they started to appropriate land in order to create large-scale plantations. This process was accelerated after the definitive "pacification" of the Bakweri in the next decade. The Bakweri themselves were confined to reservations higher up in the mountains, and the Germans hoped to force them to come and work on the plantations. However, right from the beginning, the Bakweri showed little enthusiasm for this. After 1914, when the British conquered this part of Cameroon, the Bakweri continued to keep their distance from the plantation sector. The consequence was that they were marginalized in their own area. The plantations attracted ever more laborers from elsewhere, and especially after 1940, the Bakweri rapidly became a minority in many villages. The "strangers" profited much more from these new economic opportunities, and colonial reports began to record these strangers' spirit of enterprise in contrast to Bakweri "apathy." The Bakweri did not seem capable of defending their own lands or even their women. They sold or rented their last lands to strangers, and their women left them to live in concubinage or even as prostitutes among these same strangers, who seemed better able to maintain them. In 1952, when the Ardeners arrived in the region, the Bakweri seemed to be threatened with extinction. This was often blamed on their laziness and apathy, which became fixed elements of the ethnic stereotype of this group.

The Bakweri themselves tended to relate their restraint in the face of new economic opportunities to their fear of a novel form of witchcraft, called *nyongo,* that was closely linked to wealth. The new rich were especially suspected of being *nyongo* witches. Like all witches, they were supposed to kill their own relatives. But the novelty about *nyongo* was that these witches did not eat their victims; instead, they turned them into *vekongi* (zombies). *Nyongo* witches were supposed to transport their victims in a lorry to Mt. Kupe, more than sixty miles to the north of Bakweriland, where they had to work on "invisible plantations." A *nyongo* man could be recognized by his modern house with a tin roof, which he was only able to build thanks to profiting from the zombies' labor. But a *nyongo* man was always in danger. He had to go on "selling" his intimates to the other witches. If he was no longer able to offer someone, his colleagues would kill him and reduce him to slavery.

Ardener indicates that these ideas constituted a real obstacle to economic initiative. The villagers hardly dared to build modern houses. The few that were built by Bakweri clerks and other "carpetbaggers" remained empty. Nobody dared to pass the night there for fear of the *vekongi*. These new forms of wealth were considered dangerous since they automatically made one fall under the suspicion of *nyongo*.

The *nyongo* belief seems to be a good example of the role of witchcraft as a traditional obstacle to development. Therefore, it seems relevant to stress that, for the Bakweri, this *nyongo* was anything but traditional. On the contrary, they insisted that their ancestors had not known *nyongo* before the arrival of the Europeans. It had been introduced by the Duala, who were the first traders to come into contact with the Europeans. It was the Duala who had taught Bakweri witches how to turn their victims into zombies and become rich by their labor.[11]

The *nyongo* is, therefore, a sign of the dynamic of this sorcery discourse and not a "traditional relict." But other, even more spectacular changes were to follow. In 1951, several Bakweri intellectuals founded the Bakweri Cooperative Union of Farmers. The cooperative's main aim was to stimulate the cultivation of bananas in order to profit from new opportunities provided, most notably, by better means of transport to Europe. In 1953, the first sale of bananas under the auspices of the cooperative clearly showed how much money could be earned in this way. Under these circumstances, the Bakweri proved to be far from apathetic. More and more villagers started to cultivate bananas, and ever more money flowed into the villages. As Ardener (1970, 149) puts it, the "banana boom" created an "embarrassment of riches."

These economic changes reinforced witchcraft tensions. Ardener describes how, in 1955, *nyongo* accusations rocketed. With much drama, young men accused the elders of attacking them with their *nyongo*. Finally a "*nyongo* doctor" in Lysoka village made the village council look for support elsewhere. Money was collected to send a delegation to the Banyangi near Mamfe, 150 miles to the north, in order to buy a new juju (powerful spirit) strong enough to resist the *nyongo*. The delegation returned with the message that the Banyangi wanted more money. But even this extra sum was rapidly collected. Finally, with sufficient inducement, the Banyangi agreed to come with their famous Obasinjom.[12]

Seven weeks later, the Banyangi made a triumphant entry into Lysoka: a group of wild dancers in long robes, in their midst a fearsome crocodile mask—Obasinjom himself. Ardener (1970, 152) describes the following events in lyrical terms: "The marvels of the succeeding days passed expectations." Witches were flushed out and disarmed in large numbers.[13] The Banyangi trained thirty doctors to perform Obasinjom, and they left a powerful fetish to protect the village. Other villages followed the Lysoka example and invited Banyangi doctors to found an Obasinjom lodge with them as well. Altogether, the Bakweri would have paid more than £2000 from the banana money to Banyangi doctors.

Ardener notes that at the same time a true building craze began. Often he could hardly hear his informants' stories about *nyongo* and Obasinjom because of the noisy construction of tin roofs. The *nyongo* ban on modern houses, and on individual enrichment in general, was broken. As one informer put it, "*Nyongo* is gone; there is Obasinjom instead."

However, the story did not end with this "happy scene," so vividly depicted by Ardener. After 1963, the banana boom ended as abruptly as it had started. Bakweri farmers lost their privileged access to the British market as a result of the unification with the former French Cameroon and the new state's association with the EEC. When prices began to fall, most Bakweri rapidly lost interest in banana cultivation. According to Ardener, this economic slump coincided with the emergence of a new form of sorcery. The new rumors concerned strangers, notably people from francophone Cameroon, who were suspected of using bewitched coins in order to transform Bakweri into zombies and put them to work on the construction of a new harbor in Victoria (now Limbe).[14]

In 1987, when I worked in the area, people no longer talked about these bewitched coins. They made me understand that *nyongo* was still there, but that it was more or less under control. Obasinjom had not danced for many years. According to several people, he was "something of the past." However, in 1988, things again changed suddenly. Obasinjom made a spectacular reappearance, especially in the mountain villages, in order to expose *nyongo* witches. Several people related this resurrection to the new austerity measures announced by President Paul Biya in 1987, the effects of which began to be felt in 1988. Others simply said that people had made Obasinjom come out again "because there was too much sorcery."

An old chief in Buea gave me a more specific explanation. According to him, Obasinjom had come out by himself because he was so angry with the old men who were his guardians: they had become too corrupt and accepted money from the *nyongo* witches "just like the policemen do." Consequently, several old witch doctors had abruptly died, victims of Obasinjom's anger. That is why hardly anybody was left who knew the juju's secrets and why Obasinjom had chosen to descend on new people. The chief commented, "Obasinjom takes anyone he wishes. If he descends on you, you cannot resist. You start to tremble and you cannot speak. It is only after they have put the crocodile mask on you, that you can speak again." [15] He added that in several villages it had been so long since Obasinjom had come out that people no longer knew the secrets. There people had been obliged to buy the juju once more from the Banyangi—again, for a lot of money. In his own village of Buea, the secrets had been kept.[16] But people had nonetheless been obliged to put up some money and send a small delegation to the Banyangi in order to buy some medicine for reinforcing the juju.

When I returned in 1992, the situation had changed once more. Obasinjom had stopped dancing again. According to several informants, mostly young men, this was because people had found out that the juju was corrupted by the elders who continued to use Obasinjom to enrich themselves. As yet, no new way had been found to combat the *nyongo*.

In these stories, the circularity of the discourse on witchcraft and sorcery is less marked than among the Maka; with the Bakweri, as noted previously, this discourse seems to be more "compartmental-ized." *Liemba,* their central notion, does not cover all the manifes-tations of the occult forces, as *evu* or *djambe* tends to do for the Beti or the Maka. When asked whether *nyongo* was a form of *liemba* or, rather, something separate, my informants gave different and evasive answers. In this case, Obasinjom seemed to break through the cir-cularity of witchcraft: introduced from outside, he did succeed in bringing the *nyongo* out into the open. According to Ardener, he thus liberated the new riches from the suspicion of *nyongo.* But one may wonder whether this rupture was indeed definitive. After all, Obasinjom himself also belongs to the shadowy world of the occult. And more recent developments among the Bakweri indicate that he, also, could be corrupted by the elders who are, here as elsewhere in Africa, considered to be the true masters of this domain.[17]

One might also wonder whether Ardener's heavy emphasis on conceptual continuity among the Bakweri, despite all the changes, is completely justified. He concluded that the innovations in the sphere of sorcery, such as the *nyongo* or Obasinjom, had to be interpreted as variable but repetitive emanations of a basic conceptual "template" that continued to determine the Bakweri's reactions. Ardener does indeed sketch a fascinating historical perspective. But his approach seems to neglect the novelty of these transformations in witchcraft discourse—the fact that they reflected a determined struggle to cope with new circumstances. This aspect is all the more interesting since the *nyongo* notion followed different trajectories in other regions.

The Temptations of Mt. Kupe: Witchcraft, Wealth, and Variations

The obsession with *nyongo,* and the idea that the new rich are witches who make their victims work for them, are not particular to the Ba-kweri. On the contrary, they are part of a broad regional configura-tion. Similar notions play an important role throughout the southern and western parts of Cameroon—among the Duala and Batanga on the coast, but also among the Bakossi and the Beti in the interior and with particular force still further inland, in the Grassfields of the West and Northwest Provinces (among the francophone Bamileke and the anglophone Bamenda). In all these areas, these ideas about wealth and witchcraft mark people's reactions to new opportunities for advancement, but their exact implications vary considerably.[18]

In these representations, two places are of special importance in Cameroon. First is Duala, the main port through which the European trade has penetrated the country since the sixteenth century, and now Cameroon's metropolis. People often say that Duala is also the place where this new form of witchcraft originated. Second is Mt. Kupe, sixty miles from the coast in the land of the Bakossi. This mountain has a sinister magical reputation throughout the country; it is there that the witches supposedly put their victims to work on their "invisible plantations."

Among the Duala, this form of witchcraft is called *ekong*. This is the vicious force which Éric de Rosny, the French priest quoted previously, confronted when he had himself initiated as a *nganga* (traditional healer). His "professors" saw it as the most dangerous form of witchcraft. Its basic scenario is vividly summarized by Bureau:

> A person who is interested in *ekong* goes to visit an *ekoneur*
> [French for "*ekong* owner," a commonly used neologism],
> who puts him to sleep by hypnosis. In his dreams, this person
> will see a land where money flows and many laborers work for
> him. An estate owner will offer him his plantations on the condition that he offers the life of, for instance, his mother in return. His first reaction will be to refuse. When he wakes up, the
> *ekoneur* will say to him: "Now you have seen, now you know
> what you have to do." His client will ask for some time to
> think about it. Some day he will make up his mind. (1962,
> 141; my translation)[19]

A crucial notion is that one has to sell a parent in order to obtain *ekong*. De Rosny (1981, 93) gives an equally vivid picture of the other side—the anxiety of potential victims: "when someone dreams that he is taken away with his hands tied toward the river or the ocean while he cannot see the face of his captors, he knows that he has to see a *nganga* [witch doctor] as soon as possible" (1981, 93; my translation). *Ekoneurs* are supposed to steal their victims' bodies from the grave and then sell them to one of their customers. In their magical pursuits, they use a huge snake, the *nyungu,* which is linked to the rainbow and brings riches.[20]

De Rosny's spokesmen made a clear distinction between the *ekong,* "where one kills and sells someone," and older forms of witchcraft, *lemba* or *ewusu,* where the witches eat their victims. The *ekong* is considered to be special to an urban setting. Nonetheless, the Duala must have known the *ekong* long before the colonial conquest of 1884. In earlier days, the *ekong* was an association of chiefs, notables, and traders: it represented *la classe opulente* (de Rosny 1981, 92). But nowadays, the *ekong* has been "democratized": it is believed to be in everybody's reach, and therefore people are even more afraid of it. De Rosny (1982, 92) connects this change with the spread of wage labor and the expansion of the money economy. The power to buy and sell is no longer a prerogative of a few family heads and notables. However, this has not made the economy more transparent. The dramatic fluctuations of cash-crop prices and the uncertainties of the labor market have become crucial to the survival of ever more people but seem, at the same time, to be utterly uncontrollable and unpredictable. One of the attractions of the *ekong* belief, still according to de Rosny, is that it has "integrated" the mysteries of the market. It continues to be so generally accepted because it can offer an explanation for the growing inequalities of wealth and poverty.

In his fascinating case studies, de Rosny describes the struggle of the *nganga* against the *ekong.* The victims are usually extremely weakened when they are brought to the *nganga:* often they can hardly stand or speak. They remain for some time with the *nganga,* who tries to restore their force by long treatments with herbs. But they are only really cured if he succeeds in breaking the spell, the real cause of their troubles. This requires a spectacular all-night ceremony during which the victim's relatives must be present. A crucial moment is a solemn procession by the *nganga* and his assistants, who walk slowly in circles around the group. This is "the march to Mt. Kupe" in order to find the victim's "double," who is believed to work there on invisible plantations that are *tristement célèbres.* The *nganga* can only cure his patients if he succeeds in liberating them far away on Mt. Kupe, but this requires a complicated and dangerous

journey. The therapy is only crowned with success if the *nganga* succeeds in safely bringing back the patient's "vital double." [21]

A clear-cut profile of either the *ekong* witches or the victims does
not emerge from these case studies. But there are some recurrent
traits. Nearly all the *nganga* clients have an urban background; they
are often girls or adult women. In general, the accused are somewhat
older. Relations to new forms of wealth are also quite ambiguous. In
some cases, the clients are relatively prosperous and are supposed to
be the victims of jealous relatives (who are apparently poorer). Other
clients are unemployed and do not succeed in gaining a stable position in the city, blaming their bad luck on sneaky forms of sabotage
by their relatives. But the clients also include people who are believed
to try to profit too much from new opportunities for enrichment,
and who are therefore suspected of having *ekong*.

De Rosny relates these *ekong* accusations and fears most specifically to tensions between a growing individualism and the continuing importance of the family in the urban context. He notes that, in
all his cases, the individuals concerned—both the victims and the
accused—have problems with their families. New individualizing
tendencies undermine ties of kinship and can lead to feelings of solitude and anxiety, which make people believe that they are the victims
of *ekong* (de Rosny 1992, 53). This is the case, for instance, for a
woman who has a good job as a customs officer but who is not yet
married and has no children; apparently, she feels that her parents
strongly disapprove of this. She is brought to the *nganga* in a terrible
state of weakness. The *nganga* "sees" immediately that she is attacked by *ekong;* yet it will take him months to set her free. There are
also persons who, precisely because of their show of individualistic
ambition, are strongly suspected of *ekong*.

The *nganga*'s therapies concentrate on finding the causes of such
problems within the family and arranging for the necessary reconciliation (de Rosny 1992, 31). This is why the presence of the patient's
family is required during the healing ceremonies. The *nganga* will
try to bring the tensions among the relatives into the open in such a
way that a reconciliation remains possible. In several examples, they
seem to consciously refrain from specific accusations in order to fa-
cilitate the victim's reintegration into the family. But de Rosny also

emphasizes that the *nganga* can never succeed if the family is unwilling to face internal problems. In one spectacular case study, the *nganga* decided to break off the therapy after only a first meeting with the patient's relatives. From this de Rosny concludes, "A *nganga*'s weapon will miss its aim if the family refuses to provide him with the ammunition" (de Rosny 1981, 70; my translation).

Although Duala is often mentioned as the place of origin of the *ekong,* its center is now clearly located on Mt. Kupe. This is a densely wooded mountain in the heart of the land of the Bakossi, who speak of *ekom* to indicate a similar new form of witchcraft. Ejedepang-Koge (1971, 200) describes this *ekom* as an "association" of witches who frequent Mt. Kupe in order to get riches. The Bakossi also believe that one can buy the *ekom* from someone who already possesses it, but for this one has to sell a close relative. Only then can one go to Mt. Kupe. There, the initiated will find "mysteriously closed bundles" that contain riches but also all sorts of misfortune (illness or even death). In the night, the *ekom* people secretly go up the mountain to steal a bundle, but they must not open it until they are safely back. If they discover misfortune in their bundle, they must immediately throw it into the river. But they can be lucky and find riches. People call this the "market of sorcery."

The missionaries of Basel, who were among the first Europeans to reach this area in the 1890s, noted already that Mt. Kupe had a strong reputation for magic throughout the area. But they also observed that this reputation differed for the Bakossi as compared to other groups. Initially, they had great trouble reaching the mountain since their carriers from the coast were so afraid that they refused to go on. The Bakossi, on their side, did everything to stop the Europeans from climbing the mountain. Evidently, they feared that the whites would appropriate the riches hidden there. In 1893, the missionary Father Authenrieth wrote, "Just as the mountain appears dangerous and ruinous to the coastal tribes, so it is a promise of good luck to the Bakossi people" (quoted in Heinrich Balz 1984, 327–28). In the 1970s, Balz (330) found that people in certain parts of Bakossiland believed that Mt. Kupe's riches were exhausted and that it was no longer of any use to go there. But he also found that, among other Bakossi groups, the belief in these riches remained strong, having incorporated all sorts of modern elements related to the colonial plantation economy. Alobwede d'Epie (1982, 80) indicates that the Bakossi even integrated the postcolonial manna of development into the *ekom*. He notes that during the secret meetings on Mt. Kupe "development projects of great significance are believed to be highly contested for among the different racial or tribal spirits, and the race or tribe whose spirits win, wins the project." But here again the segmentary logic of Bakossi society asserts itself: "for example, a fight breaks out among the spirits of the tribe that won the project so as to determine the clan in which the project would be located. Another fight breaks out among the spirits of the victorious clan to determine the village in which the project would be finally situated."

S. N. Ejedepang-Koge (1971, 202) describes the role of the *ekom* victims in more detail: "This invisible town on Kupe is something like a labor camp. First of all the ancestral spirits need people who should work to keep the fortunes flowing in such a way that they can be distributed during the *ekom* meetings. Secondly the great men have invisible estates there and they need people to cultivate them. The source of this labor supply is widespread: from all the area surrounding the mountain, from Victoria, Bakweri area, from Duala etc." Furthermore, Ejedepang-Koge says that these "invisible laborers" are "enslaved people," but he adds, quite surprisingly, that they are "very contented"; many of them are recruited among the victims of "*nyongo* witches" in the South. Apparently, the fear of being sold and put to work on Mt. Kupe, so widespread among the Bakweri and the Duala, has its reverse in a kind of wishful dreaming among the Bakossi, who believe they are entitled to profit from the magical riches of their mountain. Heinrich Balz (1984, 331) speaks of a "capitalist or ruling-class dream." Maybe one should rather speak of an absentee landlord's dream. When the cultivation of cocoa spread in this area during the 1920s and 1930s, the Bakossi tried to profit from the new possibilities for enrichment in a particular way: many farmed out their land to strangers, mostly Bamileke from the western highlands, who were willing to pay a substantial rent—often one-third of the harvest or even more—to the landlord. In the following decades, it seemed possible for the Bakossi to get rich without much effort by profiting from other people's labor. The Bakossi imaginary around Mt. Kupe seems to reflect the memory of those happy days, which, unfortunately, are over.[22] No wonder that, to them, the *ekom* is certainly not unequivocally evil: if someone is believed to have enriched himself through *ekom*, this is (according to Balz 1984, 331) "not criticized, but seen as just good luck." There is indeed a clear contrast here with the general fear or even panic about *nyongo* or *ekong* among the Bakweri and the Duala.[23]

A striking aspect of these representations in all these regions is a close association with the whites. This is what de Rosny discovered, to his distress, when he visited an old *nganga* (witch doctor) and a chief in a village near Duala and offered them both a bottle of whiskey. When he wanted to leave, he found to his surprise that the road was blocked by the village youth who abused him and refused to let him pass. Apparently, both the chief and the *nganga* were suspected of having the *ekong*. The rumor that a white stranger had come to offer them a present was enough to resurrect old fears of people being sold to the whites (de Rosny 1981, 93). After a few unpleasant hours, de Rosny succeeded in getting away. But on a later occasion, the people in another village made him understand that they had heard rumors about *un blanc* who had secret dealings with an old witch and a chief in order "to buy people" (88). Nearly a century earlier, the first Swiss missionaries had similar problems among the Bakossi: the chief who received them during their first visit died soon after they had left; on their return they were immediately accused of "stealing souls" (Balz 1984, 115, 332).

Apparently, the *ekong* belief relates to the traumatic memories of the slave trade: that is why it is so easily associated with the whites.[24] The dream image of the *ekong* victims previously quoted from de Rosny—of being taken away, their hands tied, toward the ocean, without being able to see their captors' faces—reflects similar traumas. But this does not explain why Mt. Kupe plays such a central role in these nightmares. It might reflect the realization that, nowadays, the accumulation of new forms of wealth is taking place inside the country as well as overseas. Other elements seem to be part of the colonial legacy. The Bakossi associate *ekom*, as indicated above, with labor camps, and the Bakweri believe that the *nyongo* victims are transported in "lorries" to the "invisible plantations" on Mt. Kupe. Such images seem to evoke the more recent traumas of the forced levying of labor during colonial days. These historical ramifications can explain why an expression like "I'll sell you"—especially when there is an implicit association with the whites—has a particularly ominous ring in these areas.

Famla and Modern Entrepreneurs in the Grassfields

The variations become even more marked if one includes the Grassfields of the West and the Northwest in the comparison. This area is of particular interest since it is from here that, especially after independence, a new bourgeoisie of entrepreneurs emerged who are generally thought to dominate the national economy of present-day Cameroon. Similar notions on the new witchcraft of wealth, here mostly referred to as *famla* or *kupe*, spread somewhat later in this area, where they acquired particularly strong capitalist overtones.[25] They are often associated with notions of debt and with rotating credit associations, the *njangi*, which have recently aroused much attention since having gained particular momentum in this area.

Nowadays, people talk about *njangi* of big businessmen where billions of francs CFA are accumulated. So much money is circulating, particularly in the Bamileke *njangi*, that this endangers the cash flow through the official banks.[26] These *njangi* are believed to also have a more sinister side. People tell horror stories about how, through a *njangi*, one can be recruited into a *famla* coven without knowing it: a man goes to town and accepts a beer from some strangers; suddenly he realizes that he is dealing with a *famla njangi*, but by then it is already too late; he has contracted a debt that he can only pay off by selling a close relative.

Famla has become a major issue of debate in present-day Cameroon, precisely because of its supposed link with the success of the Bamileke, and to a lesser degree Bamenda, businessmen. But, unfortunately, it has hardly been studied in a more systematic way.[27] It is

clear that, in these societies as well, this sorcery of the rich is considered to be a new and highly shocking phenomenon. Here also *famla*
or *kupe* rumors can create true outbursts of panic. Patrick Mbunwe-
Samba (1996), for instance, cites several cases from villages in the
Grassfields where such rumors triggered a true avalanche of accusations. It is striking, however, that in other contexts the fact of being
associated with *famla* does not seem to have serious consequences
for the people concerned. Notably the big businessmen seem to be
immune to such insinuations that do not have concrete effects, at
least not in the world of the day.[28] Young Bamileke often complain
that the *famla njangi* have become so strong that it would be futile
to try to attack them.[29] The only way to escape them would be to
migrate. In many respects, the *famla* rumors seem rather to affirm
the success of the big entrepreneurs.

The discourse on sorcery and witchcraft in these societies reveals
the same basic traits as in the forest societies. Here as well, witches
are supposed to eat their parents, to have two pairs of eyes, and to be
motivated by jealousy and individualistic ambition. But there are two
important differences. The first is the role of the chief (*fon* or *fo*). In
contrast to the segmentary societies of the forest area discussed
above, the chief was, and is, the linchpin of any form of social organization in the Grassfields. The strong accent on hierarchy makes the
whole structuring of these societies markedly different from the segmentary forest societies, with their strong egalitarian ideology. Of
special interest for our topic are the concerted efforts to separate the
chief as much as possible from negative expressions of the occult
forces. In many respects, the powers attributed to the chief seem to
break through the circularity of the sorcery discourses emphasized
above. The chief can distinguish between acceptable and unacceptable expressions of these forces and has highly concrete sanctions at
his disposal, notably the *kwifon* (the police association of the court),
which are more or less outside the realm of sorcery.

Another crucial point is the close link between the chief and trading. In his historical study of these societies, Jean-Pierre Warnier
(1985) showed how, prior to the colonial conquest, the chief exercised strict control over the wealth and economic success of his subjects. It was he who permitted, or forbade, them to engage in com-

merce. Even in precolonial days, trading was the main venue for enrichment and prestige. But a trader's success always depended on the support of the *fon*. Even today people firmly believe that any form of enrichment needs the *fon*'s consent. Due to their special link with the ancestors, the *fon* and his notables have occult powers that permit them to fertilize the land and to enrich their dependents. The Nso say, for instance, that a wealthy man must have received "the power [*sem*] of the *fon*." This expression directly refers to the occult powers—one can even say "the sorcery"—of the *fon*. He has shared his power with his dependent and thus permitted the dependent to accumulate riches (Goheen 1993, 1996).

As in the preceding examples, the more constructive and more destructive uses of the occult powers are often difficult to distinguish in practice. These forces can be used in different ways, and one is never sure if someone who has received "the power of the *fon*" will be tempted to indulge in nightly excesses. However, in this region, the *fon* and his court are there to guarantee that these forces are indeed "tamed." By offering opportunities for social elevation, the *fon* encourages the more positive manifestations of these powers.

The introduction of new riches in the form of money was at first difficult to integrate into this configuration.[30] The old forms of wealth were based on the accumulation of persons and goods that were administered by the elders in the name of the family. The new forms of wealth had more individualistic implications. By its very nature, money eroded the familial organization. It was associated with new forms of sorcery that alarmed the people.[31] The following case study offers an example of the ambiguous perceptions in the Grassfields villages of new forms of wealth and accompanying witchcraft threats. It also illustrates the particular ways in which these societies attempt to cope with such threats:[32]

> During the school year of 1975–76, order at the village school of Lassin-Noni (Bui Division) was disturbed by persistent rumors that a group of boys from the fourth grade (ten to twelve years old) had formed a secret *njangi* (association) called *kupe*. People whispered that the boys were planning to sell their own kin—"especially those who had taken good care of them"—in order to get

rich. Every morning around ten o'clock the class would hear the sound of money as if a stream of coins was falling down. Then the entire class would shout, "Kupe, kupe, kupe."

When these strange happenings continued for more than a week, the class master alerted the head of the school, who "fortunately," was a prince from the local palace. He asked to be called for immediately, any time the sound of falling cash was heard again. He did not have to wait long, for the next day the strange phenomenon repeated itself. The moment the children shouted, "Kupe, kupe," the headmaster rushed in, "raided" the classroom, and grabbed the big boys sitting at the back. He discovered that they had a list of seven boys who were apparently members of their group.

The headmaster immediately alerted the local *kwifon* (disciplinary society) whose inner core of "seers" had to solve the problem with the help of their occult powers. The seven children had to appear before the large assembly in front of the palace and were asked to tell their story. But they all kept quiet, despite threats mingled with appeals. At this point, the "hooded judge" appeared and started to beat the boys. Then finally one of them cracked and told his story.

He claimed that the organizer of their *njangi* (association), who had initiated them to the *kupe,* was a young man (early twenties) from the neighboring village. He had promised them "money and enormous wealth" if they agreed to be initiated. These confessions hardly surprised the people: the young man concerned was already suspected for some time since "everybody" knew that he was born with a particularly powerful sorcery in his belly. But people were shocked that he even wanted to recruit little children. Apparently he would not stop at anything in order to become a powerful witch doctor. Moreover, this *kupe* was something new to the people. The idea that individuals tried to enslave other people in order to make them work on Mt. Kupe was so shocking that all agreed that this evil had to be eradicated at any price.

The experts of the *kwifon* association gave the boys an anti-witchcraft concoction which neutralized their powers. All the school children were warned to alert the elders as soon as the

young man from the neighboring village ever set foot in Lassin
again. Again, they did not have to wait long. During the next market day he turned up. The *kwifon* members were indeed alerted,
and the "hooded judge" came out also. When the young man
heard they were looking for him, he ran for his life. Back home in
his village, he only stopped to grab some luggage, and then he left
as quickly as he could for the Southwest Province (more than
three hundred miles away). He subsequently settled in Buea and
there he became a traditional healer of great renown.

This story had a surprising sequel in 1980. In this year, the
young man, who in the meantime had accumulated considerable
riches due to his success as a witch doctor, returned to the village.
This time, he was received with great honors. He was even elected
president of the Village Development Committee and made an
extremely generous donation during the fund-raising that followed. Nobody wanted to remember that he had been chased
away only a few years previously. All that was history now. "He
had changed."

The end of this story is especially surprising. This new form of sorcery
was at first attacked by all means. But only five years later the instigator of these frightening practices was received by the people "as a
hero."[33] Several factors help to explain this drastic change. In these
societies, the fact that one succeeds in gaining money among
strangers is generally considered as a new equivalent to heroic acts in
the outside world—kill a beast of prey, come back with an enemy's
skull—by which, in the olden days, a young man could establish his
reputation in his village. But the most important thing is, no doubt,
that, on his return, the witch doctor concerned had "offered" his
wealth to the chief (through his donations to the court and other
local associations). In the Grassfields, as said before, any new acqui-
sition has to be "tamed" by presenting it to the *fon* (chief). Thus the
witch doctor was offered the opportunity to legitimate both his new
wealth and his secret powers.

This example illustrates, again, the *fon*'s capacity to break through
the circularity of witchcraft discourse that is so marked in the forest
societies discussed earlier. In the Grassfields, on the contrary, the *fon*

and his court can decide which manifestations of the occult forces are acceptable and which are not: they first chased the young sorcerer from the village but later chose to "whitewash" his sorcery. It is especially this later possibility that gives the *kupe* belief in this area specific implications. The highly hierarchical structures furnish a framework to integrate—or, as Fisiy says, to "whitewash"—the new riches and corresponding occult powers. As long as new wealth remains outside the local power structure, it is associated with sinister forms of sorcery that have to be eradicated by all means. But as soon as the new wealth has been presented to the *fon,* the same secret forces have become legitimized. In this sense, the recent comment in a newspaper interview of His Highness Chief Njika Kanga of Bandjoun (a Bamileke chieftaincy) that "the wealth of all Bandjoun citizens is my wealth" can be read as an indirect legitimation of certain forms of *famla* sorcery.

If someone is accused of being a member of a *nyongo* or *famla* association, he can whitewash his new wealth by presenting it to the *fon*. From this perspective, one can understand why the nouveaux riches in this area are so keen on buying "traditional" titles with the money they have earned in the outside world. The majority of chiefs seem to be as keen to profit from this.[34] The old hierarchical structures of the West and the Northwest offer special opportunities to "domesticate" the secret forces of Mt. Kupe. Apparently, notions of occult powers can thus serve to affirm and protect new forms of accumulation.

Yet one might wonder how long the chiefs will retain enough moral authority to whitewash new forms of wealth. Even the chiefs are now deeply involved in the money economy. They try, in their own ways, to profit from new opportunities for enrichment. The chiefs are not only exploiting their control over the traditional title societies by selling pseudotraditional titles to the new elite, but they also try, for instance, to make money through their customary land rights by selling off large tracts to strangers, notably Fulbe pastoralists, often to the detriment of their own subjects.[35] Thus the chiefs seem to be more and more assimilated with the new elite. Jean-Pierre Warnier characterizes the present-day Bamileke chieftaincies as a "shell, emptied of its substance" since the UPC riots of the 1960s, but "reconstituted" by the new urban elite of businessmen and civil servants in accordance with their own interests.[36] In his interpretation, these "neonotables" have saved the chieftaincy mainly because the chief could play his role in the socialization of their new and suspected wealth. However, among the Nso of the Northwest, as elsewhere in the region, people seem to no longer be sure whether the *fon* will indeed succeed in whitewashing the new wealth and the concomitant occult powers of the new elite. Miriam Goheen, in her book on the Nso (1996), evokes a striking image that forcefully expresses people's doubts about their chief's alliance with these new titleholders: they wonder whether these businessmen and civil servants will indeed prove to be the new "leopards" of the *fon* with whom he, at night and transformed as a lion, will prowl the countryside in order to protect its inhabitants against evil; or will these nouveaux riches turn out to be themselves "sorcerers of the night" who will corrupt the chief and his court from within?[37]

The *Kong* Spreads Panic in the South

More recently, the forces of Mt. Kupe manifest themselves in the southern forest area of the country. Among the Beti (around Yaunde and further to the south), for some time now, people make reference to the *kong*. Again, it concerns a new form of witchcraft that is associated with the selling of relatives but also with the whites and their new forms of wealth.[38] Until very recently, this occult force was still hardly known among the Maka in the East. But over the past few years, it has become assumed that the *kong* is at work among them, too. In those regions, unrest is even greater because of striking uncertainty about which sanctions to apply against this new threat. Above, I emphasized the strong circularity of the witchcraft discourses in these areas. In line with this, people seem to suspect that the *nganga* (healers), who are in principle the obvious protectors against the *kong*, are involved in the *kong* themselves. This has resulted in great uncertainty about how to deal with this new threat: people seem to feel defenseless against it.

During a brief stay in Kribi, a small port on the coast of the forest region, a few questions were enough to trigger a true avalanche of rumors and dramatic stories about new witchcraft excesses.[39] Everybody—the village elders but also young employees in town; a catholic priest but also the state attorney of Kribi—complained about the proliferation of sorcery and witchcraft, which seemed to be out of control. People spoke of *kong* but also of similar contracts to enrich oneself on a truly international scale. The priest of Bipindi told us how he had cured a boy who had sold himself to *L'Oeil du Tigre* (the Tiger's Eye), a notorious sorcerer from Europe. The priest himself had seen how white phantoms sent from Europe by this sorcerer were attacking the poor boy because he no longer wanted to honor his obligations. Other informants made us understand that Mt. Kupe was now only a relay station in the traffic of zombies to Europe and beyond.

A striking phenomenon, revealing the great uncertainty created by such rumors, was that people had recourse to very young healers. In the Bisima—supposedly an anti-witchcraft movement that has been active in the area for about fifteen years—it is not exceptional for boys of about sixteen to begin practicing as *guérisseurs*.[40] An excommunicated priest, Father Many from Lolodorf, had founded a new anti-witchcraft movement that recruited only children, often schoolboys, who were called *zomelo'o*. Some of them had considerable renown throughout the area.[41] Our informants in Kribi were themselves also somewhat surprised by the rapid ascent of such young healers. Normally, the elders are supposed to control the domain of the occult forces. However, according to some, the elders no longer used their forces to heal, but only to destroy. Others implied that, these days, elders tend to keep their secrets to themselves and refuse to pass them on to the next generation. Others again believed that the young folks, with their modern forms of knowledge, despised the secrets of their elders. But everybody agreed that the elders' failure had created a gap, and that witchcraft thus threatened to run wild. Such somber prophecies were often accompanied by references to other groups—the Bassa or the Bamileke—where elders and chiefs are still thought to know how to restrain the occult forces.

This uncertainty seems to inspire a frantic search for ever new sanctions and forms of protection. For some time, the Bisima had seemed to be capable of combating the *kong*. But nowadays many people believe that this movement is corrupt as well. Thus, people are more inclined to invoke the help of outside agents, like the state with its gendarmes and its law courts or the churches with their priests and their exorcism rites.[42] The next chapter indicates that, in particular, interventions by the state can have quite troubling effects.

Again, there is a clear contrast here with the examples from the West and the Northwest, discussed above. There, these new forms of witchcraft also evoke great unrest, but people at least seem to know what kind of sanctions to apply.

Conclusion

A common thread in all these stories is that they hardly correspond to the stereotype of witchcraft as a traditional barrier against change and innovation. On the contrary, there is a constant proliferation of new forms of sorcery or witchcraft that seem, rather, to express determined efforts to appropriate new riches. To the Bakossi, *ekom* has become a means to arrogate development projects; to the Bamileke, *famla* has become a normal trait of modern entrepreneurship; and in the forest areas of the South where such entrepreneurship is less developed, the *kong* takes on a bureaucratic allure.[43]

Clearly, the relation between the occult and new forms of power and wealth is the leitmotif in all these examples. But it is as clear that reactions to these new forms of sorcery are strikingly different. There was general uncertainty and even panic in Kribi; an appeal to the chiefs and his notables in the Grassfields; the introduction of a juju from elsewhere to eradicate the *nyongo* among the Bakweri; a quest for healing among the Duala, where the *ekong* associations have apparently completely lost their more or less prestigious aura from precolonial times. These various scenarios represent different choices and different patterns of articulation between local societies and modern developments.

Among the Maka, new inequalities remain limited, at least within the villages, since they are circumscribed by strong leveling tendencies. Here, people still tend to integrate the new inequalities into the old *djambe* discourse. Elsewhere, new forms of wealth manifest themselves more clearly, also in the local setting. There, people tend to associate them with unknown and therefore dangerous occult forces, which seem to reflect their deep mistrust of the nouveaux riches.

The great uncertainty in Kribi suggests that, in this region, conceptions of new wealth can hardly break out of the vicious circles of the sorcery discourse. Among the Bakweri, it seemed for some time that Obasinjom, the juju imported from elsewhere, was capable of breaking through the occult ban on new forms of wealth. But recently his force seems to be corrupted by the same forces he is supposed to combat. In the Grassfields, on the contrary, the chief and his court offer a more solid institutional support for efforts to domesticate these occult forces and to integrate, or whitewash, new forms of wealth. In those regions, rumors of *famla* and *kupe* hardly seem to undermine the success of modern entrepreneurs from these societies. However, as mentioned above, there are good reasons to doubt whether these chiefs will retain enough moral authority to do so in the future as well.

One can wonder, moreover, whether it is not overly simplistic to reduce the differences discussed in this chapter to a simple opposition between societies with and those without "real" chiefs. It seems that deeper differences are at stake.[44]

This might be illustrated by a brief but interesting argument that took place during a recent Ph.D. defense at the University of Yaunde, when I had the honor of presiding over the jury. The thesis was about funeral rites among the Ewondo, a Beti group. An elderly jury member, himself from another Beti group, praised the candidate, especially because of his analysis of the precarious position of urban elites when they had to attend a funeral in their native village. The professor resumed the ambiguity of the elite's position by the following striking phrase: "C'est comme ça chez nous: celui qui émerge doit s'excuser constamment auprès de ceux qui n'émergent pas" (It is like this with us: those who ascend must excuse themselves constantly to those who do not ascend).

The jury member to my left, a colleague from the Northwest,

was clearly as struck by this phrase as I was. He bent over and whispered in my ear, "Did you hear that? That is precisely the difference with relations among us. It is because of this that those Beti have to eat the state. How else could they satisfy their own people?"[45]

A striking aspect, which might help to clarify what is at stake here, is the recurrent link between sorcery/witchcraft and kinship. In all the examples above, witchcraft originates from kinship: the witches are supposed to attack their own kin, and the therapy of the victims requires, first of all, a reparation of kinship relations. Even in cities like Duala, where family ties seem to be drastically weakened, the accusations and therapies of *nganga* always primarily address relations within the family.[46] But the everyday meanings of kinship relations—the discourses and practices—vary from one region to another. In their analysis of the ascent of entrepreneurs from the Grassfields, Michael Rowlands (n.d.) and Jean-Pierre Warnier (1993) emphasize that these societies elaborate special arrangements for protecting oneself against "the strategies of disaccumulation"—that is, against the leveling forces that characterize so many kinship systems. In the Grassfield societies as well, people are certainly obliged to share with their kinsfolk, but there are clear limits. Warnier speaks of "solidarity according to merit" and of the "embankment of kinship" in these societies.[47] To the contrary, among the Beti, the Maka, or the other segmentary forest societies, it seems that there are no limits to the leveling impact of kinship ideology.

These variations in strategies of accumulation and disaccumulation within the family, and their modern transformations, are no doubt of fundamental importance: we return to them in the conclusions of this book. They constitute the context in which not only the differing trajectories of witchcraft discourses among the various groups but also tensions between these groups at the national level can be explained. In other words, such a perspective allows us to address the extremely troubling "ethnicization" of present-day politics in a country like Cameroon.

THE STATE ATTACKS: A JUDICIARY OFFENSIVE
AGAINST WITCHES

In Cameroon, as in other countries of the continent, the state is increasingly inclined to intervene directly in the unstable terrain of sorcery and witchcraft. As mentioned above, newly devised judiciary proceedings are a key element in this governmental offensive. Since the end of the 1970s, the official tribunals of the East Province, home of the Maka, sentenced supposed witches with some regularity. This is a dramatic shift in jurisprudence. Under the colonial government and during the first decades following independence, the state courts pursued cases related to witchcraft only when concrete proof of physical aggression could be established. Now accused "witches" are condemned without any concrete proof and, moreover, often without their own admission of guilt. Very heavy sentences are issued; they include fines and imprisonment for periods of up to ten years.

Another remarkable change—and no doubt as surprising to Western observers—is that the *nganga* (healers) now appear before the courts as witnesses for the prosecution. Under the colonial regime, judiciary action was for the most part directed against the *nganga* under the pretext that they were a threat to social order since they accused supposed witches and were guilty of defamation. Now their services are apparently quite useful to the courts. In many instances, their testimony is the basis upon which the accused are sentenced. It seems that the judges deem these specialists essential for the establishment of witches' guilt.

These dramatic intercessions of the courts in the East Province are part of a wider context. As was previously noted, there are complaints about the recrudescence of witchcraft everywhere in Cameroon, as well as in many other parts of Africa.[1] Even members of the modern elite now increasingly ask the state to intervene against this threat that seems to overwhelm society. Numerous Africans are of the opinion that Western laws from the colonial period have left dangerous lacunae with respect to this issue. The colonial authorities are criticized for having protected witches since, during this period, judges refused to pursue them without "tangible proof" (see Fields 1985). As a Maka friend who was then municipal counsellor of Abong-Mbang told me in 1973, "With decolonization, all this will change. You whites, you think witchcraft does not exist. But now Africans occupy positions of authority, and they know that witchcraft is too real here. Soon we will change the law so that judges can confront the witches."

Anxiety about witchcraft is now so widespread in Africa that the courts cannot afford to be indifferent. To take up the terms of a high-ranking Zairian judge, "citizens [should not] experience a psychological schism" because state courts treat witchcraft as an "imaginary offence" while the customary judges take such accusations very seriously and impose heavy punishments (Kimvimba 1978, 311). The problems encountered by judges in the face of witchcraft and the question of the establishment of convincing proof are now common themes dealt with by African authors writing in legal journals.[2]

These witchcraft trials raise all sorts of questions. The first is, of course, who took the initiative that inspired this abrupt change? When I worked among the Maka in the 1970s, nothing indicated that the state would suddenly intervene against witchcraft. Was this, then, a determined effort by the state to establish control over elusive occult forces? This proposition is in keeping with the administrators' diatribes cited above and their denunciations of the villagers' witchcraft as an omnipresent form of subversion. However, analysis of these trials also brings to light the role of more modern figures within the villages—teachers, relatively rich farmers—who, it seems, feel particularly threatened. And a critical part is played by the healers who furnish "proof" against the witches. Often, they are the ones who drag the accused before the law. The judges are willing to collaborate with these experts of the occult for good reason: how else could they establish proof of forms of aggression that are, by definition, hidden? One might add that this alliance between healers and judges is nothing new. As stated earlier, modern elites tend to ask the *nganga* for help with all sorts of problems.

Another question is whether this new state offensive will succeed in breaking the vicious circles of witchcraft discourses. Will the new sanctions applied by the tribunals really mean a breakthrough in the field of witchcraft and sorcery? The role of the healers could have problematic consequences in this respect. As we saw, these specialists are ambiguous persons in the eyes of the villagers. They are the representatives *par excellence* of *djambe*, and one can never be sure that they will use their dangerous force only to protect or heal. The healer might be a sort of Trojan horse, and the judges, by engaging these specialists in their attack on the witches, might implicate themselves in the ambiguities of local discourses on the occult. It seems that recent state interventions against witchcraft might occasion unforeseen and contradictory effects.

In this respect, as well, regional variations in the articulation between local witchcraft notions and changes in the broader political economy result in markedly different trajectories.

The Witchcraft Trials in Bertua

The heart of new judicial action against witchcraft is Bertua, the capital of the East Province. This is where the first sentences against witches were pronounced and where the tribunals' interventions have been particularly wide-ranging.[3] These trials have attracted much attention in other parts of Cameroon. It is often said that it is not by chance that they are taking place in the East; everyone seems to agree that witchcraft abounds in the East Province and that, therefore, the state is obliged to act.

The files that were made available to me indicate that these cases correspond to a general model, at least with respect to judicial procedure.[4] The judges based their sentences on Article 251 of the 1967 Penal Code of Cameroon: "Whoever commits any act of witchcraft, magic or divination liable to disrurb public order or tranquility or to harm another in his person, property or substance, whether by taking a reward or otherwise, shall be punished with imprisonment from two to ten years and with a fine of five thousand to one hundred thousand francs."⁵ The accused were not assisted by legal counsel in any of these cases.⁶ They were briefly interrogated by the public prosecutor and the judge. Then the latter pronounced his judgment. In most cases, the accused were condemned: in our sample, for a total of thirty-eight suspects, only eight were acquitted (for four suspects, the documents are not clear as to the outcome of the trial). In all cases, concrete proof of physical aggression was lacking. Only eight of the accused made clear confessions.⁷

The suspects in these cases were mostly charged with having perpetrated one or several homicides by means of magic or, more generally, by having used magical objects to disturb the village. In the twenty-two files I consulted, moreover, there were three affairs concerning love relationships, two of which involved women who supposedly had rendered their ex-lovers impotent. In these latter cases, the judge imposed by far the highest fines. It seems the court takes such threats to virility more seriously than homicide.⁸

The accused in the various cases present no common profile. The majority were middle-aged men.⁹ But there were also several suspects about twenty years old (or even younger) and a few very old men.¹⁰ The number of bachelors without children was quite high (twelve of thirty-eight suspects). However, here also, there were a few counterexamples: one of the accused boasted before the tribunal about his twenty children.

In spite of this diversity, a common tendency emerges from the files. Most of these cases involve, more or less explicitly, supposed attacks against eminent villagers of a more or less modern allure: teachers, local party leaders, richer farmers. At first glance, witchcraft appears in these cases as an anti-modern force. The tribunals seem to act against what we previously referred to as the leveling aspect of witchcraft: most notably attacks made by the weak against the nouveaux riches, who seek judicial interventions. The following case offers an illustrative example:

> On 14 June 1983, the Court of First Instance of Abong-Mbang judged a serious case against four young men of the village of K—— who were accused of having tried to kill "by *sorcellerie*" Mr. Mpoam, a teacher in the village school.¹¹
>
> The whole affair had been triggered by the confessions of Nkal,

a young man who was still a pupil despite his twenty years. Mr. Mpoam, the teacher, noticed that Nkal left the classroom several times without asking permission. When Mr. Mpoam asked him to explain himself, Nkal responded that his *patron* called him. When questioned further, he made it known that he was a member of a band of *sorciers* with three companions (young peasants, somewhat older than he) and that Medumba, their leader, wanted to kill Mr. Mpoam.

After his arrest, Nkal made the following declaration in front of the gendarmes: "Last year, Medumba told me that he wanted the school to leave the village of K—— for M——, his natal village. He said that, in order for this to happen, a teacher had to be killed. He himself designated Mr. Mpoam as the teacher to be sacrificed. Thus, on 8 April 1982, he took us in *la sorcellerie de la nuit* (night witchcraft) to the teacher's house. He operated on Mr. Mpoam and took out his heart. Medumba split it into four parts; he took his part and gave us each a part. He ate his part and told us to do as he did. The others ate their parts as well. But since it was my teacher, I did not eat my part so as to try to save him. This part of the heart is still hidden in the bush. Mr. Mpoam should die on the spot when he is transferred to another school. At present, he does not have a heart, and if he moves for a transfer he will surely die. . . . As for me, I can put back my part of the heart, but the others consumed their parts—I do not know if the entire heart can return."

Apparently, Mr. Mpoam was profoundly shocked by Nkal's horrifying statements. He immediately lodged a formal complaint with the authorities. The tribunal took his complaint as well as the repeated confession of Nkal very seriously. The judge hardly took account of changes in the statements of Nkal, who, once in front of the tribunal, gave new hope to his teacher when he indicated that the teacher's heart could, after all, be reconstituted: "The teacher has a heart, but it's full of holes in the places where it was eaten . . . to give him a normal heart, each person who has eaten must give his blood, and then the holes can be filled." [12]

The judge was even less impressed with the denials of the other accused.

They flatly denied that they were witches. Medumba insisted that this was already the third time that Nkal tried to drag him into witchcraft affairs by such confessions. He added that he had already asked the village authorities to take him to a diviner "to determine what lies between this boy and me." [13] But the tribunal put its faith in Nkal's allegations, which asserted that Medumba had threatened him "by way of witchcraft" even after his denunciation. The judge affirmed that Medumba, like the other accused men, had tried to "mislead the tribunal with his vain and ridiculous denials." He continued that "by affirming that Mr. Mpoam no longer has a normal heart due to their witchcraft practices, the accused . . . break his morale and thus cause him enormous moral injury."

Mr. Mpoam demanded compensation of 5 million francs CFA ($12,500 at the time) for damages. The judge deemed this amount to be exaggerated. But given the "enormous moral injury," he was willing to accord Mpoam some compensation, which he fixed at 25,000 francs CFA. One of the accused, whom Nkal had described as the "neophyte" of the band, was sentenced to two years in prison. The leader, Medumba, and Nkal—in spite of his confession and his attempts to show that he had saved the teacher from death—were condemned to heavier sentences: five years in prison. The fourth accused received four years. All of them also had to pay fines of 30,000 francs CFA and the "entire expenses" of the trial. On 29 November 1983, these severe verdicts were confirmed by the Court of Appeal at Bertua. [14]

In this case, three of the accused admitted nothing but were nonetheless condemned. The only "proof" against them was Nkal's confession—he claimed they had conspired with him to kill the teacher. Among the Maka, people are often implicated in witchcraft through the confessions of others. Normally, one can defend oneself against such allegations by invoking the expertise of the *nkong*. The latter can "see" if someone has in fact "left" his or her body. If necessary, the *nkong* can consult an oracle (*lundu*). In the case described above, Medumba, the supposed leader of the band, tried to defend himself against Nkal's allegations in this manner. He had already asked the village notables to take them both to the *nkong*, and he repeated this demand before the tribunal. In the court documents, his last word is: "I want a witch doctor [*féticheur*]." But the judge did not take heed of this request, and there is never another mention of a *féticheur* in the remainder of the file. This is all the more remarkable since these specialists play a primary role in other cases brought before the courts; then, however, they are witnesses for the prosecution. Evidently, judges are more willing to consult witch doctors to confirm accusations than to challenge them.

Nkal's confession might seem improbable or even outrageous to the Western reader. But, for the Maka, it conforms to an extant model. The idea that witches work in bands, the image of their nocturnal meetings where they eat their victim's heart, and the certainty that the victim will fall ill and die unless the witches are forced to lift the spell all constitute fundamental elements of Maka discourse on *djambe*. One aspect of Nkal's horrid scenes is, however, surprising: the witches are young and attack older men; the elders even seemed to have no idea how to defend themselves against these youngsters. Normally, of course, the elders are supposed to be all-powerful in the realm of occult forces.

Indeed, Nkal's allegations correspond to a new model. This is the *gbati*, referred to above. It is a new form of witchcraft that the Maka have known only since the 1960s and that inspired true panic in the villages, especially at the outset (Geschiere 1980). What scared people about *gbati* was that boys had a monopoly over it. Only boys who have not yet slept with women are supposed to be able to hold the *gbati* in their bellies. This tenet seems to reflect the fear that young men who do not have access to women can become jealous and hence dangerous.[15] Clearly, the term *young* must be taken in its most extensive sense: one affair involved a fifty-year-old bachelor who confessed to the gendarmes that he had the *gbati*.[16] His confession made a clear link between the *gbati* and access to women. He explained that because of his *gbati*, he had no wife in the daytime world. But he added, "With my powers, I fly away into the night and I sleep with any woman who pleases me, even if she is in bed with her husband. When I sleep with a woman like this, she can never have a child again."

Gbati also has a strong anti-modern quality. People say that it "prevents progress in the village." The fifty-year-old "gbatician" mentioned above claimed that all the shops in the village closed because of his *gbati*. In another instance, someone's *gbati* supposedly stopped the construction of a Protestant church in the village and blocked the road to prevent the Catholic priest from visiting the village.[17]

In several cases brought before the courts, a central role is played by more "progressive" persons in the village who, apparently, feel seriously threatened. The case of a well-to-do farmer and the fifty-year-old "gbatician" offers a particularly telling example:

> This case was brought to justice by a fairly rich farmer. He told the judge that each year the income from his plantations surpassed 600,000 francs CFA but that this wealth brought him nothing. All his investments were unprofitable. He was especially bothered by the fact that his children had poor results at school in spite of all the money he paid for their schooling. Hence he consulted the witch doctor (*féticheur*) Aliguéna to uncover the cause of these setbacks.[18] Aliguéna told the tribunal that he immediately "saw" that the farmer had been bewitched by his neighbor, who was jealous of his wealth. The farmer, with the support of the witch doctor, issued a formal complaint against this neighbor. The latter was arrested by the gendarmes and confessed that it was indeed his *gbati* that was bothering the farmer. But once in front of the tribunal, he retracted his confession, asserting that the gendarmes mistreated him. He was nonetheless condemned to five years in prison and a fine of 50,000 francs CFA.

Increasingly, those who are relatively well off fear the jealousy of the other villagers. This seems to reflect growing economic differentiation within the village. The spread of cocoa and coffee cultivation not only created new income disparities between villagers but also caused a "closing off" of families. In the past, every family elder was eager to adopt young men in order to reinforce his own group and increase his prestige. However, especially since the 1970s, people have become increasingly aware of the permanent value of the cocoa and coffee plantations, which are now primary elements in inheritance. The sons of the family are thus generally opposed to the adoption of new members who might make claims to a part of their birthright. In consequence, the number of youth from broken families who are not integrated into other family units—wandering elements, one might say—is on the rise in the village. Many of the accused in witch-craft trials appear to come from this category of persons, and often the more well-to-do villagers are the ones who bring them before the courts, being encouraged by the healers.

The Healer as Broker between the Population and the Courts

The case of the rich farmer bewitched by his neighbor is a prime example of how healers mediate between suspicious villagers and the tribunals. The healer Aliguéna "saw" that it was the neighbor who frustrated the farmer's efforts to profit from his wealth. This is cer-tainly not new: the typical role of the *nkong* is, and was, to discern such hidden attacks.[19] But what has changed is that, in this case, the healer then encouraged the farmer to bring the matter before the court. In other cases, the healer's role is even more pronounced.

On 17 May 1983, the tribunal of Abong-Mbang condemned Mentanga (fifty-seven years old, widower, without children) to five years in prison, a fine of 30,000 francs CFA and damages to the plaintiff, the healer Baba.[20]

Baba (forty years old, native of A——) told the tribunal that he returned to his native village in 1980 and immediately began to purge it. With the support of the local authorities, he "gave an ultimatum to all the killers, demanding them to give over their evil objects." Eighteen people complied, and he treated them. But Mentanga "never wanted to declare himself." That is why Baba decided, in May 1982, to armor the entire village with "his means." This had immediate results: "The following month, the above named [Mentanga] came to give his fetishes over to me in the presence of a curious crowd that started to hoot at him. Over-come with shame, Mentanga tried to kill himself by swallowing some panther whiskers, but I quickly slapped him, causing the whiskers to fall to the ground; I collected them and gave them to the village chief. The chief decided to bring this matter before the Court." [21]

Mentanga told the tribunal an entirely different story. He did not know if he was a witch "because I am not God." The packet of panther whiskers was given to him by a friend when they returned from the plantations together, half drunk. The friend did not disclose the contents of the packet, and he did not ask his friend. The next day, when Mentanga awoke, he could not find it. Hence he had called Baba to ask him to find them. Mentanga concluded, once more: "I know nothing of sorcery."

But here again the judge payed little attention to the denials of the accused. He insisted that Mentanga had in fact tried to sabotage Baba's acts. Furthermore, he had the packet of panther whiskers in his possession and could not explain how he had obtained them. The judge concluded, once again, that "the vain denials of the accused, along with his contradictory statements, only tend to mislead the court." The accused was condemned.

As a plaintiff, Baba had asked for compensation of 500,000 francs CFA ($1,250 at the time). The judge found that he did in fact have the right to damages since "a healer provoked by a witch and prevented from doing his work is subject to great difficulties, and hence suffers moral injury." But the judge deemed the amount requested excessive and reduced Mentaga's fine to 5,000 francs CFA in damages. On 6 December 1983, the Bertua Court of Appeal confirmed this judgment on all its points.

This case gives insight into the extent to which judges are willing to support the healers. The argument that the healer has the right to compensation from any witch who disrupts his or her work is open to very broad interpretations.[22] In this instance, once again, the denials of the accused were to no avail. But concrete proof was upheld, in the form of panther whiskers. The significance of this proof was, however, unclear; it was not certain, for example, that Mentanga had used them. Also, Mentanga insisted that it was Baba who had found the packet, seeming to suggest that the latter could have planted it—a feat of which healers are regularly accused.

In other cases, the healer's role is even more spectacular. One file includes a dramatic description of the way in which Baba searched the house of a suspect with the aid of his assistants. He planted himself in the middle of the house with his right hand raised and a "flat iron full of fire" in his left hand. From this remarkable position, he began "making his incantations before the group of petrified notables and onlookers." The meaning of the flat iron escapes me—I know of no other healers who use this prosaic tool—but the *onkong* are generally great *bricoleurs* (inventors).

There are good reasons why healers play a central role in these trials. For the villagers, it is only normal to turn to the *nkong* when one fears being bewitched. But the *nkong* now brings such accusations before the courts. For the judges who wish to take witchcraft accusations seriously, the healer is an obvious ally. The cases cited herein demonstrate that they hardly dispose of other proof; the *nkong* appears to be the only one able to help them settle these difficult cases.[23] As noted above, the new elites (civil servants and politicians) tend to consult the healers with respect to personal problems, especially in relation to difficult political issues, when their careers seem threatened, or in order to resolve thorny questions. It is, then, hardly surprising that the judges are willing to collaborate with these *onkong*.

Nonetheless, the prominent role the healers now play in the courts is an innovation of great consequence. It constitutes official recognition of their expertise, and thus strengthens considerably their positions, especially when compared to earlier periods in which healers were in fact the targets of judiciary interventions. The villagers are highly conscious of this change. They say that bringing a witchcraft matter before the tribunal without obtaining the support of a renowned *nkong* is a useless endeavor. Without the testimony of a healer, confirming the accusation, the judges will hardly take interest. It seems the *onkong* now even control access to the courts.

One wonders whether this new role as broker between the population and the tribunals has consequences for the general position of the *onkong*. Indeed, there are signs that important changes are taking place. Official recognition of their expertise has led to the emergence of a new type of healer, more "modern" and surely more aggressive. The *onkong* I knew in the Maka region during the 1970s were true

villagers. They hardly spoke French and their knowledge of the ex-
terior world was limited. Some were considered to be rich, but one
always said that the wealth of witches is based upon "delight without
sweat"—which seems to mean that it is easily acquired but does not
last long. Most of the *onkong* lived in simple earthen houses, often
situated slightly outside the village, not far from the bush. Generally
speaking, they remained in the background: they were thought to
operate in secret.[24]

But *onkong* like Baba or Aliguéna have an entirely different allure.
They present themselves emphatically as modern figures. Often, they
have worked for some time elsewhere, sometimes in public service.
They speak French fluently and use, with certain ostentation, French
books on magic, occult forces, and secret knowledge. They brag
about their modern education. One *nkong* (thirty-five years old) told
me, for instance, that he had just been admitted to a Swiss medical
school when his ancestor "took" him. He remained paralyzed for six
months. Then he started as a traditional healer. But he still considered himself a "doctor." These modern *nkong* often emphasize that
they work with the government as members of the new association
of traditional healers. Their membership card is used as a sort of li-
cense and, more generally, as a symbol of their modern prestige.[25]

The contrast with healers of the 1970s should not be exaggerated.
A *nkong* like Mendouga, my friend from the village who offered me
"a second pair of eyes," also tried to give herself a modern allure. She
liked to visit whites (not only the author but also the priests of a
neighboring village) and often boasted of her contacts with the new
urban elites. But a healer like Baba is in much closer contact with the
modern world.

Baba now lives in the middle of the village, on a very visible
site (an important crossroads). His house is indicated by several
large signboards: "Traditional Healer," "Astrologer," and "*Rose-
Croix*" (Rosicrucian). This last sign truly underscores the modernity of this healer: the Rosicrucians are thought to be very active
among the new elites (President Paul Biya is an affiliate). Baba often speaks of his brother, who has an important position in the
president's office in the capital. He himself has the solemn and

assured air of a functionary, which is hardly surprising since he served in the army for a long period. According to the villagers, he was sent home because of "problems"; it is said that he even spent some time in prison. But this rumor only serves to reinforce his renown since people believe that in prison one meets the really dangerous sorcerers who may teach you very deep secrets. Baba himself emphasizes the scientific nature of his expertise: before the tribunal, he often explained how he applied "his science" to uncover witches. He calls himself a "doctor."

It is these modern *onkong* who have apparently become the judges' preferred collaborators.[26]

Many of these modern *onkong* display quite direct, if not outright aggressive, behavior.[27] In the 1970s, the Maka *onkong* were often fairly discrete. They appeared in public only during special events, such as when the notables invited them to perform a ritual or an oracle. They were often hesitant to advance specific accusations, no doubt for fear of difficulties with the authorities, but also because vague allusions seemed more useful to their own forms of therapy. The treatments of such *onkong*—as the case of Madame Mendouga reminds us—were mostly aimed at repairing familial relationships.

A *nkong* like Baba has a different manner: in the case described above, he took it upon himself to purge the village. Then he was the one who captured the evildoers, handed them over to the chief, and ordered the latter to bring the matter to court. In general, this type of *nkong* has few scruples when it comes to hurling direct accusations.[28] An example may illustrate the aggressive manner in which these *onkong* approach potential clients.

In 1991, I discovered Zjé, an old friend from a Maka village where I had lived for some time, in a very serious bind. He felt threatened by witchcraft from all sides. He had been married two consecutive times, but both his wives died young, which led to a series of conflicts with his in-laws. More recently, he married for a third time. But, soon after, his wife lost her mother; she accused her uncle (her father's brother) of having killed her mother by witchcraft. Zjé was profoundly affected by this affair as well.

During a burial, he met a *nkong* from another village who
warned him that he had "seen" that Zjé's home was "mined"
with witchcraft; if Zjé did not immediately "clean" his compound,
he would be hit with more misfortune. Zjé was impressed by this
man and invited him to come purge his camp. And, indeed, the
nkong found a small basket filled with dangerous objects (such as
a bone within a bone, nails, hair) under the entry to his house.
The *nkong* told Zjé who had planted the basket. He then insisted
that the entire village be cleaned. Zjé thus went to the village chief
and asked him to authorize the *nkong* to do so. But the chief
bluntly refused despite the protests of Zjé and his family, and in
spite of the *nkong*'s other sinister predictions.

The chief had good reasons, in fact, for refusing his authorization. He had been at odds with Zjé and his family for a long time,
and the *nkong* had alluded that certain of the chief's male family
members were in a plot against Zjé. It was not impossible that the
chief himself would be swept up by the avalanche of accusations
once the affair was launched. Zjé was extremely angry with the
chief's refusal and even said that he might submit the matter to
the *sous-préfet* in order to obtain his authorization to purge the
village.

This example reveals that village authorities are not always ready to
collaborate with the *nkong*. In fact, in contrast to the judges and
other members of the urban elites, they are not sheltered from the
onkong's accusations. But this story especially illustrates the new
boldness of the *onkong*'s interventions. Evidently, the *nkong* in question had developed a very direct method of recruiting clients. Indeed, Zjé was terrified of his "visions." By gaining the authorization
to purge the entire village, the *nkong* hoped, perhaps, to hoist himself
to the ranks of Baba, who had just established his reputation by
cleaning a series of villages.

Collaboration with the tribunals offers the *onkong* new possibilities for renown, which they are evidently eager to exploit. But such
collaboration also has an impact on their role as healers and protectors and the way they undertake this role. One of the modern *onkong*
I interviewed in the Maka region had the habit of calling his clients
"the accused." One wonders whether the collaboration with the

courts truly helps the *onkong* to better protect the people. In principle, *onkong* are supposed to heal: they must free the witch by "neutralizing" his or her witchcraft when it becomes dangerous. This is how they restore family solidarity. But the modern *onkong*, who work with judges and gendarmes, seem to be intent, instead, on punishing the witches. In this sense, the *onkong* become disciplinary figures. Is this compatible with their role as healer?[29] An important question raised by the Bertua witchcraft trials is to know whether the *onkong*, by delivering the accused to the tribunals, really help cure them and neutralize their forces.

Comparisons:
Regional Variations in Cameroon

One of the most remarkable aspects of the witchcraft trials of Bertua is that they constitute a brutal reversal in jurisprudence. When I conducted research in the Maka region during the 1970s, nothing indicated that the courts would soon intervene so directly in witchcraft affairs. To be sure, from time to time the gendarmes would thrash a villager accused of witchcraft, but this was infrequent. In those years, such affairs were mostly settled within the village. They were rarely brought before the courts since everyone knew that they would be considered only if "tangible proof" could be produced. Why such an abrupt change, then, around 1980? Was it inspired by the state, in an attempt to better control witchcraft? Or was it, rather, inspired by the villagers, who had become panic-stricken by the supposed proliferation of witchcraft? To respond to these questions, it is useful to briefly compare developments in other regions of Cameroon. It is striking that there have been quite important regional variations with respect to the state's engagement in witchcraft affairs.

During the 1980s, Cameroonian colleagues often told me that these trials were specific to the East Province. A brief episode going back to the beginning of my research among the Maka illustrates the extent to which this region is associated with witchcraft.

In 1971, Minister of Territorial Administration M. Ayissi Mvodo, on a visit to the East Province, started his speech in one of the towns with these arresting words: "Before coming here, I thought the people of the East were above all engaged in drinking *arki* [local spirits] and practicing witchcraft."

He evidently wished to add that he had been able to observe that this was not the case. Unfortunately, the master of ceremonies gave the signal for applause just after the first sentence. The remainder of his remarks were lost in the din. Nonetheless, the minister had aptly summarized standing opinion on the situation in the East.[30]

This association plays into the Bertua witchcraft trials. Administrators serving temporarily in the East Province are almost always natives of other parts of the country. They often complain of feeling threatened by the proliferation of witchcraft in this region. This is also true of the judges involved in these trials. The idea that this "backward" region—another typical connotation of the East—is being overrun by witchcraft inspires their haste in sentencing the accused in these affairs.

However, it remains to be seen whether such trials are in fact limited to the East. Recently, similar actions have been repeated in the Center and South Provinces.[31] In 1992, during a brief stay in Kribi on the coast of the South Province, it became apparent that, here as well, there is rapidly mounting panic about the supposed proliferation of witchcraft, which is aggravated by deep uncertainty about how to contain it. Several informants said that earlier anti-witchcraft movements in the area had lost their force. People were increasingly turning to the church for protection. As mentioned previously, a Cameroonian priest, Father Many of Lolodorf, was even excommunicated for being too implicated in witchcraft problems. However, his attempts to combat and exorcise witchcraft generally commanded much respect in the region. In an interview, the priest of Bipindi, who had no contentions with his ecclesiastical superiors, emphasized that Many was in principle on the right track; given the increasing anguish, the church had to find some sort of solution. According to him, it had its own answers, which included prayer as well as ancient practices of exorcism. The priest himself, who emphasized that he had pursued in-depth studies in parapsychology, regularly exorcised demons with, as he said, considerable success.

But the population, in general, seemed more inclined to have re-course to the state.[32] In Kribi, several witchcraft affairs were cited that were brought before the tribunals. A spectacular example took place in the village of Ntdoua, about twenty miles to the northeast of Kribi. In 1991, the population of Ntdoua dragged an elderly man to the gendarmes for having killed several villagers with his witchcraft. The state prosecutor started an investigation, but several days later he ordered the gendarmes to release the old man for lack of tangible proof. The consequences were dramatic. A few months later, the villagers set afire the house of the alleged witch, and the old man perished in the flames. The gendarmes then arrested seventeen young men.

We had occasion to discuss this matter with Mr. Ela, the new prosecutor at Kribi (the successor to the one who set the old man free). For him, the affair posed an insolvable dilemma. In his opinion, his predecessor had tried to expedite the matter too rapidly. He should have kept the man in prison at least until spirits were calmed. Mr. Ela did not have a clear idea as to how to treat the youngsters who had killed the old man and were still incarcerated. In principle, they should have been condemned: Mr. Ela emphasized that the state could never allow the population to impose its own law, especially in a case of summary execution. But, at the same time, condemning them would also be dangerous since this would confirm the general idea that the state was inclined to protect witches. People might even think that he, the prosecutor, was himself in the witches' pay.

To the prosecutor, this dilemma was a typical consequence of popular pressure being put on judicial authorities to intervene. He insisted that, in these affairs, the initiative did not come from him or his colleagues. They were rather inclined to adhere to the positivism of the law. The big problem was, however, that "the letter of the law does not correspond to our culture": the state cannot elude the pop-ulation's pressing demand that witches be pursued. Mr. Ela insisted that recent witchcraft trials were certainly not the result of the delib-erate actions of the state.[33] Nor had he or his colleagues received clear directives from his superiors in this regard. The Supreme Court at Yaunde, still according to Mr. Ela, would consider witchcraft accu-sations inadmissable without tangible proof; these judges still would hold to the "positivist" letter of the law. Before the Yaunde court, judgments made by the Bertua Court of Appeal would certainly be overturned, but the people of the East did not know how to make an appeal.[34] The Kribi prosecutor also signaled considerable differences between the interventions of the tribunals in the East Province, on the one hand, and those of the South and Center Provinces, on the other. In the latter regions, there had been a few witchcraft trials in which the tribunals had indeed condemned those charged with witchcraft. But in these areas—in contrast to the East—there were also many countercomplaints of libel made by those accused of witchcraft, and often the judges decided in their favor. Also, here people were generally less eager to bring witchcraft accusations before the courts.[35]

During the interview, the prosecutor finally proposed a stunning solution to the problem of the young men of Ntdoua. Despite his declarations of positivism, he contended that the state must, in the end, accept the community's opinion. If the whole village was determined to expel someone due to their witchcraft practice, the state was obliged to accept this. How could peace be otherwise restored? This conclusion is indicative of how strong the pressure is on bureaucrats to intervene. Despite his skepticism of traditional healers, his antipathy for collaboration with them, and his doubts about witchcraft accusations in general, the prosecutor did think that the government had to intervene against witches in order to stem the rising tide of anger.[36]

In other regions of Cameroon, different attitudes prevail. There is, again, a clear contrast between the forest zone of the South and the more hierarchical societies of the West and Northwest. In the latter regions, rumors about new forms of witchcraft (*famla, kupe*) have inspired great anxiety as well, but there are hardly any witchcraft trials like those in Bertua. People from these areas express doubts as to the efficacity of such trials. They question, for example, if the state is really capable of treating such problems: Can the tribunals in fact cure the witches and neutralize their witchcraft? Are prison sentences or fines the most effective means to do this? In their view, the struggle against witchcraft should be left to the chiefs and their associations since they are better equipped in this domain than the state officials. The very fact that witchcraft accusations are rarely brought before the courts in these regions suggests that people still have confidence in traditional sanctions for controlling occult forces.

Apparently, the general contrasts identified above between discourses on witchcraft in the forest societies, on the one hand, and those of the Grassfields in the West and Northwest, on the other, have concrete effects on state action. I have attempted to show how, in the West and Northwest, efforts are made to place the chief outside the vicious circles of witchcraft discourses. He has the necessary authority to distinguish between acceptable and unacceptable manifestations of occult forces, and he has concrete sanctions at his disposal against undesirable manifestations. In contrast, in the societies of the forest, the circularity of discourses on witchcraft seems to efface all clear distinctions. Here, one is therefore more inclined to call on the state and its tribunals to escape this circularity. One wonders, however, if the courts in fact succeed at this. The central role of the healer as mediator between the population and the tribunals increases the risk of implicating the judges in the ambiguities of local discourses. We later return to this point, but there is evidently a clear contrast with the West and the Northwest.

Several authors note that the societies of the West and Northwest have always been inclined to maintain a certain distance from the state and to trust, instead, the forces of their own institutions—such as the authority of their chiefs or the economic force of their savings' associations (*tontines*).[37] This evidently also applies to witchcraft affairs. The contrast with recent developments in the East and, to a lesser degree, the South and Center Provinces, is clear. There, the population seems no longer inclined to keep the state at bay. To the contrary, people are willing to encourage state intervention even in the highly private domain of witchcraft and family quarrels. It remains to be seen whether the state is indeed capable of bringing this treacherous field under its control.

Comparisons:
Witchcraft Trials in Europe at the Beginning of the Modern Era

It is difficult to compare developments in eastern Cameroon with state interventions in witchcraft affairs elswhere in Africa. This is not to say that the acts of the Cameroonian tribunals are exceptional: previously, I quoted several authors from other African countries who insist, like some of their Cameroonian counterparts, that governments have to act against the recrudescence of witchcraft. And elsewhere, as well, the state has effectively intervened. It appears, for example, that during the 1970s the Marxist-Leninist regime of Benin's President Kerekou unleashed a real witch-hunt by radio, inciting the population to take action against secret conspiracies against government development policies.[38] But there are still few other in-depth analyses of these interventions. Until recently, the main trend in anthropology was to study witchcraft in local contexts, ignoring the role of the state.

Potentially interesting comparisons are found, then, on an entirely different terrain: in the historical studies of the European witchcraft trials that took place at the beginning of the modern era.[39] Indeed, the historians more than the anthropologists were forced to analyze external influences on local conceptualizations of occult forces. In Europe, it was obvious that the brutal persecution of witches (most of whom were women) spread like true epidemics in certain regions and was closely linked to the encroachment of the state and ecclesiastical authorities on local communities. It was only in the context of this large-scale historical process that direct interventions by the secular and ecclesiastical tribunals in the domain of witchcraft became possible.

In their analyses of these dramatic events, historians are often inspired by the works of anthropologists, especially those on Africa. This is an effect, no doubt, of the recent, but already waning, proclivity for anthropology among historians. It is surprising, however, that exchanges between these two disciplines seem thwarted by the appropriation of more or less outdated ideas and by a striking neglect of more recent criticism issuing from the discipline in question. Many historians, even in very recent publications, make use of rather dated studies of African societies, which are marked by an ahistorical structural functionalism. Hence they evoke an image of "African witchcraft" (sometimes in the singular, with no specification of time and place) that appears atemporal, more or less static, and linked to societies "in equilibrium." Such interpretations—which suggest that belief in witchcraft is normally "eu-functional" and that local communities are in a state of "magical equilibrium"—are then applied to the peasant societies of Europe prior to the great changes of the sixteenth century.[40]

A striking example of such a time lag in borrowing from anthropology is found in a recent contribution by R. Rowland (1990).[41] It is rather shocking that Rowland speaks systematically of African societies as "primitive" (an adjective that no anthropologist would use today). But it is even more disturbing that he compares themes from witches' confessions in Europe to the general characteristics of "African beliefs" in witchcraft, basing himself on a study by Lucy Mair from 1969 and without bothering to ask whether beliefs common to all of Africa even exist. Since he hardly refers to specific societies or periods, he can only establish a static representation of these "African beliefs."

His "structural" approach—another borrowing from anthropology?—forces him to establish rigid binary oppositions (Africa versus Europe; or day-witches versus night-witches, an opposition he thinks is characteristic of Africa without further explanation). In some respects, he even succeeds in surpassing structuralist anthropologists at their own trade: when statements from people involved in these trials or other contemporaries fail to correspond to his distinctions, he deems them "confused" or even "muddled" (rather than questioning the foundations of his own distinctions).

Such appropriations from anthropology by historians are all the more curious since, for Africa, it was historians who admonished anthropologists about the dangers of reproducing atemporal and ahistorical representations of African village communities and of neglecting profound and constant changes experienced by these societies long before colonization. This static image of local society—which anthropologists working in Africa now try to leave behind, not without difficulty and with constant admonishment by historians—thus emerges elsewhere, in historical studies of Europe. No surprise, then, that several historians now profess disappointment with the relevance of anthropological interpretations for the analysis of witchcraft trials in Europe.[42] Doubtless, they might find more inspiration in historical studies of religious change in Africa than in structural-functionalist anthropology.

Thus some pilfering by historians in the anthropological arsenal may be surprising. But it is perhaps even more disconcerting to note that anthropologists are so little inspired in their studies of witchcraft by the flow of historical publications on similar phenomena in Europe.[43] Historians have, for some time already and very convincingly, demonstrated that the vicissitudes of witchcraft at the local level can be understood only in relation to larger historical processes. The French historian Robert Muchembled, for instance, relates in an evocative way the sudden proliferation of witch-hunts in Europe to the disciplinary action of political and ecclesiastical authorities, closely linked to the rise of the absolutist state, and the Reformation and Counter-Reformation. He views the great witch trials from the sixteenth century as an emanation of the "forced acculturation" of popular culture and a process of "triumphant centralization." The absolutist state, often in collaboration with the ecclesiastical tribunals, unleashed a "civilizing offensive" with the intent of obtaining nothing less than the "submission of souls and bodies," the repression of popular culture, and the "political and religious conquest of the countryside" (Muchembled 1978a, 225–27; 1978b, 30). It is in this context that he explains the obsession of political and ecclesiastical elites of the time with the sinister forces of witchcraft. The elites linked local representations of evil witches to the image of a heretical sect of devil worshipers striving to undermine the prevailing order. This fusion of local representations with the theme of the black mass presided over by the devil rendered witchcraft a major stake in the struggle for the submission of popular culture and the disciplining of local communities.

Other historians had already noted the relatively recent nature of this fusion, pointing out that only this association of the devil with local witchcraft belief allowed for the great witch trials of early modern times. Along these lines of interpretation, Muchembled distinguishes between two forms of discourse in the files of these trials. First, there is the discourse of the witnesses in the village, who do not seem to incriminate witchcraft as such, but who accuse particular witches (which sometimes, but rarely, include men) of threatening the harvest, cattle, and even the lives of villagers. Second is the discourse of the judges and other members of the elite, who force the witnesses to link these popular beliefs with the figure of the devil and his attempts to undermine the church and official faith.[44] This op-position suggests correspondences, but also, and more interestingly, contrasts with recent judiciary actions in the domain of witchcraft in Africa.

Another variant in historical studies of witchcraft trials in Europe places less emphasis on an offensive from above, seeking rather to explain these trials in light of tensions internal to local communities. This work is inspired by the well-known studies of Alan Macfarlane (1970) and Keith Thomas (1971) on witchcraft in England at the time of the Tudors and the Stuarts. They remark that in England, in contrast to the continent, the idea of a diabolical sect was hardly significant. The trials were not foremost the result of the actions of the elites, but stemmed instead from increasing economic differentiation within the villages—most notably from the fact that the nouveaux riches tried to avoid community obligations. Neglecting long-standing obligations of solidarity, they began to accuse their indigent neighbors of witchcraft in order to protect themselves against the jealousy of the other villagers and to free themselves of guilty sentiments. To affirm the new distance that separated them from the others, they were increasingly apt to bring these accusations before the tribunals.

Similar interpretations are relevant not only to England. This same pattern is found in the study by P. Boyer and S. Nissenbaum (1974) of the famous Salem witch trials that took place in New England in 1692. For these authors as well, the sudden wave of witchcraft accusations can be understood only through detailed analysis of rising tensions in the village. Because of their painstaking research into this small society, their study became an impressive example of the degree to which historians are capable of reconstructing daily life in a community belonging to a distant past. Boyer and Nissenbaum are able to demonstrate how the fear of witchcraft was amplified by intense factional struggles around the "church"—that is, the congregation that constituted the center of local organization in New England—and especially around the figure of the pastor. At first sight, the factions in Salem-Village seem blurred. And yet, through close analysis the authors reveal how these factions logically arose from socio-economic developments that had dire consequences for at least part of the population. One faction, which more or less constituted the old Salem elite, felt threatened by the rapid rise of the neighboring commercial center of Salem-Town. Other villagers were in a position to profit from the situation. For the old elites, encouraged by the pastor, this threat could only be apprehended as the work of the devil himself. Thus the struggle among the factions suddenly led, in 1692, to an onslaught of accusations of witchcraft, aimed mostly at women (but also at a few men): a total of 142 people were accused, and 19 were executed. In Boyer and Nissenbaum's intepretation, the Salem witches were victims of the tension between Puritanism and commercial capitalism that poisoned rivalries between local factions.

In a more recent study devoted to the "last pyres" in northern France, Robert Muchembled (1981) is equally influenced by this approach. He attempts to explain why, as late as 1679, four "witches" were burned in Bouvignies, a small village near the border with Flanders, even though the authorities in Paris had become more reluctant to bring witchcraft cases to trial. As in his earlier publications, Muchembled continues to explain the development of the Bouvignies trials in relation to the influence of the superior magistrates—in this case, the judges of Douai who translated popular accusations into demonological discourse, linking them to the figure of the devil. But in his study of Bouvignies, Muchembled locates the direct cause of these trials in internal village conflict, which manifested itself in tenacious charges against certain women. Like Boyer and Nissenbaum, he attempts, through detailed analysis of the socioeconomic context, to reconstruct the struggle between local factions so as to explain why certain people became targets of accusations. While the contours of the factions remain unclear in his analysis, Muchembled nonetheless believes that he has located the true instigator—the innkeeper, Mr. Gilles Fauveau, whose intention was to surpass his rival, the "mayor" of the village, by attacking his clients.[45]

These micropolitical interpretations of witchcraft trials in the West approximate another strain in anthropology: "transactionalism"— most notably associated with the Manchester school of Max Gluckman. Striking parallels can be drawn with studies of Central Africa (Zambia, Zimbabwe) in British anthropology of the 1950s and 1960s; these also offered detailed microanalyses of witchcraft accusations as weapons in factional struggles within village societies.[46] Once again, though, the historians neglected earlier criticisms of these works in anthropology. One criticism was that these analyses overestimated the possibilities offered to "big men"—the primary subjects of these monographs—to manipulate their environment. Mary Douglas noted in 1963 that "witchcraft accusations were a clumsy and double-edged weapon" (1963b, 126). Other critics observed that, in this style of anthropology, cultural themes such as witchcraft beliefs risked being reduced to simple reflections of socioeconomic tensions.[47] For the people involved, the reality of witchcraft was evident. Their action patterns and decision making can only be understood within the logics of this conceptual framework.

For our comparison, it should be noted that, from this micropolitical perspective, the role of the state in European witchcraft trials seems more limited. Several historians have recently observed that, in many parts of Europe, the courts were hardly inclined to persecute witches and tended to ignore accusations coming from local communities. One historian even marvels that there were relatively few trials, given the peasantry's extreme fear of witchcraft.[48] In his more recent publications, Robert Muchembled also refines the idea of a totalizing offensive emanating from above. He now posits the pivotal position of the village notables, which might explain why an "infernal circle" of accusations unfurled in some regions while others remained untouched by such "epidemics."[49] Evidently, in Europe as well, there were significant variations in the ways in which interventions from above and tensions internal to villages articulated in actions against witches.

The fact that European witchcraft trials lend themselves to varying interpretations renders a comparison with contemporary interventions by the Cameroonian courts all the more interesting. On the surface, it seems that, in Cameroon as well, a sort of "civilizing offensive" has been enacted, with witchcraft becoming the centerpiece in government efforts to discipline local societies. This view corresponds to the idea of a "hegemonic project," which, according to Jean-François Bayart, defines the logics of the Cameroonian state.[50] He argues that the regime strives, in a "totalizing" way, to dominate all domains of society. In such a perspective, it seems only logical that witchcraft becomes an issue. Being difficult to control due to its hidden and diffuse nature, witchcraft must seem to present a direct challenge to such a hegemonic project. No wonder Cameroonian officials tend to characterize it as one of the most dangerous forms of subversion. Such ideas must encourage judges to act against witches: the examples above offer morbid but nonetheless clear illustrations of this.[51]

However, for Cameroon as well, this interpretation of witchcraft trials as the effect of an offensive "from above" is not entirely convincing. If this was a case of a government-coordinated operation, one would expect more uniformity in court actions across the country. At present, the courts seem prepared to intervene directly only in certain regions: in the East, less so in the South and Center, and hardly at all in the West or the North. But it is precisely in the East, South, and Center that popular pressure on the tribunals to act against witches is particularly strong. This is rather in keeping with the second mode of interpreting the European trials, which posits that tensions internal to village communities are the key factor. From this point of view, the central question is to what extent the various regional communities are disposed to appeal to the tribunals.

The distinction established by Robert Muchembled between two discourses on witchcraft in the European trials—that of the village witnesses and that of the judges and the elites in general—is also suggestive of comparisons and contrasts with the Cameroonian examples. In the files of the Cameroonian trials the judges introduce also their own shades of meaning, which differ from popular discourse. The judges' perception of witchcraft is profoundly influenced by their modern legal education, as well as by Christian representations. For them, at least in their official statements, witchcraft is always evil; there is no place for the idea that these forces can be used in a positive manner; withcraft is instead equated with the "moral injury" it causes to others. However the judges' discourse is constantly tainted, "creolized," by popular conceptions—perhaps more than in the European scenario. One can hardly expect otherwise, given the elites' continuing engagement with traditional healers.

The language of the files of the Bertua Court of Appeal reveals what kind of confusions can follow from this. In these documents, *sorcellerie* is evidently a key term, but this term clearly lends itself to various interpretations. For the judges, it is strongly associated with evil: someone who confesses to being a *sorcier* is sure to be condemned.[52] However, in several files, the healer begins his testimony by presenting himself as "Mr. So-and-so, *sorcier*." For the judges, this is not even a reason to challenge the witness. To the contrary, their judgments are based explicitly on the expertise of this *sorcier*. Similar contradictions outline the difference between the judges' language, which objectifies *sorcellerie* as always evil and hence to be completely eradicated; and local discourse on *djambe* as a special force that can be used for various ends. Confusion surrounding the term *sorcier* also indicates that local conceptions penetrate and corrupt the offical discourse of the judges by way of the ultimate intermediary, the healer.

The central place of the healers in the Cameroonian examples constitutes another distinguishing mark—a significant one—from the European trials. The general willingness of the judges and the Cameroonian elites to call on the healers' expertise is indicative of the extent to which they are still implicated in local discourse on witchcraft, with all its ambivalence and vicious circles. Once again, this raises questions about the efficacy of the tribunals' actions against witchcraft.

Conclusion

The Bertua witchcraft trials condense all the problems and ambiguities inherent in the state's relation to witchcraft. One understands why the government is inclined to intercede. Many officials strongly believe that occult forces do undermine government policies and its "hegemonic project." But more important, at least in certain parts of Cameroon, seem to be the pressure put on the state by people and their demands that the state act against the spread of witchcraft.

Yet it also seems that there are good reasons to question the efficacy of judicial action in this domain. In the first place, even from the population's point of view, the tribunals' ability to cure witches is

doubtful. As we have seen, local healers are thought to control witchcraft because they are able to neutralize the forces of witches; they
can persuade witches to confess and can free them of their occult
powers. But a confession has an entirely different effect when enun-
ciated in front of the tribunal: it does not lead to a cure but, rather,
to fines and lengthy prison sentences. The big question is whether
these measures will help neutralize the supposed witchcraft of the
accused. The reverse seems to be the case. As indicated before, it is
generally believed in Cameroon that people can learn the most dangerous secrets in prison. There, one meets *marabouts* and evildoers
from all over the country; someone who has done time is therefore
endowed with an aura of danger. It is, then, highly unlikely that the
"witches" from Bertua, once liberated, will be considered cured
and relieved of their dangerous powers. To the contrary, they will
inspire even greater fear than before. The tribunals can punish the
accused, but they do not have the means to neutralize their occult
powers. Furthermore, we saw that the engagement of local healers
in judiciary action may counteract, in popular opinion, their healing
capacities.

There are, then, good reasons to doubt that the courts will rupture the vicious circles of the witchcraft discourses.[53] Due to the central role of the healer, judiciary action becomes implicated in the ambiguity and circularity of local representations. As noted, the judges
are willing to base their judgments on the healers' expertise. In the
absence of tangible evidence (which is most often the case) or confessions, this becomes the only possible means to establish "proof."
I already evoked the image of the healer as Trojan horse: by bringing
him into the court, the judicial offensive drags in all sorts of popular
conceptions and hence acquires, itself, unintended consequences.

For the population, the *onkong* (healers) are the personification of
djambe (witchcraft). They can only "see" and overcome the witches
because they themselves are "witches who have beaten all the records." This also signifies that healers are always highly ambivalent
figures: they can only heal because they have killed. One is, in the
end, never sure that healers will use their redoubtable forces only
to cure. Because of their reliance on healers, the tribunals' initiatives seem, therefore, to encourage, and not weaken, belief in occult

forces. Moreover, the judges' confidence in the expertise of specialists who are seen as highly ambivalent by the population implies that the tribunals will sooner or later become embroiled in the ambiguities of local witchcraft affairs.

In order to avoid the more problematic aspects of their collaboration with local specialists, the judges and other members of the elite try to make a distinction between *bona fides* and *mala fides* healers. The government evidently claims to collaborate with only the former; these would be the only ones admitted to the national association of traditional healers. But from the people's point of view, especially in the forest zone, such a distinction between "good" and "bad" *nganga* is always problematic and relative. The *nganga* is the symbol *par excellence* of the ambiguity of witchcraft.

Over all, then, the courts' interventions may reinforce, rather than weaken, faith in the efficacy of witchcraft.[54] The judges themselves become entangled in the conspiracies and the traps of the occult forces. The judicial offensive seems to encourage the emergence of a new type of healer, an emboldened figure of modernity with a highly aggressive approach. We saw how these *nganga* are avidly exploiting problematic situations to establish their reputations. And we saw their strident confidence in launching direct accusations. New possibilities for collaboration with the government offer them opportunities to obtain official recognition, but they also strengthen the punitive aspects of their behavior. Thus the *nganga* risks becoming more of a disturbing element than a healer.[55]

There are good reasons, then, to doubt that the judiciary apparatus, and the state in general, are equipped to intervene in the dangerous terrain of witchcraft.

BALANCE

I t is not easy to draw general conclusions from the preceding chapters. The modernizing capacities of witchcraft discourses—their potential to incorporate and address modern changes—is expressed in a dazzling array of appearances and manifestations. In the preceding chapter, the more frightening effects of these discourses and their dynamics in postcolonial Africa came especially to the fore: the judges of Bertua who condemned alleged witches to heavy sentences on the basis of very shadowy evidence; the emergence of a modern type of *nganga* (healers), heavily armored with novel attributes—sunglasses, books on "Eastern magic"—and extremely aggressive in their ways of approaching potential clients. But these troubling manifestations should not disguise the real wisdom and consolation contained in these discourses, even in the changing contexts of present-day Africa. A *nganga* like Mendouga could, indeed, if she wanted, reassure frightened patients and restore solidarity within the family. Éric de Rosny's studies of the *nganga* in the slums of Duala offer even more striking examples of how they use their powers to bring consolation and restore well-being. In their implications for power and politics—our central topic—these discourses prove to be equally ambiguous and confusing: they can express leveling efforts vis-à-vis the new elite's arrogance, but they can also confirm the elite's power and self-assurance.

Firm conclusions are therefore very risky in a field so bogged with ambiguities and vagueness. Nonetheless, it is possible to discern certain general tendencies.

Witchcraft and Distrust of Power:
The Dialectics of Secrecy and Publicity

A central question of this study is whether these notions on the occult inspire specific modes of political action. In the introduction, I
referred to the Cameroonian historian Achille Mbembe and his wor-
ries over the stalemate of the democratization processes on the continent. In his view, real political renewal requires nothing less than
the forging of "other languages of power," better rooted in "the
everyday life of common people." We saw also that power is a central
issue in discourses on sorcery and witchcraft. The question becomes,
then, to what extent do the latter provide elements for the language
Mbembe evokes?

The link between witchcraft/sorcery and politics is close by definition—if only because these discourses relate everything to human
agency. They tend to personalize the universe and explain every event
in terms of interventions of human actors, even if these actors remain
hidden behind witchcraft's mysteries. Our analysis of these discourses in the forest societies of southern Cameroon—among the
Maka, but also among the Beti and other groups—suggests that
these representations do inspire specific images of human agency.
Each man and woman can acquire the capacity to double himself or
herself. This is seen as a crucial step: one enters into another world
full of dangers, but also full of promises. By "going out"—*wos*, a
central notion in the Maka discourse on witchcraft—one exposes
oneself to terrible dangers, but one can also access unknown powers.
There is a strong temptation to use these powers for evil ends, most
notably for joining the cannibalistic banquets where the witches offer
each other their own kin to eat. But one can also learn to control
these forces and use them in a constructive sense. The best example
of this is the *nganga*, who can heal only because they have such an
extremely developed *djambe* (witchcraft). The same applies to the
djambe idjuga (witchcraft of authority) that allows the elders to
dominate the turbulent palavers in the *kaande* (village council). But,
no matter how highly respected such an elder may be or how great
the fame of a *nganga* is, there is always the danger that the basic
instinct of the *djambe*—that is, to kill and eat one's kin—breaks

through. Even when it seems to be controlled and is used in a positive sense, *djambe* remains an utterly dangerous and ambiguous force.

The close link between witchcraft and political power expresses, therefore, a deep mistrust of politics and power that is characteristic of these societies. But this is combined with the insight that power, and therefore the occult forces, are indispensable to the very functioning of society. Discourse on the occult reinforces power but serves to limit it at the same time; it encourages personal ambition but serves also to restrict it and force ambitious figures back into line with the egalitarian ideology. Or, to continue with the terms used above: in these societies, witchcraft discourse seems to interpret power in terms of a highly delicate balance between "leveling" and "accumulative" tendencies.

Such notions do, indeed, suggest a specific view of human agency and politics. But it is important to stress that there is not an absolute discontinuity with modern ideas on power and politics. Indeed, post-colonial developments in Cameroon, as in other African countries, show that the imaginary of power in terms of witchcraft and sorcery dovetails very smoothly with modern state institutions and the new relations of dominance imposed by the state. The uncertainties of modern politics and state authoritarianism—the abrupt and often unpredictable decisions of the political summit and the secrecy with which it is surrounded—create a political climate in which rumors on witchcraft blossom as never before. The fact that such rumors penetrate the very heart of the process of state formation is not just an exotic rarity. It is inevitable with the Africanization of the state, in view of the close conceptual link between power and occult forces.

However, there is not only continuity with old ideas on the secret roots of power. In these new contexts, the ambiguity inherent in witchcraft discourses—the precarious balance between "leveling" and "accumulative" tendencies—seems to shift. In the postcolonial situations analyzed above, accumulative tendencies become more pronounced; in the present circumstances, discourse on the occult emphasizes the distance between the new elites and the people. It is nowadays a common idea that the elites dispose of such terrible weapons in witchcraft—because of the commercialization of the occult domain, the best "medicine" is available only to those who can pay dearly—that the people can no longer get to them. In the new arenas of national politics, the cut-throat competition among ambitious politicians offers fertile ground for witchcraft rumors. But the people hardly play a role in those rumors. The belief in *famla* (the new witchcraft of wealth) among the Bamileke in western Cameroon has the same implications: it confirms the success of the new entrepreneurs whose wealth inspires such strong fears among other ethnic groups.

However, as suggested by the diatribes of civil servants against the villagers' *sorcellerie*, seen as a dangerous subversion of the government's development policy, the leveling side of these notions is also present in new relations of domination. It is true, moreover, that these representations inspire a certain fear among the elites who are afraid to maintain too close contact with their former fellow villagers. If relations became too intimate again, jealousy could easily turn into the "witchcraft of the house," the most dangerous of all forms of occult aggression. But it is even more striking how the elites use the witchcraft discourse so effectively in order to reinforce new inequalities and affirm their having taken a definitive lead over the villagers. Moreover, the leveling impact of these discourses seems to get weaker when applied outside the kinship setting. On the whole, the impact of the leveling side of witchcraft discourse on new relations of domination seems, therefore, to be restricted. Within the family, in relation to urban elites, it still constitutes a leveling pressure. But its political impact outside this limited setting is much less evident. In this sense, one can hardly call it a "popular mode of political action" (for a general critique of this notion, see Geschiere 1995b).[1]

One consequence—especially when new relations of domination centered on the state are concerned—is that discourse on the occult seems to inspire a cynical view of power and the way it is used. In the context of the village, these discourses do express a certain mistrust of power, but this is balanced by the idea that these dangerous forces are also necessary to the functioning of society. To repeat Philippe Laburthe-Tolra's brief characterization of the relation between witchcraft and power among the Beti in the forest of central Cameroon: *evu* (witchcraft) expressed a deep suspicion of power, viewed as "a kind of original sin," but it was also recognized as indispensable to the organization of society (1977, 1080). Moreover, the *evu* discourse itself indicated how to contain these occult forces and the dangerous ambitions they inspired—in other words, how to control power.

However, in more modern contexts such restrictions seem to disappear. Witchcraft is especially associated with personal ambition and accumulation. The wealth and power of the new elites largely surpass old frameworks. The supports of which the new *Grands* can dispose seem no longer balanced by the egalitarian ideology. Moreover, their power appears to be personal; it is no longer linked to the norms of the community but seems to be completely determined by individual ambition. No wonder, then, that, in the popular view, modern forms of power of the new state elites are equated with the "politics of the belly."[2] But one should add that this is not only the popular view of what is normal; it is also, and this is even more dangerous, the view of the elites themselves.

In a recent article on the "banality of power" in the "postcolony," Achille Mbembe (1992) criticizes the tendency—which inspires many studies of present-day politics in Africa—to look for resistance "from below." He maintains, on the contrary, that "a logic of conviviality" has developed around the postcolonial state "which inscribes both dominant and dominated groups in the same *épistémè*." He enumerates the more striking aspects of the "politics of the belly"—its vulgar and arrogant expressions in the pursuit of wealth and power—in order to show that it is not only the elites but also the "common people" who are eager to participate, each in their own fashion. Thus, everyone is included in "an illicit cohabitation." Mbembe warns that most studies of the postcolony tend to start from a conceptual opposition between resistance and collaboration and thus risk overlooking that both the elites and the people are mutually engaged in the practices of the politics of the belly.[3] One can add that witchcraft and sorcery conceptions play a key role in the "vulgarization of power" evoked by Mbembe. This discourse locks the whole population—the rich and the poor, the powerful and the weak—into one conceptual framework. This makes it very difficult indeed to characterize the discourse as "a popular mode of political action" against new relations of domination. It is, rather, a cynical discourse shared by the elites and the people, which implies that the politics of the belly is something normal.

It is, therefore, highly doubtful that the discourses on the occult can contribute to the emergence of the new language of power that Mbembe evokes, in one of his more optimistic publications, as a precondition for relating more positively state power to the dreams and the ethics of the people.[4] Yet, it is clear these discourses do matter in the crystallization of a new political culture centered around the postcolonial state and its institutions. The general tendency to interpret new forms of power in terms of the occult indicate that a cynical view of modern politics has rapidly taken root. This should not be surprising: after all, Africans have had little reason to develop a more positive view of the forms of power that were imposed upon them since the colonial conquest and largely continued after independence. Moreover, such a cynical view on power is certainly not particular to Africa. It emerges everywhere when power seems to be no longer subject to manifest controls. Even in countries with longer democratic traditions, people display growing disappointment and cynicism in relation to politics since power, despite formal democratic appearances, seems to escape control, thus obfuscating its true dimensions.

Yet, it is clear that the explicit association of power and the occult in Africa—especially since it is emphasized not only by the population but also by the new power holders themselves—has specific effects. It creates a climate in which the use of official powers by a civil servant in the service of private interests risks becoming a normal practice, not to say a legitimate one. In modern contexts, witchcraft and power, still closely linked, seem no longer contained by communal values. The politics of the belly become not only a popular representation of power but also the principle upon which state elites are acting. From such a perspective, it is only normal that anyone can eat the state (an expression, current in Africa, that directly refers to witches and their obsession with eating). The other version of power that is certainly as much present in African tradition—of the elders or the chief whose legitimate powers are, at least formally, under strict communal control—seems to be less applicable under new forms of domination, despite the efforts of several heads of state to "authenticize" their novel powers.

A promising perspective for understanding the more problematic aspects of the link between sorcery/witchcraft and modern forms of power in Africa today is offered by the explorations of Bill Murphy, Rosalind Shaw, and other recent authors into the delicate balance between secrecy and publicity, which in their view is inherent to these discourses as such.[5] It seems indeed that the more frightening aspects of the role of witchcraft in postcolonial Africa—the general idea that it is running wild, the unbridled nature of the fantasies involved, the ever more draconic punishments meted out not only by the state but also by *nganga* of the umpteenth witch-cleansing movement—all these aspects, as they were sketched above, are related to a changing balance between secrecy and publicity in people's perceptions of how the occult should be managed.

The relations between secrecy and publicity—or, to borrow Murphy's terms, between concealment and revelation—in these discourses is indeed highly complicated, not to say paradoxical. By its very nature, witchcraft presupposes secrecy and mystery. Yet it can only play a role in society if the secrecy is, at least to some degree, unveiled—if witchcraft is, at least at times, brought out into the open. This balancing act between veiling and unveiling determines the way in which these discourses affect society and processes of change. Witchcraft is a good example of what Michael Taussig so aptly calls a "public secret": its power stems from it being both secret and public.[6] The varying situations described in this book show that its effectiveness requires both secrecy and at least some sort of publicity—especially when its implications for power are at stake.

In this view, the general readiness in the East Province of Cameroon to bring witchcraft affairs before the state courts seems to stem from a determined search for new public spaces in which witchcraft fears can be acted out and resolved. Of old, the Maka did have such a public space. The *kaande*, the great village council, did serve as an open space where witchcraft fears could be expressed and acted upon if people felt the situation was getting out of hand. As noted above, the first aim of the *kaande* was, and is, not so much to punish wrong-doers but rather to bring as many complaints as possible out into the open. If necessary, a *nganga* could be invited to publicly neutralize the occult powers of tenacious witches. Thus the *kaande* served to reproduce the belief in witchcraft itself as well as its restrictions.

However, recently, the villagers seem to feel more and more that the *kaande* is no longer effective in dealing with the new transformations of witchcraft that clearly surpass the world of the village. Hence the search for new public arenas, such as the state courts, that might be better equipped to balance witchcraft's secrecy in its new transformations. However, it is also clear that the state is not very effective in dealing with these dark threats: it can have the "witches" locked up, but this does not mean that their powers are neutralized; and the *nganga*, recruited by the courts as witnesses for the prosecution, become disciplining figures to the detriment of their healing capacities.[7]

Indeed, one may wonder whether the state can offer the type of public space needed—whether its brand of publicity is effective in counteracting witchcraft's secrecy.[8] It is quite striking that the opening up of politics due to recent democratization has not led to a decline in references to witchcraft. In the 1970s and 1980s, I was inclined to relate the omnipresence of witchcraft rumors in national politics in Cameroon to the heavy authoritarianism of the regime that tried to settle all conflicts and differences of opinion behind closed doors, thus creating a political climate that indeed reminded one of the stories about the nightly escapades of the witches. After 1989, democratization and the imposition of a multiparty system did create a new kind of "public space"—of *Oeffentlichkeit* in Habermas's sense.[9] Yet, as we saw above, the concomitant uncertainties offered new scope for rumors on the decisive role of witchcraft in politics. Apparently, witchcraft notions easily invade such new and more open types of public spaces. Therefore, one can indeed wonder if other types of publicity are needed—other public spaces than the state can offer—to rob witchcraft of its self-evidence.[10]

The rapidly increasing popularity of Pentecostalist and Spiritual churches in many parts of Africa might be related to this search for a public place to deal with witchcraft. Indeed, this popularity seems to be based to a large extent on the supposed success of these movements in dealing with witchcraft. And this seems to be related, again, to their effective public rituals of witch cleansing. In her fascinating study of German missionaries and Pentecostalists, and their struggles against the devil and witchcraft in southern Ghana, Birgit Meyer (1995) gives several reasons for the strong appeal of Pentecostalism. In contrast to the Mission churches, Pentecostalists do take witchcraft seriously: they equate it with the devil and, during services, encourage their followers to act out their shocking fantasies. Moreover, they developed elaborate and highly physical rituals to exorcise these weird forces.[11] Or, to put it differently, they succeed in creating their own public space in order to deal with witchcraft. And in this, they seem to be much more successful than the state. With their public rituals they appear to succeed in neutralizing these dangerous forces, and that is certainly more satisfying than the state's solution of simply locking up the alleged witches. Indeed, in Cameroon as well, Pentecostalism—after a much later start than in Nigeria or Ghana—is suddenly spreading very rapidly, presumably because of its ability to deal with witchcraft. During my last visit to Yaunde, in 1995, I found that a popular bar where we used to drink until late at night had been transformed abruptly into a Pentecostalist church. The Pentecostalists' way of both affirming the existence of witchcraft (by taking the "confessions" extremely seriously) and offering the means to combat it will make them a redoubtable force in postcolonial Africa for the future as well.

Regional Variations:
Circularity and the Struggle for Classification

In the preceding pages, the emphasis was on the deep distrust of power, as expressed in the witchcraft discourse. But this is only one possible scenario. In earlier chapters I tried to square this scenario—prevailing in the forest societies of southern Cameroon (Beti, Maka, and others)—with developments of a different tenor in the Grassfields chiefdoms of the West and Northwest Provinces. As noted in the introduction, there is good reason for modesty here. The relation between witchcraft and politics is by itself a highly elusive topic, and this makes regional comparisons (mainly on the basis of literature) all the more risky. Moreover, these two regions—southern forest area and western Grassfields—should certainly not be compared as two homogeneous blocs.[12] And important links are missing from our comparison.[13] This is, then, only a first comparative attempt.

But even if this comparison risks being overschematic, it does highlight different regional trajectories in the articulation of witchcraft, power, and modern changes. The forest societies seem to be deeply marked by what I called the "circularity" of witchcraft discourse. Here, sanctions against *evu* or *djambe* are to be found with these same occult forces. The *nganga* can offer protection against the witches only because he or she is a "super witch" who has "beaten all records." The distinction between acceptable and unacceptable uses of occult forces is always highly relative. In this region, new forms of wealth and power also became ensnared in the vicious circles of *sorcellerie*: they are suspect since they are supposed to be related to witchcraft; but they also evoke jealousy, which makes them inevitable targets of the deadly "witchcraft of the house"; and yet they can be protected and reinforced by the same witchcraft forces.

Among the Bamileke and the Bamenda of the Grassfields, this circularity of witchcraft discourse seems to be broken (at least to a certain degree) by the chief and his associations. In these societies as well, these discourses do express a certain distrust of power as such. Yet, among the Nso, for instance, one of the largest chiefdoms of the Grassfields, *sem*—a force as dangerous and ambiguous as the *evu* of the forest societies—constitutes the very basis for the chief's authority. However, the Nso try to separate the chiefs in all sorts of ways from the darker manifestations of *sem*. The chief has the power to impose a clear distinction between tolerable and intolerable manifestations, and he guarantees that his secret societies will use their deadly secret powers only to protect the people against witches (Goheen 1996). To the Nso also, new forms of wealth have a suspect aura since they are related to new, and therefore particularly dangerous, forms of witchcraft. But the nouveaux riches can dedicate their wealth to the chief and thus have it "whitewashed." As sovereign of the community, the chief can "domesticate" their wealth by coopting the new elites into the title societies of his court.

The association of new forms of wealth with the occult has, therefore, varying implications in these regions. In the forest, rumors about *kong*, the new witchcraft of wealth, seem to create a general panic. Here, new inequalities are hard to reconcile with the basically egalitarian ideology of these segmentary societies. In many respects, new forms of wealth and power still constitute an unresolved problem both for the new elites and their former fellow villagers. The general uncertainty seems to translate itself into the increasingly current idea that witchcraft is becoming rampant and out of control. The old controls no longer seem capable of containing its proliferation, and, therefore, one tends to invoke the help of outside agencies like the state. In the West and the Northwest, people seem to be rather intent on keeping the state at bay. Here also, new forms of witchcraft like *kupe* or *famla* evoke general anxiety, but the customary authorities are still supposed to be able to socialize these dangerous forces. Witchcraft rumors hardly seem to disturb new forms of accumulation in this area; sometimes the rumors even reinforce them.

These regional variations help explain why references to witchcraft have such different implications in the ethnic stereotypes that pervade the new political space for democratization in Cameroon. The expression of my old Beti colleague quoted above—"It is like this with us: those who ascend must excuse themselves constantly to those who do not ascend"—refers as directly to the occult forces as the current association of the success of the Bamileke entrepreneurs with *famla*. But in the first instance, it is the "leveling" side that is referred to; it is the fear of their kin's jealousy and ensuing witchcraft that makes the new Beti elites "eat" the state. In the second case, it is the "accumulative" side of these representations that is at stake— the secret forces of the *famla* supposedly allow entrepreneurs from the West to dominate the national economy.

These references to witchcraft seem to make such stereotypes self-evident, as some kind of inborn qualities. Above, I tried to demonstrate that these variations have to be understood, instead, in terms of different historical trajectories. In the West and the Northwest, the strong institutional basis of the chiefs, and the way they are able to relate to modern developments, are such that they have retained the moral authority to whitewash new and suspect forms of wealth. In contrast, in the segmentary societies of the southern forest areas, where local relations of authority have been undermined by the impact of the state, such crystallization points seem to be lacking. As a consequence, there is much greater insecurity in the face of new inequalities that appear to be directly related to novel forms of witchcraft. It is this insecurity that makes people turn to the state. The new elites use the state to satisfy the demands of the family; hence a "privatization of the state" and extreme manifestations of the "politics of the belly." The people turn to the state and its judicial apparatus in order to find protection against these new dangers, which come from inside society itself. Historically, there is a tragic paradox here. At the time of the colonial conquest, it was these segmentary societies that put up a fierce resistance against the state. In the South and especially in the East, the colonial authorities had great trouble in imposing new forms of domination that were so strikingly different from the kind of authority these societies had known until then. Today, these same societies seem to be prepared to call upon the state in order to solve their most intimate problems. In this way, the state seems to penetrate into the heart of domestic relations.

It is important to situate such regional variations in time: they are certainly not timeless "givens" but have emerged in specific historical constellations and will evolve as history goes on. One might wonder, for instance, whether the chiefs in the West and the Northwest will retain, in the future, sufficient moral authority to legitimate new forms of wealth. Their eagerness to profit in their own way from new opportunities for enrichment by selling pseudotraditional titles might undermine their prestige. Their efforts to incorporate the new elites into the traditional structures of their courts correspond to their age-old duty to control the ambitions of their subjects and assure that they are not endangering the prosperity of the community. However, at least some people seem to fear that the chief's association with the new elites might have the reverse effect—that it might corrupt not only the associations of the court but even the chief himself.[14]

Such a comparative perspective might demonstrate that the ethnic contrasts that now dominate political debate in Cameroon are certainly not self-evident. True, one can distinguish different regional models. But these contrasts, far from being constant "givens," stem from specific historical articulations in the interactions between state, market, and regional principles of organization.

A more general point that follows from such comparative explorations is the broader importance of the tension between what was indicated above as the "circular character" of these discourses versus the struggle to impose classifications—a certain compartmentalization—upon the domain of the occult. This drive toward classification is certainly not only an anthropological preoccupation (as was suggested somewhat rashly above). Nearly everywhere, the people involved are also obsessed with making distinctions between various types of occult forces: for instance, between more and less dangerous ones; or, more often, distinctions with a clear moralizing tenor, such as between permitted and illicit ways of using these forces. But there is also a basic circularity—one might also say a basic amorality—in these discourses that creates these vicious circles, from which it is so hard to escape. For instance, protection against these forces is procured through the very same forces; a more constructive way to use them—to get rich or to reaffirm one's authority—is never completely separated from their dark sides; there is always the danger that the basic instinct—that is, to kill—will break through.

This basic circularity is such that all classifications and distinctions in this field turn out to be extremely precarious and relative. They never are definitive. Instead, there is a constant, difficult struggle to impose and maintain certain classifications. It is also clear that some societies succeed better in this than others. To understand differences in this respect, it might be important to focus on the materiality of such discourses. For instance, if we return to the comparison above, it is clear that the Grassfields societies dispose of a whole array of institutions—the chief, their courts and associations, their rituals—to reproduce the "traditional" distinctions within the domain of the occult forces. But even with this impressive apparatus, it seems that the maintenance of certain distinctions—for instance, among the Nso, between "good" and "bad" *sem*, and its relation to the chief—is always precarious and situated in time. What is labeled "traditional" by the Nso seems to be the product of difficult adaptations to changing circumstances. It is also clear that in the segmentary forest societies, the institutional infrastructure of discourse on the occult is less elaborated and more easily undermined by modern changes. Here, the circularity and the basic amorality of these discourses seem to prevail over any attempt to make moralizing distinctions.

A general conclusion might be that, in this field of study, it is less expedient to engage in polemics over the relevance or the true meaning of certain *emic* distinctions, as anthropologists often tend to do. The issue is, rather, how are certain distinctions in specific societies maintained? What kind of institutions play a role in this respect? How are such distinctions protected from, or adapted to, changing circumstances? Such questions can help us understand how regional variations such as those sketched above can develop and how they are reproduced.

Witchcraft and the Stretching of Kinship

The preceding comparison must be complemented in yet another way. These regional variations should be explained not only with reference to the differences—quite manifest, also to the people involved—in the role of chiefs. As indicated above, deeper variations in the relation between witchcraft and kinship do play a role as well.[15] Above, I quoted Michael Rowlands (1993) and Jean-Pierre Warnier (1993), who explain the relative success of entrepreneurs from the Grassfields societies by referring to the special protection these societies offer from the "strategies of disaccumulation" by poor kin against ambitious persons in their midst. In the forest societies, in contrast, such protection against disaccumulation pressures from inside the family seems to be lacking completely.[16] Apparently, kinship can have highly variable implications for modern changes, being related to different patterns in the articulation of the domestic economy to the modern market.[17] The varying role of witchcraft discourses in relation to processes of accumulation or disaccumulation must be understood against this background.[18]

Consequently, the close link between witchcraft and kinship is the true leitmotiv of this study. This link is crucial if one wants to understand why witchcraft remains so pertinent, despite all the modern changes. It stands out in all the regions discussed, as well as in highly urbanized contexts. Among the Maka, the *djambe le njaw* (witchcraft from inside the house) is the most dangerous form of witchcraft; this is also true for the urban elites. And even among people who have been living in a metropolis like Duala for generations, the source of witchcraft is invariably sought within the family. Éric de Rosny (1981, 1992) shows that his fellow *nganga* always try to unite the patient's family before organizing a healing session. To them also, healing primarily means restoring trust within the family.[19] If the parents refuse to cooperate, the *nganga* feel unable to heal and have to drop the case.

Witchcraft is still the dark side of kinship in several senses. It expresses the frightening realization that aggression threatens from within the intimacy of the family—that is, from the very space where complete solidarity and trust should reign without fail. But this discourse also expresses the effort to maintain relations despite this terrible threat—after all, your parents are by tradition the only people you can really trust. As the Duala proverb, already quoted, states: "One must learn to live with one's sorcerer."[20] The deep power of these representations stems from the family. They express the frightening consciousness that there is jealousy and therefore hidden aggression among those with whom one necessarily has to live and collaborate. Nearly everywhere in Africa, it is inconceivable, still today, to formally refuse maintaining family ties: the family remains the cornerstone of social life, and one cannot live without its intimacy. Yet it is precisely this intimacy that harbors deadly dangers since it is the very breeding ground of witchcraft. The continuing force of this discourse is that it expresses the permanent struggle of living with this dark threat from inside.[21]

In the local context, witchcraft discourse suggests clear possibilities for repairing disturbed relations: the *nganga* can try to redress solidarity within the family. But this aspect seems to get lost in the broader settings of the modern world. As said before, the general conviction that witchcraft is on the increase confirms the idea that the old countervailing powers are no longer of avail. People tend to look for new sanctions that surpass the old kinship frameworks. In some areas, this leads to the rise of *nganga* of a new type, less intent on healing—that is, on repairing family relations—than on disciplining the "accused," often in close collaboration with the state and its fearsome coercive apparatuses.

The background to this frightening vision of witchcraft tearing itself loose from its moorings—*la sorcellerie en liberté*, as Georges Dupré (1982) puts it—is general: it is the stretching, or even the overstretching, of kinship relations. Modern changes—politico-economic developments but also the dreams and fantasies of modernity—bring an increase in the scale of human relations and foster new inequalities. Yet people continue to try to fit these increasingly complex networks into the framework of kinship. Kinship terms are literally stretched in order to bridge new inequalities—that is, in order to include as many urban elites as possible in one's personal network—and kinship norms are redefined and adapted in order to meet changing circumstances. We saw that all this creates terrible tensions. The Maka *évolués* try to keep their distance from the village, but ever more villagers ostentatiously claim in all sorts of ways to be their relatives, often invoking highly complicated kinship constructions. Kinship has to bridge the gap between village and city; it also has to incorporate ever wider personal networks. One result is that, to the *évolués*, the number of kin and the consequent dangers of *djambe le njaw* are multiplied to a staggering degree indeed.

Éric de Rosny's fascinating case studies similarly highlight the role of the family. A well-to-do woman, a customs officer, does not dare to emancipate herself from the pressures of her family; a *fille libre* who goes for the swinging city life is brought to heel by her family. Even the *famla* rumors about the Bamileke entrepreneurs relate these nouveaux riches, albeit in a perverse way, to the kinship framework. There are good reasons for this strong and continuing emphasis on kinship. Even in the modern sectors—in a metropolis like Duala—kinship still constitutes the primary form of social security for the great majority of the population. The solidarity between parents may be put under heavy pressure by urbanization and the emergence of new inequalities, but kinship still dominates social life. Even for the elites, the ultimate source of social security appears to be in the village—where one plans to retire and where one has to be buried—rather than in the city.

It is this stretching of kinship relations, putting them under heavy strain, without kinship as such loosing its grip on people, that is reflected in the general anxiety about the proliferation of witchcraft. Here also lies a possible answer to the difficult question of when the belief in witchcraft might finally subside. As long as the family remains the main basis of social security, the enigmatic discourses on witches and their secret forces will continue to mark people's reactions to modern changes in Africa.[22]

AFTERWORD:
THE MEANDERINGS OF ANTHROPOLOGICAL
DISCOURSE ON WITCHCRAFT

It is quite remarkable that the topic of witchcraft and modern changes in postcolonial Africa has been neglected for so long by anthropologists. As observed in the introduction, sorcery and witchcraft have always been favorite topics of anthropologists. The occult forces are, moreover, a true obsession—and a highly conspicuous one—to people in postcolonial Africa, most notably in the modern sectors of society. However, when Cyprian Fisiy—my distinguished coauthor whom I recently lost to the World Bank—and I began to publish on this topic at the end of the 1980s, we found that there was hardly a comparative literature, at least not by anthropologists or other social scientists. It is equally remarkable that this has suddenly changed. For about two or three years now, there has been a real stream of studies by anthropologists, including articles and even books, on witchcraft and modernity in contemporary Africa.

The aim of this brief afterword is to look into the question of why anthropologists in Africa avoided the topic of the modernity of witchcraft for so long. Apparently, this has to do with quite particular twists and turns in the development of anthropology's discourse on witchcraft and sorcery.

A good starting point for trying to understand the vicissitudes of this discourse is Mary Douglas's introduction to a set of papers by anthropologists and historians, discussed at a conference to commemorate the thirty-year anniversary in 1967 of the publication of Evans-Pritchard's *Witchcraft, Oracles and Magic among the Azande*, a classic in the study of witchcraft in Africa. In her introduction (pub-

lished in 1970), Douglas tried to draw up the balance sheet of the
1950s and 1960s—a period that was in many respects the heyday of
anthropological witchcraft studies, marked as it was by a series of
monographs by British anthropologists on the role of these representations in African societies.[1] Douglas observes with some apparent
surprise (or irony?) how wide the gap is between the contributions
in the book by anthropologists (mainly on Africa and Melanesia) and
those by historians (on the witch-hunts in early modern Europe):
"The anthropologists of the 1950s developed insights into the functioning of witch beliefs which seemed about as relevant to the European experience as if they came from another planet. Dangerous in
Europe, the same beliefs in Melanesia or Africa appeared to be tame,
even domesticated; they served useful functions and were not expected to run amuck" (Douglas 1970, xiii).

Today, qualifications like "tame" or "domesticated" for the role
of occult forces would be quite surprising for both Africa and Melanesia—unfortunately so, one might add. A recurrent theme in the
preceding chapters was the increasing anxiety among Africans today
about witchcraft becoming rampant. In many parts of postcolonial
Africa, this anxiety triggers panicky reactions and a desperate search
for new protections to contain novel and therefore all the more
frightening witchcraft threats. We also saw that this search for new
protections—for instance, the popular pressure on the state authorities to intervene—can have truly shocking consequences. This raises
the question of how, only a few decades ago, anthropologists could
form such an image of witchcraft as "tamed" and "domesticated."
Have things really changed so rapidly in Africa?

Of course, there have been important changes in the role of the
state due to decolonization. It is a moot point whether popular anxiety about witchcraft was less pronounced in colonial times. But it is
clear that the role of the colonial state was very different in this respect. The colonial authorities were primarily intent on containing
manifestations of witchcraft (or anti-witchcraft): their overriding
concern was to maintain law and order.[2] Postcolonial authorities, in
contrast, are much more sensitive to the popular pressure to intervene against what is perceived as an unprecedented spread of witchcraft. As my Maka friend, quoted above, remarked in 1971: "Now

we Africans are in charge, and we know that witchcraft is real." The consequence is that witchcraft—not only specific accusations but also general anxiety about its proliferation—is brought out into the open much more. Thus, it becomes clear that it is anything but tamed.

However, the colonial context is not the only explanation of the anthropological image of witchcraft as "domesticated." There were, after all, many signs of anxiety and unrest in those times as well. Clearly, this image was a direct product of the then prevailing approach in anthropology, an approach that influences witchcraft studies even today. Anthropologists were then especially interested in the role of witchcraft beliefs in the maintenance of social order. They studied its relation to power, but only within the local context, notably inside the village. The general tenor of the monographs quoted above is that witchcraft beliefs served to denounce overly ambitious leaders and neutralize changes that threatened to undermine the local order. Witchcraft thus appeared to be a primarily conservative force.

In this respect as well, Mary Douglas has interesting things to say. In her 1970 introduction, she repeatedly refers to Evans-Pritchard's Azande book, which was the occasion for the conference. But she notes that, even though generations of anthropologists pretended to take this book as some sort of guide, in reality a striking reorientation had taken place. Evans-Pritchard wanted to study Azande beliefs from an epistemological perspective: how could these beliefs remain acceptable to the Azande despite their skepticism? But among his supposed epigones, the study of witchcraft became the study of micropolitics:

> First and foremost this [Evans-Pritchard's Azande book] was
> a book about the sociology of knowledge. It showed how
> Azande, clever and skeptical as they were, could tolerate dis-
> crepancies in their beliefs and could limit the kinds of questions
> they asked about the universe. It might have been expected to
> stimulate more studies on the social restraints upon perception.
> Instead it fathered studies of micropolitics. The relation be-
> tween belief and society, instead of appearing as infinitely com-
> plex, subtle and fluid, was presented as a control system with a

negative feedback. Anthropologists strictly limited the questions they asked and restrained their natural curiosity. The
assumptions of their model were no more critically examined
than those underlying the Azande theory of witchcraft. (Douglas 1970, xiv)

Indeed, the anthropologists to whom Douglas is referring concentrated notably upon accusations of witchcraft, trying to relate their
tenor and frequency to sociopolitical tensions within village societies.
According to Max Marwick (1965), these accusations had to be
studied as a "social strain-gauge," especially in relation to the threat
of fission of the village community. Witchcraft, and especially the risk
of being accused of it, seemed to serve as an effective mechanism of
social control.[3]

A quotation from the guru of this school, Max Gluckman, can
show how difficult it is to reconcile the perspective of these anthropologists to situations such as those described above for contemporary Africa:

> An Anglican anthem demands "See that ye love one another
> fervently." Beliefs in the malice of witchcraft and in the wrath
> of ancestral spirits do more than ask this as an act of grace; they
> affirm that if you do not love one another fervently, misfortune
> will come. . . . Though a charge of witchcraft . . . may exagger-
> ate and exacerbate a quarrel, the belief emphasizes the threat to
> the wider social order which is contained in immoral senti-
> ments. Hence the beliefs exert some pressure on men and
> women to observe the social virtues, and to feel the right senti-
> ments, lest they be suspected of being witches." (Gluckman
> 1955, 94; see also Douglas 1970)

This attempt to reduce witchcraft to some sort of Anglican church
service abstracts very effectively from the thrill and excitement witchcraft rumors can evoke among the people, which is certainly one of
the reasons why these ideas are still so popular. This quotation is
striking, moreover, for its highly moralizing tenor: witchcraft is defined as basically evil and is therefore the very antithesis of social order as such. We saw that this perspective is difficult to reconcile with
the relations described above.[4] For the Maka, for instance, the

djambe is an essential part of social order. The same applies to the *evu* among the Beti: people may regret that these forces exist, but they are so closely linked to any form of power that they are indispensable to the proper functioning of society.[5] In this view, witchcraft is basically ambiguous: it is in principle an evil force, yet it must be canalized and used for constructive aims in order to make society work. Moreover, this ambiguity is essential for an understanding of why witchcraft remains so pertinent in modern contexts: it not only offers ways of resisting change and concomitant inequalities, but it can also inspire efforts to gain access to new resources. This is precisely why my friends were often thrilled by the newest rumor about the witches' escapades.

Such considerations not only influence the general view of witchcraft; they also have specific implications for how it is to be studied. It is characteristic that the British anthropologists quoted above focused on witchcraft *accusations*. This presents, no doubt, clear methodological advantages since accusations are often the most concrete manifestation of the occult forces. Yet a problem is that this focus automatically relates witchcraft to the reproduction of the social order. After all, there is a fair chance that only those accusations that do not attack the social order as such are expressed in public. Or to put it differently: normally, it is quite dangerous to publicly express accusations against those in power. However, if one wants to understand the ambiguity of these representations—their ramifications into all aspects of daily life and their ambivalent implications for modern changes—it is not sufficient to study only accusations. Therefore, one is obliged to venture into more vague spheres and try to make sense of the turmoil of rumors or the highly ambivalent and elusive role of the healers and how they affect social relations.[6]

A creative critique from French anthropology came from Marc Augé (notably Augé 1975). With the help of detailed analysis of several texts from British functionalism, he shows the limits of the approaches of these anthropologists, with their concentration on accusations in a strictly local setting, trying to distill a clear tendency from them that was supposed to be specific to the society concerned.[7] In contrast, Augé places his study of witchcraft among the Alladians (on the beach of southern Ivory Coast) in a larger context, linking it to broader historical changes in lineage organization, but also to the emphatical development policy of the new national government. He concentrates on the anti-witchcraft movement of the "prophet" Atcho, who tries to posit himself as a sort of mediator between the coastal population and the Ivorian regime.[8]

Anglo-Saxon authors have also paid increasing attention to such anti-witchcraft movements, especially since the 1970s.[9] These studies certainly contribute to a more dynamic and broader vision of witchcraft, showing how these movements have changed local beliefs and how these changes are related to broader politico-economic developments. But several of these authors tend to take for granted the strict separation between witchcraft and anti-witchcraft forces, as it was propagated by the movements' leaders themselves. We saw that, for the societies studied above, such a separation is always highly precarious. There is the danger that, by adopting this conceptual separation, attention is focused on anti-witchcraft experts and the changes they effect while the witchcraft belief itself continues to be viewed as a traditional residue without its own dynamics.

It is significant that the most promising impulses for renewing the study of witchcraft and understanding its potential modernity come from authors who distance themselves from a moralizing discourse, and to whom the distinction between good and evil is not self-evident. Michael Taussig's book (1987) on the Indian shamans from the Amazonian forest in southeast Colombia is a fascinating example of this. Taussig tries to understand how conceptions of occult forces affect modern changes. Because he shows that the shamans are in many respects beyond a good/evil opposition, he is especially able to convey some of the thrill and excitement brought by the images these shamans evoke. To Taussig, discourse on the occult is to be analyzed as a complex play of reflections and mutual appropriations of images between the whites and the "savages." The Indian shaman is the prototype of the savage that obsessed the colonials at the end of the nineteenth century. In Taussig's view, the ever more gruesome image of the savage played a crucial role in the justification of the "rubber terror" unleashed by the colonials in this area. But surprisingly enough, this same savage, in the person of the Indian shaman, becomes the preferred healer for the descendants of the colonials. Taussig gives a vivid picture of how they come down the steep slopes of the Andes and venture into the frightening forest, looking desperately for a cure for the tensions within their own society. As Taussig concludes: "Going to the Indians for their healing power and killing them for their wildness are not so far apart." The consequence is that the success of World Bank projects in the highlands now seems to depend on the forces of these "wild" shamans who have to armor peasants willing to participate in these projects against the jealousy of the people around them. In such a view, the distinction between good and evil becomes, indeed, relative and even of minor importance. It is also from such a perspective that one can understand how these beliefs can play a role in modern development projects.[10]

For Africa, similar impulses have come from the margins of anthropology. In his study of the Sundi region near Brazzaville, the sociologist Dominique Desjeux (1987, 178) included a brief but seminal chapter on *la sorcellerie*. His emphasis on the "dimension of uncertainty" of these discourses is of special interest. This makes him propose to study them as attempts to "manage insecurity." In his view as well, it is precisely because witchcraft addresses uncertainty that it remains the preferred discourse for interpreting modern changes.

The same relation between witchcraft and the uncertainties of a modern way of life mark the work, already cited above, of Éric de Rosny, the Catholic priest of Duala who had himself initiated as a *nganga* (healer).[11] He analyzes the work of his *nganga* colleagues as a continuous and fierce struggle to prevail over the vicissitudes of urban life. Typically, he does not restrict himself to the study of accusations and is wary of oversystematizing these beliefs—by, for instance, introducing clear-cut oppositions between good and evil. He indicates, rather, how these notions—precisely because they are so open and therefore allow for different interpretations—remain relevant in everyday life despite all the changes. It is because of this openness that these beliefs can incorporate the mysteries of the market economy. In his view, witchcraft discourse does not express an opposition to modern developments as such; rather, it is a concerted attempt to make life in modern circumstances more livable.

As noted above, over the last few years, there has been a sudden abundance of publications by anthropologists on witchcraft and modernity. It is, as yet, too early to say whether a dominant paradigm—like the "homeostasis" paradigm deduced by Mary Douglas (1970) from the witchcraft studies of the 1950s and 1960s—is emerging from these more recent studies. However, it is clear that most of these studies have two related accents in common.

First, there is the emphasis on the historicity of these discourses and practices—witchcraft is seen not as a more or less fixed, traditional residue but, rather, as a constantly changing set of notions reflecting and reinterpreting new circumstances. A striking example is Rosalind Shaw's forthcoming book *The Dangers of Temne Divination: Ritual Memories of the Slave Trade in West Africa*. By her subtle analysis, Shaw succeeds in relating the self-evidence of witchcraft as a major factor in politics and new forms of enrichment in present-day Sierra Leone to the terror of the Atlantic trade and colonialism. She shows that these large-scale historical processes are, indeed, crucial for understanding the role these notions play in contemporary relations of power and violence.

A similar perspective is developed in more general terms by Ralph Austen's article on "The Moral Economy of Witchcraft" (1993). Again, he explicitly tries to place the evolution of these ideas in a global context—notably the relation between Africa and Europe and the growing inequality between the two. To Austen, the different evolution of witchcraft notions on both continents is related to different views on the reproduction of the life force. In the same collection (Comaroff and Comaroff 1993), Misty Bastian offers a fascinating example of how to study the historicity of witchcraft over a shorter time span. She links changing ideas on witchcraft among the Igbo (Nigeria) to the increasingly complex relations between urban elites and their village of birth. Both parties, by following their respective reinterpretations of witchcraft, succeed in stigmatizing the other as witches.

A second common aspect, closely related to the first, is the emphasis on the impact of broader configurations as crucial for understanding the specificities of local witchcraft fantasies. In chapter 6, we saw that another difference between historians and anthropologists was that the former were much quicker in realizing how local witchcraft events—for instance, the large-scale witch-hunts in early modern

Europe—were directly affected by changes in the role of outside agencies like the state or the church. Anthropologists long continued to study witchcraft in strictly local contexts. However, this is rapidly changing now as well. In their introduction to their collection, Comaroff and Comaroff (1993) explicitly relate witchcraft to modernity: "witchcraft is a finely calibrated gauge of the impact of global cultural and economic forces on local relations, on perceptions of money and markets, on the abstraction and alienation of 'indigenous' values and meanings. Witches are modernity's prototypical malcontents." [12] Most contributions to this collection follow this emphasis on the impact of broader processes of change. [13] Mark Auslander (1993), for instance, relates the upsurge and passing of anti-witchcraft movements in eastern Zambia to "the moral geography" of the road and the changes it brought in the conditions of human reproduction. Of interest in this respect is also the sudden flow, after the end of apartheid, of studies on witchcraft in South Africa—for instance, Isaac Niehaus's seminal analysis of witch-hunts in northern Transvaal as part of the struggle against apartheid (Niehaus 1993 and 1995) or Adam Ashforth's forceful study (1996) of the uncertainties of witchcraft in the highly urbanized context of Soweto.

Common to all these studies is their emphasis on the uncertainties and the continuing relevance of witchcraft discourses in the face of modern changes. These discourses do not express a traditional refusal of change; rather, they try to address modern developments and make sense of them. This focus on the dynamics and the ambiguity of these notions allows one to study the specific implications of witchcraft in a particular setting without, however, falling back on a discourse about the Other as radically different and reducing witchcraft to an odd or exotic obsession. Authors like Michael Taussig or Éric de Rosny succeed indeed—as, I hope, the present study may do—in showing that these notions, now translated throughout Africa as "witchcraft," reflect a struggle with problems common to all human societies.

NOTES

CHAPTER 1. INTRODUCTION

I have used pseudonyms for names of individuals mentioned in the sections of this book that refer to my fieldwork among the Maka. However, I made an exception for public figures—like the great *nganga* (witch doctors) or the regional and national politicians from this area—and retained their real names.

1. Below I deal with problems of terminology, which are particularly prominent in the field of "witchcraft" or "sorcery." Here, it suffices to say that I retain these terms only because the people concerned use them. Indeed, these Western terms are often unfortunate translations of local notions with a much broader range of meaning. However, they are now appropriated by Africans throughout the continent. I do not follow the conceptual distinction between "witchcraft" (as an inborn quality) and "sorcery" (as the use of acquired means) proposed by Evans-Pritchard on the basis of his Azande material. For unclear reasons and despite a long series of critics (for instance, Turner in 1964 and Pool n.d.), many anthropologists have tried to generalize this distinction. I use the two terms interchangeably since the distinction does not apply very well to the Cameroonian societies studied here (nor does it in many other parts of Africa). For a different way of contrasting "sorcery" and "witchcraft" in Melanesian studies, see Stephen 1987, 6.

2. Below we shall see that anthropologists played their own role in reinforcing this stereotype.

3. The reverend Ayuk concludes this testimony by asking for the development of a "theology of witchcraft . . . not dominated by foreign theological models." His statement is included in an appendix to "African Culture and Christianity" in Mbuy (1994, 39). I thank Sally Chilver for showing me this text.

4. As Comaroff and Comaroff (1993, xxix) express it: "Witches . . . embody all the contradictions of the experience of modernity itself, of its inescapable enticements, its self-consuming passions, its discriminatory tactics, its devastating social costs."

5. See, for similar examples, Offiong 1991, 51.

6. To my Maka spokesmen, soccer more or less replaced the ancient practices of *doomb* (war) between the villages. As in the old *doomb*, the support of the occult forces was seen as an indispensable condition for victory. See also Hebga (1979, 85): "The belief in magic in sports is general. . . . It relates to an old tradition in black Africa."

7. Similar examples are reported from various parts of Africa; see, for instance, Ciekawy (1989), who describes a scene from the coastal region of Kenya that is remarkably similar. The last phrase of the *sous-préfet* quoted above is a good example of the ambiguity, elaborated upon below, of discourses on the occult. His remark that he could "see" the witches is certainly interpreted by the villagers as an allusion that he, too, has "a second pair of eyes," which, in this part of Africa, is a first and indispensable phase in one's initiation into witchcraft.

8. We see below that democratization and multiparty politics did not lead to a drastic change in this respect. These developments created more openness, at least to a certain extent, but also provided new scope for rumors about the use of occult forces in politics.

9. See Sulikovski 1993, 1995; Elwert-Kretschmer 1995; Tall 1995; all emphasize the ambivalence of the state toward *vodun* and *sorcellerie*—the rapid succession of official persecutions and attempts to use these forces.

10. *Jeune Afrique*, 30 July–5 August 1992, 20.

11. This title is, of course, somewhat sensational. It remains to be seen whether there was indeed such a sharp increase in "witch" killings in South Africa, as compared to earlier periods. It is striking, however, that there has been a sudden spate of historical and anthropological articles on witchcraft and witch-hunts in South Africa since the official end of apartheid (see, for instance, Ashforth 1996; van Kessel 1993; Niehaus 1993, 1995). Ashforth, however, convincingly shows the centrality of witchcraft in daily life in Soweto for a much longer period of time. He also notices the surprising lack of attention to this issue in the work of social historians of South Africa, who are rightly famous for their detailed attention to daily life in the townships but who apparently wish to avoid, in the context of apartheid, this more "ugly" side of daily life.

12. *Challenge-Hebdo* 79, 22 July 1992, 9 (my translation). Adopting a similar perspective, John Lonsdale (also a historian) affirms that in order to solve Africa's political crisis, the first thing needed is "an effective political

language." He adds: "A common political language and its inventive usage by the divided members of a political community can be produced in only one way, by historical process. Historical awareness is the only force of self-knowledge there is" (Lonsdale 1991, 205). This premise inspires Lonsdale to try to reconstruct the evolution of political thought among the Kikuyu of Kenya. His aim is to show that even so-called stateless societies had their own forms of political thought that provide elements for forging new discourses on power in the face of modern changes (see also Copans 1991).

13. The same applies, for instance, to debates on "development." In this field also, it has become commonplace to insist that notions of development should be expressed in people's own terms, in relation to their own language. This reorientation is certainly necessary, not to say overdue. But, in this field again, one must then be prepared to take ideas about the occult seriously. For it is in those terms that people tend to discuss development and the new inequalities it engenders.

14. In his beautiful collection of life histories from Zaire, Jewsiewicki (1993, 12) characterizes discourse on sorcery and witchcraft as an essential element in the class consciousness of the petty bourgeoisie: "Urban sorcery and the countersorcery of Christian words and gestures constitute the Zairian equivalent to the 'common sense' that Barthes qualifies as the class consciousness of the petty bourgeoisie" (my translation). Jewsiewicki's book convincingly shows the advantages of a life-histories approach: it gives at least some historical depth to such statements. It is interesting that these life histories show that this obsession with *la sorcellerie* is not something new. In the memories of these early representatives of an upcoming petty bourgeoisie, the threat of the occult dominated their lives from the time they were young (that is, long before independence). Writing about the Igbo of eastern Nigeria, Bastian (1993, 133) equally emphasizes the modernizing tenor of witchcraft discourse that is not "withering away" but rather "becomes a medium for describing the complexities of Nigerian urban and rural relations for Nigerians themselves." Most interestingly, she points out that people often prefer to use English when they address such questions so as to give their words more weight. For an interesting contribution on Melanesia, which equally emphasizes the close link between "sorcery" and new forms of accumulation, see Lattas 1993.

15. In a very interesting historical comparison of witchcraft discourses in Europe and Africa, Austen (1993) tries to show that the varying trajectories of similar notions on each continent reflect their different positions in the evolving world economy. African witchcraft beliefs are then not just something particular to Africa but rather reflections of its external relations.

16. See, for instance, Clifford 1988; Appadurai 1990; Anderson 1992.

In his explorations of the "reinvention of capitalism," Bayart (1994) finds such ideas consistent with those of Braudel, notably in his book *La dynamique du capitalisme* (1985, 16). Bayart adds that "globalization" is inextricably intertwined with "the reinvention of difference."

17. In this book I study discourses on sorcery and witchcraft in relation to politics. This is no doubt a choice for a specific perspective. Pool (n.d.) rightly emphasizes that such a perspective runs the risks of reductionism (witchcraft/sorcery being reduced to politics). In chapter 3, I return to this point. Here, it may suffice to say that these discourses indeed address other than purely political preoccupations; they serve to explain surprising or shocking events and to find a remedy against illness and other setbacks. However, they tend to explain such setbacks or unexpected events in relation to social inequalities. There is nearly always a direct link between witchcraft interpretations, on the one hand, and jealousy or ambition, on the other. Sorcery/witchcraft is by definition associated with inequality—that is, with power. If one wishes to explore the world of witchcraft, one must be prepared to find issues of power and politics in unexpected corners.

18. Vansina 1990.

19. This link between witchcraft and kinship is not universal. Élisabeth Copet-Rougier (oral communication) is now working on an interesting comparison between, on the one hand, New Guinea, where the witch is usually supposed to be a stranger (that is, nonkin) and, on the other, West and Central Africa, where people generally believe that witchcraft attacks come from inside the house. It might be necessary to refine this contrast somewhat. For instance, for the Abelam of New Guinea, Forge (1970) notes that the sorcerer is indeed someone "from outside," but he adds that the sorcerer "from outside" can only succeed with the help of an ally "from within" (that is, a relative). Yet the contrast Copet-Rougier makes is highly interesting since it indicates that the relation between witchcraft and kinship can be arranged according to different scenarios.

20. See the afterword on the problems of classical anthropology in dealing with the dynamics of witchcraft discourses and their impact in new walks of life; the chapter also discusses certain promising perspectives opened up by more recent studies.

21. Notably Marwick 1965; Middleton and Winter 1963; Mitchell 1956; Turner 1954; see also the afterword.

22. One may wonder whether this confusion between good and evil is not an almost universal trend of discourses on the occult. Doubtless, societies do differ as to the degree to which the good-evil opposition is central to their worldview. (This observation by itself might caution anthropologists

when applying Western Manichean classifications to other societies.) But it seems that, when sorcery or witchcraft are involved, it becomes particularly difficult to maintain a clear distinction between evil and good—often much more difficult than anthropologists make it appear to be (see Geschiere 1994 and the afterword; see also Hebga 1979, 262).

23. See Guyer's strong emphasis (for instance, in Guyer and Eno Belinga 1995) on the mobilization of multiple forms of knowledge, dispersed over many, more or less autonomous persons, as a crucial characteristic—unfortunately neglected in comparative anthropology—of the societies of Equatorial Africa. Guyer's stress on personal "composition" of different strands of knowledge places the present-day obsession with witchcraft in these societies in a long-term historical perspective and corresponds well to the view, developed in subsequent chapters, of "witchcraft" as highly plastic and subject to personal creativity. It is striking, however, that Guyer consistently avoids terms like *evu* or *djambe*, which, at least today, serve as overarching notions for integrating various forms of personal knowledge (and may have done so in the past).

24. This dilemma is certainly not special to the field of sorcery/witchcraft studies. Rather, it is inherent to the social sciences since they must develop a scientific discourse on the very object from which they are a product (see also Olivier de Sardan 1993, 1995). But the moralizing tenor of such terms as *sorcery* and *witchcraft* makes such problems of terminology particularly acute in this field.

25. See, for instance, Crick (1979), who asserts that anthropology should completely abandon a concept like witchcraft because it contains too many specific associations, determined by the history of Europe. De Rosny (1992, 28, 105), on the contrary, prefers to retain the term *sorcellerie* despite all its disadvantages and for reasons similar to mine. See also Hebga 1979, 262. Recently, Meyer (1995, 338) formulated a spirited and interesting rejoinder to Crick. While granting Crick's plea for more attention to local concepts, she adds: "On the other hand, it does not seem to me fruitful to deal with culture in a particularistic way. For cultural translation is not only the praxis of Western anthropologists. Africans themselves actually translate terms from one African language into another or into a European one, thereby establishing the similarity of phenomena occurring in different cultures. It seems to me that many of the concepts from different cultures brought together under the umbrella of 'witchcraft' do indeed have something in common."

26. Thoden van Velzen and van Wetering 1988, 401. These authors, in contrast, insist on the modernity of the prophetic movements they studied:

"[These] collective fantasies are more than harmless 'thought experiments' about modern conditions. They enhance the readiness of disciples to try new courses of action."

27. See also the interesting remarks on this topic in the *Thèse d'Etat* of Mbembe (1989). See also de Rosny 1981; Hebga 1979; Ongolo 1986.

28. Cf. Ardener 1970; Geschiere 1982; Goheen 1996; Laburthe-Tolra 1977; Mallart-Guimera 1981, 1988; Ongolo 1986; de Rosny 1981; Warnier 1985.

29. Van Wetering 1973; see also van Hekken and Thoden van Velzen 1972; Thoden van Velzen 1977.

30. See the critique by Pool (n.d.) to this effect.

31. This perspective is obviously related to debates in African studies, during the 1970s and early 1980s, on the "articulation of modes of production." I realize that these theoretical schemes have rapidly lost their popularity (certainly in France, their country of origin). In my opinion, this demise has been too hasty. It is true that the concept of mode of production turned out to be of limited value in African studies. Therefore, it is all the more regrettable that the debates concentrated on this notion, which led to fairly sterile polemics on the definition and the classification of various modes. Unfortunately, this led to a relative neglect of the notion of articulation (see, however, Laclau and Mouffe 1985). Yet this notion was quite promising since it encouraged the exploration of the possibility of various patterns of articulation between capitalism and local relations of production (or exploitation). To Rey (1971, 1973) the crucial question was how new forms of capitalist exploitation were grafted upon local contradictions. However, since those contradictions strongly vary in Africa, it is to be expected that their articulations with new relations of power will develop according to different scenarios (in Rey's terminology, different "class alliances"). It is unfortunate that this idea of diverging regional scenarios or trajectories in the articulation of local contradictions with new inequalities was not elaborated further (see Geschiere 1985a, 1985b; in general on these debates, see Jewsiewicki and Létourneau 1985). The present study may offer a modest contribution to this effect (see also Geschiere and Konings 1993; for a creative use of the notion of articulation, see Comaroff and Comaroff 1992, notably chapter 4).

32. Evans-Pritchard was explicit on this point: "Witchcraft is an imaginary offense because it is impossible. A witch cannot do what he is supposed to do and has in fact no real existence" (1937, 418). See Mair (1969, 144, 152), who maintains that people do not "really" believe in witchcraft accusations but are conscious of the fact that other motives are at stake that

are expressed in witchcraft terms. Evans-Pritchard could be so categorical about the nonexistence of witches since he made a sharp distinction—following the concepts of the Azande—between "witches" (who were supposed to transform themselves and therefore could have no "real" existence) and "sorcerers" (who used magical tools and whose actions could therefore be "real"). However, as mentioned above, many authors have denied the more general applicability of this distinction. In a recent, highly interesting thesis on this topic, Pels (1993, 202) emphasized that if this distinction cannot be maintained, Evans-Pritchard's categorical denial of the witches' existence, which has strongly influenced anthropology, needs to be refined as well. Cf., for instance, Thomas (1971, 465), who concluded that the distinction between "witches" and "sorcerers" was hard to maintain for early modern Europe as well. For Thomas also, this is a reason to doubt that one can completely deny the reality of witches: "For some of those accused of being witches really had tried to harm others. . . . In *intention* at least, witchcraft was not an impossible crime" (my emphasis). See also Comaroff and Comaroff (1993, xxvii) on postcolonial Africa: "witchcraft is not simply an imaginative 'idiom.' It is chillingly concrete, its micropolitics all-too-real."

33. De Rosny 1992, 112–113 (my translation). See also the historian Ginzburg (1990), who tries to show with a wealth of details, and against the scepticism of most fellow historians, that the imaginary of the witches' sabbath in early modern Europe did not sprout from the judges' fantasies; rather, it was based on real experiences of the initiates; this is why their "confessions" show strikingly similar traits in very different parts of Europe.

M. P. Hebga, another priest in Cameroon writing about witchcraft and sorcery, gives an interesting explanation of the tendency of nearly all scientific researchers to deny the reality of sorcery and witchcraft. In his view, this is to reassure oneself: "A first approach to magic and *sorcellerie* would be to suppose that this is symbolical language. A man who flies in the air and transforms himself into an animal . . . and other weird manifestations would then be only a coded language for which the scientist has to find the key to crack the code. Then we would be reassured: everything would happen in the real world according to nature's order; and elaborate systems of symbols would tend to protect the group's interests" (1979, 219). To Hebga, such a symbolical explanation has certain value, but he maintains that there is also need for another "realistic" approach (admitting, at least up to a certain point, the "reality of magic phenomena and witches" [251]). One can regret that, as yet, Hegba has not elaborated upon this idea of a "realistic" interpretation (he simply repeats that "at least certain phenomena would be 'real' ").

See also Appiah's virulent critique of the tendency in symbolical interpretations (for instance, in symbolical anthropology) to deny the reality of certain phenomena that for the actors concerned are very real: "It is peculiarly unsatisfactory to treat a system of propositions as symbolic when those whose propositions they are appear to treat them literally and display in other contexts a clear grasp of the notion of symbolic representations" (1992, 187).

34. A striking example of this is Stoller and Olkes (1987). Others such as de Rosny (1981) or van Binsbergen (1991) retain a more sophisticated approach to the relation between their personal initiation and the reality of the beliefs involved.

35. A similar picture emerges from many recent contributions on witchcraft in Africa. See, for instance, Meyer (1995) on Ghana; Bastian (1993) on Nigeria; Devisch (1995) and de Boeck (1996) on Zaire; Niehaus (1993) and Ashforth (1996) on South Africa.

36. See also Pels (1993, 203), who protests against the intellectualism of anthropological studies of witchcraft: their accent on meaning, not action. Pels proposes a return to Malinowski's emphasis on the close link between magic and action. For Malinowski, magic especially was an effort to contain the uncertainties of human existence: it permits one to *act* on these uncertainties. It implies, therefore, a call to action: "Magic and religion are . . . not merely an intellectual body of opinion, but a special mode of behavior, a pragmatic attitude . . . a mode of action as well as a system of belief" (Malinowski 1925, 24). Cf. Copet-Rougier (1986a): "The mystical-magical conception is not only a form of knowledge; it is primarily a form of action and as such part and parcel of social life" (my translation).

37. Several authors see this emphasis on human action as a general characteristic of African thought. For example, it is a common theme among African philosophers of recent times to contrast this emphasis on the role of human agents with Western thought, which looks, rather, for explanations in terms of impersonal causes. To Father Tempels (1949), human spiritual action is the basic principle of "Bantu philosophy." Horton (1967) sees "African traditional religion," which he compares to modern scientific thought, as founded on the belief in the reality of invisible agents. Appiah (1992, 200) maintains that Western scientific thought—"the belief in efficient, impersonal causation"—is exceptional since even in the industrialized world, only a minority really accepts it. He tries to show that it is possible for African intellectuals to accept scientific theories without abandoning "the belief in invisible agents." (Does this mean that this belief is, for him as well, basic to African forms of thought?)

38. Compare also Das's challenging lecture on "Rumour as Performa-

tive" (1996), in which she concludes: "I hope this analysis shows that the force with which utterances are endowed in this context derives from the peculiar nature of rumour—its lack of signature, the impossibility of it being tethered to an agent . . . this very lack of signature gives it the stamp of an 'endangered collectivity.' It leads to the world being transformed into a 'fantasmagoria of shadows of fleeting, improvised men' " (the last phrase is a quote from Lacan). This analysis of the force of rumor applies very well to both the omnipresence of witchcraft rumors in many African societies and the production of news around important events in the West. In both contexts it confuses the tenets of methodological individualism by conjuring up actors and making them highly elusive at the same time.

39. In one of the earliest reviews of the French version of this book, Buijtenhuijs (1995) reproaches me for too easily equating kinship and witchcraft/sorcery, thus omitting the role of occult forces in armed struggles outside a kinship context. Of course, witchcraft and kinship do not completely coincide. Below, I describe several examples of the use of these forces outside kinship (for instance, in Maka stories about the "war-magic" of precolonial war heroes). However, even in these broader contexts, there is often an ultimate reference to kinship. For instance, the Maka believe that the old war heroes could only acquire their special war-magic by betraying kin (see below). Similarly, the witch-hunts triggered by armed resistance movements in colonial and postcolonial Africa were in many cases (for instance, in Guinea-Bissau, Zaire, South Africa) related to preexisting tensions within local communities. There is a basic tendency in these discourses on the occult to refer to kinship and intimacy. This makes their impact so ambiguous in the modern sectors, where relations appear to surpass the old kinship frameworks. Buijtenhuijs is certainly right that the role of occult forces in armed struggles requires a separate book. Unfortunately, my fieldwork experience does not allow me to write such a book.

40. Mbembe 1990 and oral communication during a seminar on "Culture and Development, Questions of Consciousness," CNWS, Leiden, Netherlands, May 1990; see also Berry (1985).

41. Indeed, already in *L'Etat en Afrique* (Bayart 1989, 325), the author distanced himself from any deterministic interpretation of this concept. In his later reply to Mbembe's review of his book (Bayart 1990, 104), he repeats that the notion of "belly politics" is, to him, a concept that refers to "a field of action, a domain of possibilities and not to an overdetermination in a monistic sense" (my translation). For the present study, it is important to emphasize that this concept—even if it does not cover "the whole political imaginary"—summarizes very well a way of expressing oneself (*registre*

d'énonciation) that directly links witchcraft and politics (because of the centrality, in both fields, of notions of eating and the belly).

CHAPTER 2. A FULL BELLY

1. In a critique of anthropological approaches to sorcery, Robert Pool writes about his own research in northwest Cameroon: "What I was discussing with the [local] people during my fieldwork was, I increasingly came to realize, not a coherent system of knowledge about which they had achieved consensus. The terms whose meanings I was trying to discover were focal points in unstable and loosely articulated constellations of meaning" (Pool n.d.; cf. Pool 1994). I had the same feeling when, upon my return from Cameroon, I compared my material concerning *djambe* among the Maka with the clear and unambiguous distinctions made by numerous colleagues.

2. The Maka now translate the term *lwa* (pl. *melwa*) as "slave"; it is still a very serious insult. It seems to me that the term *client* is a more correct translation. The people referred to were mostly young captives or poor boys who had been adopted. In principle, their new "father" provided bridewealth for them; in such cases, the boys were formally integrated as full members into their new families. See Geschiere 1995a.

3. In 1992, I was able to conduct interviews in Ngumba villages around Bipindi. It was a pleasant surprise to note that here, for once, the name *Maka* did not inspire mockery. The villagers enthused over my groping efforts to make myself understood with a few Maka words; they repeated, "Ah, the Maka, they are our brothers."

4. Numerous Maka groups were also forcibly incorporated into Beti society with inferior status. See Bateranzigo 1987. Recently, under the regime of President Paul Biya, himself a Bulu, it has become commonplace to include the Bulu within the broader category of Beti (see interlude 1 below, note 3).

5. *Dresdner Zeitung*, 7 July 1910, and *Tägliche Rundschau*, 13 August 1910 (my translations), in National Archives, Yaunde, Cameroon, doss. AZ IC 51 U 1040, "Makka Aufstand in Bezirk Dume," 1910. The details related in the *Tägliche Rundschau* article must have been invented. According to all witnesses cited in the archives, the German was killed before being brought back to the village (by an arrow in the neck), and according to my informants, hands were not appreciated as particularly tasty by the Maka, who preferred the knees of defeated warriors as a sign of the latter's humilia-

tion. See also a series of testimonies on the killing of this German trader in the German colonial archives on Cameroon (*Deutsches Zentralarchiv Potsdam*, section KA4, files 4294 and 4295).

6. At the end of 1910, Dominik mentions a *Konzentrationslager* (concentration camp) that held 1,219 prisoners, mostly women and children. This is a very high figure if one considers that the population of the entire region amounted to about 15,000 inhabitants (Dominik, telegram from Gongela, 24 July 1910, National Archives, Yaunde, doss. AZ IC 51 U 1040). During the first German campaign against the Maka (1905–6), an army doctor, Külz, estimated that the Maka had lost two thousand men in one year (cited by Wirz 1972, 139).

7. Cited by Wirz 1972, 137 (my translation). Such scenes are reminiscent of the rubber terror in Zaire or the Amazon, described by Casement and Conrad (see Taussig 1987). In Maka oral history, this period is certainly traumatic. But in this region the terror of rubber was relatively brief; its exploitation began only after 1905, and by 1913 wild rubber prices began to decline rapidly, which led to a collapse in trade.

8. This old man often concluded his stories about the atrocities committed by the Germans, sighing: "Ah, those Germans were real men; not weaklings like the French." It should be added that he was very proud of having seen the Germans—and Dominik himself—with his own eyes. This attested to his considerable age and thus reinforced his prestige among the villagers.

9. The German archives confirm this transfer of Maka women to Yekkaba soldiers. Moreover, this episode gave rise to a serious incident, with Governor von Seitz himself engaged in lively protest. Dominik defended himself by claiming that he had only followed customs. This argument was not completely unfounded, even if it is surprising that Dominik dared use it. But the extent of this transfer gave it unprecedented dimensions for the Maka. See Dominik, telegrams from Gongela, 24 July 1910, and from Dume, 10 September 1910, National Archives, Yaunde, doss. AZ IC 51 U 1040; see also Wirz 1972, 139; and Kaeselitz 1968, 53.

10. See also the afterword on "The Meanderings of Anthropological Discourse on Witchcraft."

11. See Geschiere 1982. Anthropophagy evidently had symbolic signification for the Maka and was surrounded by ritual prohibitions (adult men, above all, were permitted to eat human flesh; certain parts—knees, according to some informants—were reserved for the elders and confirmed champions of war). But in that respect, there was no radical difference from chewing other kinds of meat (especially that of big game). One might wonder

why Western observers had so much difficulty believing the "reality" of anthropophagy. See Arens (1979), who attempts to reduce accounts of anthropophagy to inventions of missionaries and other Westerners. Brown and Tuzin (1983) demonstrate the reality of anthropophagy in Oceania. See also Copet-Rougier (1992a), on the Kako (or Kaka), who neighbor the Maka to the northeast.

12. Élisabeth Copet-Rougier, who writes about the Kako, kindly showed me copies of these documents: Fribourg, Switzerland, BA-MA-F16 N521, V18; letter from Schipper, Soppo, 17 August 1910.

13. See Hebga 1979, 221, 232, 268.

14. For the neighboring Beti people, such "colonial harems" were even larger. Guyer (1985) mentions chiefs with more than four hundred wives.

15. To the contrary, the colonials sometimes tried to brake this development for fear that peasant production would hinder the progress of European plantations in the region; see Geschiere 1983.

16. Daniel Heath, of the Summer Institute of Linguistics, Yaunde, who studied the Maka language, suggests the spelling *jaamb*, but this orthography creates problems for the villagers (whose reading is influenced by French spelling and who therefore read *jaamb* as *sjaamb*). I have consistently written Heath's "j" as "dj" when the Maka would pronounce it this way. For most other terms, I have maintained the spellings proposed by Heath; see Heath 1989.

The notion of *djambe* seems to be very old. It is related to the root word *jemba*, which, according to Jan Vansina, is widespread in the Bantu region and goes back to "Western proto-Bantu." It refers to the witch substance that is generally associated with "big men," or leaders who distinguish themselves by their personal capabilities. Vansina compares the term to the root *dogi* (*-dog*, *-lok*), which is more common, going back to proto-Bantu, and designates another form of sorcery that is linked more specifically to jealousy and destructive uses. See Vansina (1990, 299) and personal communication. For the Maka, *djambe* is associated with ambitious leaders and to power in general; a positive use of *djambe* is certainly possible. But *djambe* is also closely linked to jealousy and the utilization of occult forces to destructive ends. I did not encounter traces of the root *dogi* in Maka discourse on occult forces.

17. It is possible that the Maka borrowed this story from their Western neighbors, the Beti. Mallart-Guimera (1981) and Laburthe-Tolra (1977) recorded similar narratives among the Beti. Siret (1946–49) reports a similar story for the Djem (who live in the East Province, to the south of the Maka), but not for the Maka themselves. Élisabeth Copet-Rougier was able

to track the diffusion of this story among the Kako (that is, the Kaka, to the northeast of the Maka) during the 1970s; it was apparently unknown to them before that time; see Copet-Rougier 1986a. One might conclude that diffusion of this narrative took place from west to east. But many Maka insist that this is an ancient story that they have "always" known—but are not myths always ancient for those who tell them?. See also Koch (1968, 84), on the Bikele and the Badjué of Messaména, and Hebga (1979, 89), who give variations of this myth. The version presented by Koch begins with Zièm (God), who created Man, the Gorilla, the Chimpanzee, and *eleme* ("sorcery"). He hid *eleme* in a crack in a tree and forbid it to join his brother, Man, in the village. But the Wife of Man discovered *eleme* and brought it back in her belly; thus it arrives in the village with, of course, ominous consequences. The last detail is typical of almost all versions of the myth: *djambe/evu/eleme* refuses to be carried in the arms of woman or on her back; it insists on entering her belly.

18. In anthropological discourse, one might say that this represents a threshold between "nature" and "culture."

19. See Koch 1968, 90.

20. The Maka sometimes use *djim* for "double," but they also use the word *shishim*. The term *djim* is associated with the "phantoms" of sorcerers, and also with the spirits of the dead. The term *shishim* is difficult to analyze. From the beginning of the colonial period, it was used by missionaries to designate the "soul," in the Christian sense. Prior meanings and the former distinction from *djim* are practically impossible to ascertain. The idea of a double is also expressed by the Maka in their conceptualizations of the shadow of a person (also *shishim*), an extremely vulnerable attribute. It is said that sorcerers prefer to attack people's shadows. One must therefore be particularly prudent just before sundown, when shadows become longer.

21. On this point, significant variations are noted with respect to different societies in sub-Saharan Africa. In his classic study, Evans-Pritchard (1937) underscores, for example, how among the Azande (of present-day southern Sudan), "witches" are rather unconscious of the acts of their doubles.

22. Pseudonym. As indicated in the note on pseudonyms on the last page of the acknowledgments, I have changed the names of villagers but have retained the names of public figures, such as well-known healers and politicians.

23. See in chapter 1 the reaction of my assistant, who, in the deep forest in the middle of the night, was sorry that he was not able to "see"—like the healer Mendouga—the witches who swarmed around us.

24. In the past, the Maka resorted to public oracles (*lundu*) more often. But it is not clear to what extent this led to explicit verdicts and concrete sanctions against witches. During the 1970s, I witnessed a relatively harmless oracle: *adjel jul* (serpent's tooth), during which the *nkong* puts a serpent's tooth in the eye of the accuser and then in the eye of the accused; the *nkong* closes the eye and then opens it; if the person is lying, the tooth remains in the eye, and this person will become blind unless he or she confesses immediately. But each of the three times I observed such sessions, the test was inconclusive. My informants commented that, even if the oracle had revealed a witch, one would be more worried about forcing the witch to lift the spell or neutralize his or her *djambe* than punishing this witch.

25. It is significant that these accusations concerned a new form of witchcraft (*gbati*) that is reserved for young boys (a surprising innovation) and that, by its novelty, created a general state of panic in Maka villages. See Geschiere 1980 and chapter 5 below.

26. Since the end of the 1970s, the state (the gendarmes and the tribunals) has started to intervene in witchcraft affairs by condemning supposed witches mainly on the basis of accusations put forth by "traditional" healers. These rigorous interventions mark a dramatic departure from past practice. Refer to chapter 5 below.

27. Cf. Hebga (1979, 260), who writes about the Beti and the Bassa of the forest of southern Cameroon: "A characteristic common to African traditions concerning occult power is its ambiguity, which is due to its origins: it is at once innate and acquired." Hebga chooses a subtle formulation (which is equally relevant to the Maka) when he refers to an "awakening": the occult force present in the belly of an individual must be awakened for him or her to become a witch.

28. Toward the end of the 1970s, a new type of more modern *nkong* appeared in the region; see chapter 5.

29. It is possible that Mendouga omitted an essential link in her story here. As noted, it is sometimes said that a student *nkong* must deliver a close relative before the "professor" can initiate him or her into the world of *djambe*. Cf. Mallart (1981) on similar conditions during the initiation of a Beti healer; and Copet-Rougier (1986b, 1986c) on the Kako (or Kaka) to the northeast of the Maka; and Hagenbucher-Sacripanti (1989) on similar beliefs among the Vili and the Yombe of the Congo. In this respect, the *nkong/nganga* exemplifies the maxim that one can heal only through *djambe* if one has killed.

30. One of the standing comments about Jean Mabaya's political career was that he knew how to win elections with such threats. Mabaya was the

winner of all the large electoral campaigns in the region at the time of independence. (Afterward, under the regime of the "unified party" of President Ahidjo, elections lost political significance for the population.) See chapter 3.

31. See the remarks above on the power to "double oneself" as an essential capability of a *njindjamb* (witch).

32. The Maka believe that "mongolians" (*kiasle*, "dwarf") have their own animals (like most witches). These are giant serpents that live deep in the forest; they are very dangerous but can also protect against witchcraft.

COMPARATIVE INTERSTICE 1

1. Chilver (1990, 235), writing about conceptions of the Nso of northwest Cameroon, makes the same remark. This point brings us to a more general problem. Recently, several authors—most notably Mudimbe (1988), but see also Jewsiewicki and Moniot (1988)—have affirmed that "African" discourses are profoundly influenced by the "colonial library" and especially by the writings of missionaries, administrators, and anthropologists. The current usage of terms like *sorcery* or *witchcraft* in Africa today is a good example of this. One might question, however, the weight of colonial concepts in the domain of occult forces. Of course, there have been incorporations (for example, the story, told above, of the catechist who struggled all night against a *djim*, or phantom, like Jacob with the angel), but such borrowings are probably not new since *djambe* discourse has always integrated external elements. Certain basic elements—such as the relationship between witchcraft, kin, and cannibalism—are clearly not inspired nor taken from the West. Discourse on occult forces shows, indeed, that one must not overestimate the influence of this "colonial library." Rather, these discourses exemplify the pliability and resilience of African traditions: while there were surely colonial borrowings, these were integrated, if not corrupted, by tendencies and logics specific to local discourses (see Geschiere 1991).

2. However, there are signs that the devil's role is on the increase for the Maka as well, especially in urban settings. Elsewhere in Africa, the fusion of local witchcraft beliefs with the Christian image of the devil seems to have become more pronounced earlier on. There is a direct relationship here to the spectacular success of Pentecostalism and its ways of dealing with threats of the occult (see the afterword; see also Meyer 1995 and Marshall 1993).

3. The frightful image of the nocturnal banquet where the sorcerers eat

their own family members could be a general element of witchcraft/sorcery in Africa. See Hebga 1979, 221, 232, 268; Ortigues and Ortigues 1966, 230.

4. As elsewhere in Africa, ethnic terms are fluid. In the 1970s, for example, one referred to the Ewondo to designate the people of the region of Yaunde, next to the Eton, further north, and the Bulu to the south. As noted above, during the 1980s the term *Beti* has become the current usage for designating all the groups of people living in the Center and South Provinces of the country (the Ewondo, Eton, Bulu, and sometimes even the Fang). No doubt, this is related to political developments: under the regime of President Paul Biya, himself a Bulu, this ethnic ensemble has come to dominate the state.

5. Cf. Ongolo 1986; Nomo n.d.; Mallart-Guimera 1981, and 1988; Hebga 1979; Laburthe-Tolra 1977; Alexandre and Binet 1958. In the writings of Mallart-Guimera, the ambiguity of *evu* is a central theme, elaborated convincingly through both detailed descriptions and general reasoning of a more philosophical order. However, Mallart-Guimera seems sometimes to be tempted by the logics of binary distinctions. He retains, for example, the distinction between "social" and "antisocial" *evu* (1981, 62). He contrasts the Beti, for whom *evu* is indispensable to anyone who wants to succeed, to the Fang, who repudiate *evu* in a radical fashion (1988, 375). Mary (1983, 355–56) notes to the contrary that, also for the Fang of Gabon, all forms of political power are conditional upon *evu*. He summarizes the relationship between *evu* and power by a striking formulation: "Witchcraft . . . links power and wealth to the devouring of others." One might thus wonder whether the oppositions set forth by Mallart are valid, even if they are fairly refined. However, the title of Mallart's first book, *Ni dos, ni ventre*, underscores quite effectively how *evu*, like *djambe*, effaces all distinctions. This explains the expansive capacity of such notions, as well as their ability to infiltrate all domains.

6. Among the Maka, the sons of sisters play a similar role. Although they are direct descendants of the dead, they live separated from the latter's patrilineage. Therefore, it is incumbent upon them to vindicate their uncle, who could have been the victim of perfidious attacks stemming from the intimate sphere of the home (and hence from witchcraft). This can lead, for the Maka as well, to manifestations of aggression during burials. From my experience, this aggression only rarely exceeds the limits of a "joking relationship." I have no indications that, even in the past, the nephews went as far in their role as "terrorists" as their Beti counterparts (at least according to Laburthe-Tolra).

7. Cf. Copet-Rougier 1986a, 1986b, 1986c, 1992a, and 1992b; in general, see Copet-Rougier 1977.

8. On this point, however, there is also divergence: the Kako believe that witches "eat the blood" of their victims, whereas my Maka interlocutors indicate that they eat the heart (*lam*).

9. Copet-Rougier 1986c; 87ff. See also Burnham (1980, n.d.) on the role of witchcraft notions (*duna* or *dua*) among the neighboring Gbaya (or Baya). He equally emphasizes the ambivalence of these notions in relation to power. Moreover, the basic idea that the cure is to be found in the world of witchcraft itself—that is, the healer is a witch (or at least a sorcerer)—is certainly not particular to these groups. Evans-Pritchard (1937) reported it for the Azande, and Favret-Saada (1980) summarizes the same principle for the French countryside in a striking phrase: "for evil to be removed, one must trade evil for evil." See also Bastian's recent article (1993) on eastern Nigeria.

10. Ardener (1970, 144) asserts that *liemba* comes from an ancient Bantu root, indicating common conceptual bases for "all the forest zone of Cameroon." See also Vansina (1990, 299) and above, chapter 2, note 16. Vansina avers that the Beti term *evu* (which would have more or less infiltrated itself between, on the one hand, the terms *djambe* of the Maka and *lembo* of the Kako in the East, and, on the other, terms like *lemba* and *liemba*, more toward the West) is less ancient (personal communication).

11. See Bureau (1962) and de Rosny (1981) on the Duala; Ardener (1956, 1970) on the Bakweri. This impression is also based on my interviews among the Bakweri in 1987 and 1988.

12. Shanklin (1988) claims that, at Kom (one of the bigger chiefdoms in the Grassfields), there is no relationship between witchcraft and cannibalism. This must be an exceptional case; other authors, cited below (chapter 3, note 21) all mention cannibalism as a central theme in discourse on witchcraft in the Grassfields.

13. See also Chilver (1990) on the same notion of *sem*; this article is based on her own research as well as the unedited manuscripts of Phyllis Kaberry. On the Nso in general, see Aletum and Fisiy 1987; Kaberry 1952; Chilver 1989. I thank Cyprian Fisiy for his comments on these passages.

14. As Chilver (1990, 245) comments, "the Fon was removed by various devices from some of the contaminations of power." Michael Rowlands (1987) establishes a contrast between the position of the chiefs in the anglophone Grassfields (the Bamenda) and the francophone Bamileke. Among the Bamenda (including Nso), the *fon* is separated as much as possible from "things of the night." It is his associates—such as the *kwifoyn* at Kom or the

ngwerong at Nso—who are linked to negative occult forces and who handle
the dark side of power (executions, disciplinary actions, etc.). Among the
Bamileke, this distinction is less clear: the *fo* represents both the luminous
and dark sides of power and is not distinctly dissociated from the world of
witches. However, Pradelles de Latour (1991) concludes for the Bangwa
(francophone Bamileke) that the chief is rigorously separated from sorcery
and witchcraft.

15. Evidently, Nso discourse on *sem* is only one example of representations of the occult forces in the West and Northwest. Yet this discourse
seems to express the tendencies general to the entire region: power is closely
associated with occult forces, but notions related to these forces are more
compartmentalized than for forest societies; "witchcraft," as a negative ex-
presssion of these forces, is more clearly delimited; the chief and his associates play a key role in the differentiation between positive and negative expressions of these forces, and they have the capacity to "domesticate" them.
One must note, however, that despite such general tendencies, it is hardly
possible to reconstruct a more definite basic discourse on occult forces common to all societies of the Grassfields region (such as, for instance, the discourse on *evu* or *djambe* for the southern and eastern forest areas). Of
course, these chiefdoms were never united; even the Bamileke never formed
a historical unit. (The name *Bamileke* appears to originate from a colonial
deformation of a term used by Bali interpreters to designate "people of the
mountain.") Nonetheless, it is surprising that there is such little uniformity
between neighboring societies with similar forms of organization. As will be
made clear in the second interlude (note 3) on relations between witchcraft
and power, not only the terms given by ethnographers but also the consequences they attributed to these terms—notably for political relationships—differ greatly. This terminological fragmentation might correspond
to a certain compartmentalization of conceptions of occult forces: there is
no central notion that infuses all aspects of life (such as *evu*), and this seems
to weaken the circularity of notions on the occult that is so pronounced in
the forest societies.

CHAPTER 3. WITCHCRAFT AND LOCAL POLITICS

1. In the 1970s, the villagers had a whole array of expressions to indicate
that they had no influence whatsoever on the politics of *les Grands*. A fairly
striking saying was, for instance: "We are like women here; any time somebody from the town comes to order us around, all we can say is 'yes.' " In

the 1980s, the distance between the villagers and the state institutions became less pronounced, especially because of an increase in the number of young men who were able to obtain a position in government service. Thus the villagers had more opportunities to develop informal clientelist relations in order to defend themselves against the state authorities. Nonetheless, communication within the national political institutions continued to be top-down. This lack of formal openings for interest articulation from below confirms the existing gap between local and national politics. It remains to be seen to what extent the democratization movement in the 1990s will really change all this. There are signs that the ruling party—the RDPC, the former one-party—now pays somewhat more attention to the region in order to maintain its dominant position there. But it is not very probable that the top of the party will be ready to drastically change its way of approaching the *masses populaires*.

2. For further commentary on the Maka palaver, see Geschiere 1982 (chapter 6A).

3. See Geschiere (1982, 423) for an overview of forty-seven palavers before the *kaande* in one Maka village. Of this total, there were only three cases in which the notables clearly ascribed the wrong to only one of the parties and imposed a one-sided punishment (in the form of fines). It is no doubt typical that in all three cases the party put in the wrong was a stranger. It is probably as typical that the fines were never paid in all of these cases.

4. See also Mebenga (1991) on the funeral among the Ewondo (the Maka's neighbors).

5. Among the Maka, kinship excludes marriage. One must therefore always marry outside one's patrilineage (see Geschiere 1982, chapter 2 and appendix 2C).

6. Anthropologists use the term *joking relationships* to indicate such relations, marked as they are by a hostility that is, however, expressed in ritualized form; such "canalized" expressions of tension are supposed to reaffirm relations. The Maka will indeed say that, for instance, a daughter-in-law is *obliged* to dance even though she is sad about her father-in-law's death. Her group is supposed to rejoice about the other family's loss since it concerns a nonrelated group (or else a marriage would have been impossible) and therefore a potential enemy. By dancing at the old man's funeral, a daughter-in-law demonstrates that the two families, although potential enemies, have become related through her marriage.

7. See also Mebenga (1991) on the role of the *zomelo'o* (an old man with a great reputation as a speaker and often called in from elsewhere) during the funerals with the Ewondo (the western neighbors of the Maka).

8. Their ascendancy is also confirmed by the *choga* (or *chouchoga*)—that is, the secret council of elders that, at least according to some of my spokesmen, would still regularly meet. The elders themselves tend to deny that the *choga* is still functioning, but the younger people are not so sure. As one young man explained to me: "Who pays attention to the old people? They can meet in daytime, when everybody is in the fields, or in the dark of the night. Nobody knows what they discuss, but what they decide will surely happen." It is this secret aura of the *choga* that makes it so frightening to the younger people. The reference to the dark of the night clearly associates the *choga* to the *shumbu* (the nightly meeting of the witches). After all, the elders are supposed to be the true masters in the world of *djambe* (witchcraft).

9. For a similar perspective on the role of kinship in African forest societies, see Vansina 1990; Harms 1981. See also Meillassoux (1975) and Rey (1971) for an analysis of kinship, not as the source of power but rather as its expression. As indicated above, a problem of their Marxist perspective was the linking of their view on kinship to the cumbersome notion (cumbersome at least in African studies) of mode of production. But these authors, as some of the first in anthropology, did object to a general tendency in the discipline of taking kinship as just a given of social life.

10. The position of the *lwa* (slave) appears to be an exception in this respect. In former days, a *lwa* did have an inferior position, and it still is a serious insult to suggest that somebody descends from a *lwa*. However, the *melwa* (pl.) did not form a separate group. In principle, the new "father" had to treat his *lwa* as his son (he had to arrange for the lwa's marriage, etc.), and people were supposed to forget about this stigma once the *lwa* had married (which is why it is so shocking to refer to someone's supposedly humble origins). Moreover, a common theme in old stories is that of a poor youngster (often adopted and therefore some sort of *lwa*) who succeeds ultimately in founding his own village.

11. Compare what was said previously in chapter 1 about the individualizing tenor of the *djambe* discourse and its implications for the conception of personhood among the Maka.

12. See also chapter 2. I talked mostly about Maka history with old men on the north bank of the Nyong (in Ayong-Yerap and the Ndjonkol)—that is, in regions that had been terrorized by Nkal Selek and his Mpang in the late nineteenth century. On the south bank of the Nyong, the Maka had been subjected instead to invasions of the Yebekolo and their chiefs (for instance, Evina—see below).

13. Nowadays, the Mpang Sekunda, for instance, speak Maka rather than Mpang.

14. In other versions, Ivinidu or Evina Eloga.

15. The Maka use this term in a fairly general sense to indicate Beti groups to the northwest of their own region.

16. That is, he promises to treat her as his mother if she accepts to treat him as her son.

17. This is the crucial moment in the ceremony: she asks for one or several persons in exchange for the fetishes.

18. Apparently, Evina did not even guess that Nkal's treason was the cause of his death.

19. Once again, it is clear how deceitful the *djambe* is. The Yebekolo are beaten by the very *djambe le doomb* (war magic) that their chief bought from the old Mpele woman.

20. One can deduce from the stories that other, more concrete factors also must have played a role in confirming the Mpang ascendancy over the Maka—for instance, the fact that, since they lived to the west of the Maka, the Mpang must have had somewhat earlier access to European trade goods (notably guns), which began to penetrate this part of the forest in the course of the nineteenth century (see Geschiere 1982). When I suggested to my Maka informants that such concrete factors (and also the fact that the Mpang succeeded in organizing themselves on a larger scale) must have played a role in Mpang ascendancy, people did not contradict this. But the emphasis remained on Nkal Selek's *djambe le doomb*. To the Maka, only such personal occult powers could explain how a man could thus far surpass the basic equality among people.

21. In line with this is the fact that the position of the notables is certainly not hereditary. There are no special status marks that qualify somebody as a notable. It was, for instance, striking that two of Mpal's colleagues—who generally played second fiddle to his performance but who nonetheless had a definite prestige in the *kaande*—had no children. In general, this is quite shameful in Maka culture. And indeed, there were nasty rumors about these men (that they were impotent and so on). But the fact that they showed, time and again, their rhetorical talents and their sound judgment in the *kaande* was enough for them to be generally recognized as respected notables.

22. Several studies of matrilineal societies in Congo-Brazzaville strongly emphasize the role of witchcraft/sorcery as a support of the elders' authority (Hagenbucher-Sacripanti 1973; Dupré 1982; Bonnafé 1988). However, among the Maka—where the principles of discourse on occult forces are more or less the same—this link is less unequivocal: to them, the *djambe* is an ambivalent force, even in relation to the elders. It certainly can strengthen

their authority, but it also makes the elders more vulnerable to leveling forces. Is this leveling aspect of witchcraft, present in many societies, neglected by the authors quoted above? Or the conclusion should be that the matrilineal framework of these Congo societies encourages the exploitation of the young by their elders (that is, by their uncles), even in the occult world?

23. This is, for instance, the case for the *gbati*, the new form of witchcraft mentioned above, that spread like an epidemic throughout Makaland around 1970. Surprisingly, it was reserved for boys. However, at least some of my informants told me that, even in this form of child witchcraft, there was often an older person in the background who was the real leader of the children (Geschiere 1980).

24. Laburthe-Tolra (1977, 1073). The author adds that the ambiguity of *evu* is to be understood in relation to the paradox of "an ethos that is fundamentally egalitarian in a society that is objectively inegalitarian." In this respect, as well, there is a striking parallel with relations among the Maka.

CHAPTER 4. WITCHCRAFT AND NATIONAL POLITICS

1. At the start of the 1970s, the wealthiest farmer in the village where I lived earned about 200,000 francs CFA ($500 at the time) per year from his plantations. Other "big farmers" made 150,000 francs CFA a year from their harvests. By comparison, "category A" civil servants (e.g., medical doctors) earned approximately 100,000 francs CFA per month, and those of "category B" (primary school principals) earned about 60,000 francs CFA monthly. Real differences were, and still are, even greater when benefits and supplements are taken into account (housing, transport, family support).

2. The concept of *popular* seems to have had an ephemeral renaissance in different disciplines of the social sciences toward the end of the 1970s—doubtless a result of the disappointment with the "usefulness" of the notion of class (see Olivier de Sardan 1992 and 1995 on scientific populism as the heritage of Maoism). This is true not only in African studies but also, for example, in historical studies of the *ancien régime* in Europe (see Burke 1978 and Muchembled 1978a, who contrast popular culture with elite culture). In this field also, such oppositions have inspired critique (see Clarke 1983 and Frijhoff 1985).

3. Two pioneering studies in this field, both with regard to Nigeria, are Aronson (1971) on the Yoruba and Gugler (1971) on the Ibo.

4. They still are. The Maka themselves explain this situation by monopolies, even within the Maka region itself, held by other groups (once the French and Greek, and now the Bamileke) on retail trade.

5. Over the last few years, the Biya regime's consistent policy of maintaining or even raising salaries for the police and army while lowering others has led to a recalibration of the scales. Again, many elites complain that, at the time, they had not deigned to take the entrance exam for the army or the police. (These competitions were generally considered the obvious choice for less intelligent youngsters.) "And now these people earn much more than we do."

6. Enquête ZAPI de l'Est, Bertua, Cameroon, 1970.

7. The collapse of cocoa and coffee prices over the last years has completely shaken the cash-crop economy of the villages. The consequences are not yet clear, but the urban elite will probably have even less opportunities for profitable investment in the village economy.

8. For a more detailed analysis, see Geschiere 1982 and 1989.

9. In the East, the number of retired *évolués* is still rather limited. The future will tell whether the idea of retiring to the village is, in fact, actualized. Another related factor in the continuing involvement of the urban elites with their village in many parts of Africa is the notion that one must be buried in one's home village. In 1988, there was a widely disputed case of an important businessman from the Northwest who died abruptly in the city. He had not constructed a house in his village and, therefore, could not be brought home for burial. It would have been "too shameful" for a man like that to be buried in the city, so his body was frozen for the time it took to construct a house. Only then was he buried among his people with appropriate ceremony. Evidently, such conditions force the urban elites to take seriously their relations with the village. However, in this respect as well, there are regional variations; the belief that one must be buried in one's home village does not prevail everywhere. In Maka villages, there are already a few examples of imposing tombs (with photos of the deceased) erected for the elites who had lived in the city. This is a new development; according to the elders, in the past, the actual location of the tomb was not very important. At that time, the Maka were semi-nomadic, so villages moved regularly. Today, the elders can still indicate the areas of the forest where the ancestors are buried, but there are no tombs.

10. In the 1970s, these were especially objects distributed by mail-order businesses in France mentioned above: the house of "Madame Mylla" in Paris and that of "frère Bernard" in Pau. De Rosny (1981) recounts how one of his colleagues visited Madame Mylla in Paris. She was a well-dressed,

petty bourgeois woman who believed she had a mission in Africa to protect people "against evil." For the Maka, the stars and rings ordered from her—for substantial sums of money—were not only to be used in defense. They were thought to be charged with a particularly efficient but ambivalent power which offered protection but also served to attack one's adversaries.

11. It should be noted that this commodification of occult forces is not new. There are significant precolonial precedents. Guyer (1986) demonstrates the extent of commodification in the case of the Beti during the nineteenth century. Janzen (1982) indicates that, in the Congo, these processes also touched upon the health sector and occult therapy. However, the deeper impact of the market since the colonial period reenforced the commodification of "charged" objects and the world of occult forces in general.

12. According to Levine (1964, 244), there were more than one hundred political organizations active in Cameroon by the end of the 1950s.

13. On the ascension of Ahidjo and the suppression of the UPC during the 1950s, see Mbembe 1989; Chaffard 1967; and Joseph 1977. On the formation of hegemonic relations under Ahidjo's regime during the 1960s and 1970s, see Bayart 1979.

14. Ahidjo 1968; 44. See also the analysis of UC/UNC ideology in Bayart 1979 and Geschiere 1982.

15. See Kwayyeb (1967, 127): "[T]he candidate entrusted by our party should not mount a personal election campaign. [. . .] However, once elected, some think it necessary to create 'popularity,' or to create an electoral clientele. By doing so, they give themselves over to demagogy. [. . .] This inevitably leads to friction with the administrative authorities since the latter never fail to bring the situation to their superiors' attention" (my translation). The message is clear: politicians owe their positions to the summit of the party, and administrative authorities will report every attempt by politicians to create popular support.

16. National Archives, Yaunde, Cameroon, APA 10784/C, *rapport semestriel*, 22 January 1932, Abong Mbang, under *Situation politique*.

17. Some of my informants even maintained that Mabaya first had been a member of the UPC. But during the 1970s, when I interviewed him, this affiliation had to be denied at all costs, even if it had occurred in the relatively distant past.

18. Apparently, this is now less the case.

19. The two Mimbang men were not from the same family. In the early 1960s, François Mimbang had to step aside to give the mayorship to Pierre Mimbang. Since then, open hostilities existed between the two.

20. The regulations in the 1967 law concerning such associations were

not meant to encourage them but rather to bring them under government control. In 1966, Ahmadou Ahidjo finally succeeded in integrating the political parties from former British Cameroon into his one-party, which, to commemorate this success, was rebaptized *Union Nationale Camerounaise* from *Union Camerounaise*. This fusion meant, however, that henceforth the party top had to deal directly with relations in former British Cameroon, where a tradition of forming local associations under the aegis of the elites was much more established. One of the aims of the 1967 law was to deal with this.

21. Biya won the election, at least according to official figures, with 38 percent of the votes, just ahead of his main rival, John Fru Ndi of the SDF (the main opposition party). However, most UN observers contested the results. Initially, only France, among the main donors, was prepared to recognize Biya's victory. Many people in Cameroon still believe that Fru Ndi actually won.

22. In more concrete terms, the party provided leaders of the associations with money to do their campaigning in the villages. One of my spokesmen, the president of one of the new associations, talked bitterly about this episode and the ensuing fight among the elites over these funds. He saw this as typical of the "unorganized nature" of Maka politics.

COMPARATIVE INTERSTICE 2

1. See also the novel by Laburthe-Tolra on the Beti (1986); and see Ombolo (1990) and Mallart-Guimera (1981).

2. See Copet-Rougier (1986b, 67). "However, in former times, it is plain that the war leader who wished to maintain the position he had secured by means of physical violence in external affairs had to concentrate in his hands invisible powers of violence available in internal affairs. Operating within a feedback system, he had to become a warrior in the invisible world in order to remain a warrior in the visible and external world of physical violence."

3. I already emphasized (in the first comparative interlude, note 14) the great variations in the ethnographic literature on this region with regard to the central notions of occult forces. Jean Hurault, in his book on the Bamileke (1962, 119), speaks of *ke* or *ka*, a "magic force" that is both good and bad and can be used to protect or destroy. According to him, everyone—especially the chief—must take part in this force. De Rosny (1981, 238) gives similar connotations to the notion of *tok*. These authors seem to rec-

ognize a similar circularity of notions of witchcraft as was highlighted above with respect to the societies of the forest. An entirely different opinion is put forth by Charles-Henry Pradelles de Latour, who writes on the eastern Bangwa (francophone Bamileke). Their central notions of witchcraft are *ndip* and *sue*, which, he states, are radically separated from the social use of occult forces by the chief and the healer. Warnier (1993, 202) follows this, concluding that the Bamileke chiefs are kept "out of *la sorcellerie*." One wonders whether Pradelles de Latour is referring, above all, to norms, and if he does justice to the ambivalence of these notions in everyday life. Among the Bangwa as well, the *nggankang* (healer) seems, in practice, to be a highly ambivalent person (see Pradelles de Latour 1991, 114). Warnier speaks elsewhere (1993, 215) of a certain chief who is "right in line with the figure of the Bamileke chief, father of the village by day and panther of the bush by night." Den Ouden (1987, 6) states quite clearly that "all important men in Bamileke society are in fact supposed to be 'complicated,' to be sorcerers," and concludes that a "Bamileke big man" does nothing to discourage suspicion of witchcraft: "he manages terror in order to be feared." Den Ouden adds that this is true for chiefs as well as for many modern businessmen of the region. Is this a different interpretation of the term *sorcellerie*, or does den Ouden refer, more than Pradelles de Latour, to the role of these notions in everyday life? For the western Bangwa (anglophone Bamileke), Brain (1970) refers to *lekang* as the central witchcraft term; it is a force that can be used for good or evil and is surely employed in such a double sense by chiefs. For the people of the anglophone Grassfields, these same characteristics are found in the ethnographies of Nkwi (1976, 57) and Shanklin (1988) on the Kom (the central term here is *meso*) and in the detailed work of Pool (1994) on the Bum (where the central notion is *tv*). Shanklin (on the Kom) and Pool (on the Bum) note clear parallels with *tsav* (witchcraft) among the Tiv in Nigeria, which is equally directly linked to power (Bohannan and Bohannan 1953). In light of these many variations, one would not want to depict the West and Northwest as a homogeneous regional bloc in contrast to the forest societies. However, with much prudence, one can note certain general tendencies: in all these localities, the association of occult forces with power seems to render the power suspect; but in the West and Northwest, attempts to separate power from negative expressions of occult forces seem to be more institutionalized.

4. See Michael Taussig's very imaginative reinterpretation (1995) of his stories about devil pacts from Colombia and elsewhere (see also Taussig 1980). Following Bataille, he now tends to see these stories as a celebration of consumption—in Bataille's sense of "excessive spending" and "trans-

gression" (a tension that Bataille sees as "the cause of the agitation . . . and the entire history of society"). A parallel to the examples above is that Taussig also emphasizes the basic ambiguity of these stories (they express both "attraction and repulsion") and their fit with "the adventurous, aggressive, risk-taking, high-roller element" of capitalism.

5. See Schatzberg (1993) on the problem of power in postcolonial Africa. He also emphasizes the centrality of associations with eating and witchcraft in the *imaginaire* of power.

6. Today, people sometimes speak about the colonial period with nostalgia; it was the time when "things were better organized." But such comments seem to refer to the last decades of this period (generally after 1945), when relations had become less violent. One must remember—even if it is often neglected by certain historians—that, through most of the continent, the relative calm of this period was founded upon the draconian measures of the previous decades.

CHAPTER 5. WITCHCRAFT AND THE ART OF GETTING RICH

This chapter takes up the theme of an article published by Cyprian Fisiy and myself in *Critique of Anthropology* in 1991 (see also Fisiy and Geschiere 1993). I thank Fisiy for his authorization to use elements from this article in the present chapter.

1. See, for instance, an interesting paper by Thoden van Velzen (1996) on popular fantasies about the new forms of wealth in early modern Europe. See also Kapferer (1983) on present-day Sri Lanka and Taussig (1987) on Colombia.

2. See Hannerz 1992.

3. Warnier 1993, 163 (my translation); see also Rowlands n.d.

4. The Pajero is the Japanese car that has replaced the Mercedes as the main status symbol of the Cameroonian elite.

5. An overview of the annual income from the sale of cocoa and coffee by the farmers of the village where I used to live can give an indication of the differences at stake. The figures concern sales over the year 1971 and are in francs CFA. (See table 1.) However, it is important to note that these differences were not seen as stable. In 1971, the villagers insisted that young people still had every chance to reach the level of the richest farmers, especially because there was still enough land available to create new plantations. In the following years, this prediction did come true. In the 1980s, there

were still important differences between the farmers of the village, but positions had changed. New *grands planteurs* had attained much higher levels of income (at the end of the 1980s, as much as three to four times higher than the highest incomes of 1971—however, this rise was to a large extent leveled by inflation), whereas older farmers were no longer able to maintain their farms and thus were relegated to lower income levels. However, due to the dramatic collapse of cocoa and coffee prices after 1987, such differences have disappeared altogether, at least for the time being.

Table 1. Income from sales of coffee and cocoa in 1970–71, village of Logbood (pseudonym)

Figures in francs CFA (1,000 francs CFA = £2.25 at 1971 rate)	Village Farmers		
	Over 50 years old	Under 50 years old	Total
More than 200,000	—	1	1
100,000–200,000	5	9	14
50,000–100,000	9	21	30
25,000–50,000	5	22	27
Less than 25,000	10	19	29

6. At that time, most villagers still lived in *poto-poto* houses (walls of poles and mud with a raffia roof). But even this type of housing was not traditional; it had been introduced by the French. In precolonial times the Maka lived in much smaller houses of bark and branches.

7. This plant had been constructed under the French in Edea, near the dam on the Sanaga River, to process bauxite from Guinea-Conakry.

8. Copet-Rougier (1986b, 65) reports on the Kako (or Kaka) to the north of Yokaduma: "until the 1980s, nobody dared to build a roof in sheet-metal because to do so was a mark of great success, and was too dangerous."

9. A common, but to me quite shocking, expression of my informants was: "The sorcery of the whites (*djambe le mintang*) is to construct, but our sorcery (*djamb'ayindale* or *la sorcellerie des Noirs*) is to destroy and kill." However, some people altered this adage by pointing out that at least some blacks also had the *djambe le mintang*. As an example, the Maka often quoted, with a certain jealousy, the Bamileke entrepreneurs and their economic success.

10. In general, the villagers create cash-crop plantations gradually, using

the food plots they open up each year in the forest for their wives; when the cycle of the food plants draws to its end (after about two to three years), they begin planting cocoa (or coffee) in these fields, thus gradually expanding their farms. However, Mbon, and a few other *grands planteurs*, were able to make a sudden and much more ambitious start in cash-cropping with the help of their urban earnings.

11. Interviews by author in Buea, 1987 and 1988. Ardener (1970) also says that the *nyongo* was something new to the Bakweri. Subsequently, I discuss certain transformations that accompanied the borrowing of these notions from the Duala.

12. Edwin Ardener writes "Obasi Njom," but Ruell (1969), who worked with the Banyangi, writes "Obasinjom." Nowadays, the Bakweri tend to follow the last spelling. According to Ruell, and several of my Bakweri spokesmen, the Banyangi had bought Obasinjom only a few decades earlier from the Ejagham, who lived more to the northwest, on the Nigerian border. For detailed information on Obasinjom among the Ejagham, see Koloss 1985.

13. As Father Mbuy (1989, 7) puts it, Obasinjom "fished and tamed the witches." Ardener (1970) is not clear on the fate of the witches denounced by Obasinjom. According to our informants, the witches could be reintegrated in society on condition that they made a full confession so that Obasinjom could neutralize their *nyongo*.

14. In 1988, my informants in Buea described this practice as an alternative form of *nyongo*: through it the *nyongo* witches would have tried to get to their victims without being caught by Obasinjom.

15. Obasinjom (that is, the person upon whom he has descended) is supposed to speak Ejagham, the language of his region of origin. One has to be very strong to support him, for his dancing is extremely violent and wild: "He dances here on this spot, but then he jumps and he is already down there." Mostly young men are, therefore, possessed by Obasinjom. But the elders nonetheless play an essential role: they are supposed to "feed the spirit." One informant pointed out to me that Obasinjom also has a wife since "he follows natural laws." Without her, Obasinjom is unable to dance. However, when she has grown to womanhood, he will choose another girl. The family of this girl is very happy about this since Obasinjom brings fertility and protection.

16. The juju is, of course, kept in a highly secret place. My informants in Buea were able to indicate to me where the black mantles of Obasinjom's assistants were kept, but they were vague about the place where Obasinjom himself was hidden.

17. It is not clear how exactly Obasinjom intervened in the relation be-

tween elders and juniors (as elsewhere in Africa, a key relation among the Bakweri). At first sight, Obasinjom seems to be a weapon of the juniors against the elders. Ardener says explicitly that it was because of the juniors' accusations against their elders that the latter agreed to send for Obasinjom. But several informants gave the opinion that Obasinjom had always been controlled by the elders. According to them, the elders sent for Obasinjom in order to protect themselves against the juniors' accusations and to legitimate their wealth. It is clear, in any case, that in the course of time the elders succeeded in gaining control over Obasinjom. Such a pattern of elders gaining control over an anti-witchcraft movement—originally directed against them by the juniors—seems to occur elsewhere also. A striking example of it can be found in the monographs by Rey (1971) and Dupré (1982) on the Mossendjo area of Congo-Brazza. Rey (458) describes the emergence of a series of anti-witchcraft movements in this region in the 1950s. To him this is an initiative of wage laborers, who are mainly young men, to protect themselves against the elders. However, in Dupré's descriptions, based on research among the Nzabi in the 1960s, the same movements—called *La Mère* or *Njobi*—were appropriated by the elders who use the main fetishes in order to intensify their exploitation of the young men. See also the interesting study by Löffler (1983) of Njobi in Gabon (Haut-Ogooué and Ogooué-Lolo) and Péan's cursory but vivid reference to it (Péan 1983, 35). In both studies, Njobi figures as closely linked to the new elite of the state, in particular to President Bongo himself (who has made initiation into the Njobi in the village obligatory for his close collaborators; it is complemented by a subsequent initiation into Freemasonry in the city). Apparently, the relation between such movements and prevailing relations of power can be subject to drastic changes over time.

18. Moreover, such representations of wealth, new forms of witchcraft, and zombies are certainly not limited to Cameroon. For strikingly similar notions, with again interesting variations in the way upon which they are elaborated, see, for instance, Meyer (1995) on southern Ghana; Bastian (1993) on eastern Nigeria; Bockie (1993) on lower Zaire; and Shaw (in press) on Sierra Leone.

19. See also Mallart-Guimera 1981, 115. Éric de Rosny (oral communication) doubts that hypnosis plays a role since this practice is not current among the Duala. But in his view as well, the notion that one must "sell" a parent in order to have access to the riches of the *ekong* is the basic pattern in these representations.

20. As indicated above, the Bakweri use a related term, *nyongo*, to indicate the whole *ekong* complex (which would have been introduced among them by the Duala). Apparently the term *nyongo* or *nyungu* has somewhat

different associations for the Bakweri: to them as well, it is closely related to wealth, but I did not encounter any link with a snake or with the rainbow. The Bakweri sometimes use the term *ekongi* as a general term for this kind of witchcraft (see also Ardener 1956).

21. De Rosny 1992, 56. The witches are generally believed, to transport their victims to Mt. Kupe, but the Duala also cite cases in which victims are said to have been sold to Hausa people or even to Europeans.

22. Levin (1980 and 1987) paints a fascinating picture of a "whiskey galore" among the Bakossi during the spread of cocoa cultivation: "The period most vividly remembered is the postwar period of high cocoa prices and nothing to spend money on. People recollect buying cases of smuggled Spanish gin and brandy and consuming it in long drinking bouts. Shouting and singing echoed through the cocoa farms throughout the night; pits were dug to bury the empty bottles. No farmer had to work. For one-third of the crop, a share-cropper would tend the farm" (Levin 1980, 321). He adds that after 1960, the dream was over. Then there were more possibilities to invest money (especially in schooling, since people became aware of the potential value of school certificates), so people needed ever more money. On the other hand, they began to realize that by renting their land to strangers, they risked losing their control over it (see also Ejedepang-Koge 1971). In the postcolonial era, the Bakossi have been involved in a rather desperate struggle to keep their lands in the face of an ever stronger encroachment, especially by Bamileke immigrants. Balz (1984) explains the Bakossi readiness to have strangers work on their lands by the fact that in this area slavery had only just disappeared when the spread of cocoa began. The imaginary around Mt. Kupe and the *ekom* seems, therefore, to correspond to this practice of exploiting other people's labor, first as slaves and later as sharecroppers.

23. However, one must remember de Rosny's remark (1981, 92) that, in precolonial times, *ekong* among the Duala was associated with respected traders and notables and did not yet have "the odious character it has acquired nowadays." See also Ittmann (1930 and 1963, 668), who relates the *ekom* to notables and mentions quite positive connotations of it. See also Wirz (1972) and Austen (1977) on relations among the Duala in those days. Apparently, the interpretations of these images can also vary strongly over time. It is striking, for instance, that Henri Nicod, a Swiss missionary who worked in this area in the 1940s, can offer hardly any information on *ekong*. He describes it as a dangerous form of *sorcellerie* about which people hardly speak (1948). Again, this is markedly different from present-day Duala society, where *ekong* is much discussed.

24. See de Rosny 1981, 93; see also Ardener (1970) on the Bakweri;

Ittmann (1930) and Balz (1984) on the Bakossi; Austen (1977, 1993) on the Duala. In these regions the expression *la sorcellerie des Blancs* has therefore a much less positive ring than, for instance, among the Maka. As discussed above, the Maka often contrast the *sorcellerie des Blancs*, which is to "construct," with the *sorcellerie des Noirs*, which is to "destroy." According to Pool (1994), the Mbum of the limits of the Grassfields (near the Nigerian border) make a similar contrast. In the regions touched by the *ekong*, little remains of this positive association of whites and sorcery. For a similar, yet different, elaboration on the same basic theme, see White (1993) on vampire accusations against White Fathers in colonial Zambia. In this case the priests seemed to be suspected because they made people work for them without paying them money—while in Cameroon, and elsewhere in West Africa, it was precisely the link between labor and money that seemed to trigger rumors about people being sold as zombies.

25. The term *famla* probably comes from the name of an elite quarter of Bafoussam, the main town in Bamilekeland. However, Mbunwe-Samba (1996, 75) gives a different etymology: "*Famla* actually means abandoned compound or a . . . ghost town. The meaning of this word in the context of witchcraft is that a witch, having given all his people mysteriously to his/her witch partners to eat (these are usually seven in number) . . . the compound is empty or abandoned. The witch then will become very wealthy. *Famla* is ascribed to the Bamileke people, a group of very industrious and enterprising people. . . . One suspects that belief in *famla* has gained currency because the Bamileke are considered by many people to be mean and stingy, in spite of their wealth."

26. In the 1980s, the bankruptcy and subsequent closure of several banks were generally attributed to the large-scale withdrawal of cash from official circuits by the *njangi*. See also Warnier (1993) and Warnier and Miaffo (1993) on the role of the *njangi* in the rise of the entrepreneurs from the West and the Northwest. Warnier (1993, 198) remarks that, among the Bamileke, *famla* is sometimes described as "a *njangi* of the rich." See also Rowlands 1993 and n.d.

27. Warnier (1993), Warnier and Miaffo (1993), and Pradelles de Latour (1991) all mention *famla* but only briefly. Mbunwe-Samba (1996, 75), who produced the longest text on it, has an original explanation of why it is so little studied: "The word *famla* has gained such a mystical force that no one will dare write or talk about it lest he/she dies."

28. See Warnier (1993, 74): "Thus, the wealthy traders are suspected to have enriched themselves by magically selling persons. Indeed, the term *famla* refers to both the posh quarter of Bafoussam and this practice, which

is as old as the slave trade. However, as far as my information goes—but who will do a proper study of this topic?—such suspicions do not seem to affect them or force them to redistribute their new wealth" (my translation). See also Warnier and Miaffo 1993. Francis Nyamnjoh describes a similar ambivalence for the Bum of the northwestern Grassfields, who speak of *msa* (the market of sorcery), which they also call *Munyongo* (= *nyongo*) or *Kubeh* (= *kupe*). Here as well there is a direct link between *msa* and "modernity" (*kwang*). In principle, the modern wealth accumulated at *msa* is evil, but some people ("the sly") know how to use this secret world and succeed in enriching themselves in a sensible way. Nyamnjoh (1985, 15) describes *msa* as a kind of mirror of the daily world: "there is good more than one can imagine. And there is evil more than imagination can grasp. Good and evil are its integral parts, and a person cannot choose the one without equally having the other. Yet the most difficult thing about *Msa* is that evil seems to be enveloped by apparent goodness."

29. The *famla* can therefore be viewed as a hidden script in the epic of *le dynamisme bamiléké* (the title of a 1981 book by Jean-Louis Dongmo on the economic fervor of the Bamileke). It is clear that the massive migrations of Bamileke to other parts of the country have played a crucial role in the economic ascent of this group. But juniors often tend to associate these migrations with *famla* and with the new rich who reinvest money accumulated in the diaspora in the home country; for a junior, the only way to evade this pressure would be to migrate.

30. Long before the colonial conquest, the Grassfields were included in important regional and long-distance trading networks (kola, iron objects, palm oil, slaves—see Warnier 1985). However, as Cyprian Fisiy stresses, money really penetrated into the domestic economy much later, only after the rise of migrant labor. From 1900 on, the Grassfields provided an ever-growing number of laborers on the European plantations near the coast. But it was especially after 1945 that laborers began to bring home larger amounts of money.

31. It is interesting that in these areas as well, this new witchcraft of the rich—that is, *famla*—is associated with the whites (just like *ekong* among the Duala, *ekom* among the Bakossi, or *nyongo* among the Bakweri). This seems, again, to be a reflection of the slave trade, which, moreover, had particularly profound implications in these areas. Recently, Jean-Pierre Warnier (1989) has maintained that in the Grassfields especially, the slave trade was based on the sale of people from within the large compounds. He speaks of "la vente frauduleuse de parents et des alliés." For a long time, these regions have furnished a great number of slaves for the trade not only via Duala but

probably more importantly via Calabar. According to Warnier, an important number of these slaves were not captives but rather young, more or less marginalized men who risked being sold secretly by ambitious relatives trying to gain their own access to the commercial exchanges of prestige goods (and therefore bridewealth and women). The imaginary of *famla* would therefore reflect a historical reality: the selling of kinsfolk in order to become rich. An intriguing aspect of these representations is that they relativize the distinction between people and commodities. The Bakweri discourse on *nyongo* can be interpreted as an attempt to personalize new forms of wealth: the accumulation of luxury goods by the new rich would be based on the occult appropriation of *nyongo* victims. But this relation can also be interpreted inversely. In the Grassfields, it seems rather that the selling of people, in the slave trade or through *famla*, serves to accumulate goods in ever more shocking quantities. In such a context the notion of commodification, now so popular among anthropologists and other social scientists, acquires surprising aspects (see Appadurai 1986a; Parry and Bloch 1989). The *famla/ ekong* conceptions seem to reflect a process of commodification that transforms not only goods but also people into commodities (see Guyer and Mbembe 1992 and Guyer 1993 on the notion of wealth-in-people versus wealth-in-things). For Sierra Leone, Rosalind Shaw admirably analyzes the link between memories of the slave trade, new forms of witchcraft, and commodities. Giving specific meaning to Bourdieu's general phrases, she concludes: "Today these tropes and practices . . . are more than just 'survivals' of the terror of the Atlantic trade and of the Colony's 'legitimate trade'; anachronistic relics of the past. They are practical memories, part of an 'environment of a way of acting' in which the past is embodied as an active presence in practices and perceptions—'internalized as a second nature and so forgotten as history'—which structure the present" (in press, 32).

32. This story was written down by my coauthor Cyprian Fisiy, who originates from the area concerned (Noni, a chiefdom linked to Nso). I thank him for his permission to include this case study in this chapter. For parallel stories, see Mbunwe-Samba (1996) and also Fisiy and Geschiere (in press).

33. In some respects, the story resembles Michael Taussig's examples of peasant societies in Latin America that mobilize similar representations in order to defend themselves against the eroding impact of the money economy (1980). The emphasis on the sound of falling cash is an especially common theme. However, the Cameroonian example also indicates that such themes can have highly different implications. It is too one-sided to insist only on the ways in which peasant societies try to defend themselves

against new "exchange-values." Local beliefs can also serve to legitimize participation in new forms of wealth.

34. See Goheen (1996, 141) on the sale of titles to the new rich in Nso. See also Warnier (1985) on the close link in this area between the *fon*, the title societies, and the accumulation of new forms of wealth through trade in the precolonial period.

35. See Fisiy (1992) on the role of the chiefs from the Northwest in the application of the new land law. Instead of using their customary rights to defend their subjects' interests against the encroachments by the new po-litico-administrative elite, they seem eager to profit themselves from these reforms.

36. Warnier, oral communication; see also Warnier 1993, 220.

37. See Goheen 1996, 145, 161. See also Chilver (1990) and the extremely interesting text by Ndjio (1995) on a recent series of performances of the *Ngru*, a Bamileke purification ritual. Apparently this old ritual was suddenly revived in 1994 simultaneously in several rural chieftaincies in the West Province, but also in the Bamileke quarter in the city of Duala. Ndjio interprets the staging of the ritual as a somewhat desperate attempt by the chiefs to restore their authority, which was severely undermined by their collaboration with the RDPC regime. Typically, the chiefs are strongly supported by the "external elites" and the administrative authorities in organizing the ritual. Equally typical is the ambivalent role of the *nganga* (healers) as brokers between these groups. A somewhat confusing aspect is, however, that the new rich themselves, with their supposed *famla*, seem to be one of the common targets during the unmasking of witches. Young men play a central role in this. A year later, Ndjio returned to these places and constated that, although the chiefs and some notables were still satisfied with having staged the ritual, the people in general were more skeptical. Many talked about it as a swindle that served only to enrich the chiefs and the *nganga*. One might, therefore, interpret these events as a sign that even in the West Province the unrest about *famla* is mounting and that people are beginning to doubt the chiefs' capacity to contain it. Indeed, the monetarization of the *Ngru* seems to indicate that the chiefs are being corrupted by the new rich and their *famla* power.

38. See Mallart-Guimera 1981, 1988; Nomo n.d.; Yombi 1984; Fisiy 1990b.

39. I worked in this area with my coauthor Cyprian Fisiy. This region is populated by various ethnic groups. The Batanga, who are related to the Duala, are generally considered to be the autochthonous people of the coastal area. In the interior one finds Pygmies (or rather, Bagieli), Ngumba

(related to the Maka), and Fang. Over the last century, there has been a strong influx of Beti groups coming from the North (Ewondo and especially Bulu).

40. See Yombi 1984 and Fisiy 1990b. We did not succeed in getting a clear picture of this Bisima. According to some, the movement was related to the *miengu* (water spirits) of the Batanga; others said that it came from the Fang in Gabon and Bata, and that it was related to the Bwiti-Fang (see Mary 1983 and Fernandez 1982).

41. According to our information, Father Many had been exorcising evil spirits for some time already. He was excommunicated only when he started to use his personal powers to heal people. It is, incidentally, quite surprising that his young assistants were called *zomelo'o*. In Ewondo, this term is a kind of honorary title, sometimes translated as "Master of the Word" and strictly reserved for elders (see Mebenga 1991 and Ngoa 1968). Laburthe-Tolra (1977, 1401) mentions *zomoloo* or *zomoloa* and translates it as "*grand juge*"; he relates this title to the So ritual, a key institution in the old Beti order. The transfer of these titles to young boys might be characteristic of their increasing role in sorcery and witchcraft. Some informants from this area emphasized, indeed, that the juniors were increasingly overtaking the elders, even in this domain.

42. It should be noted that, during the last decades, Pentecostalist churches and other "independent" churches have been much more successful in the Kribi area than in other regions of Cameroon. In general, until quite recently the spread of such independent churches remained limited in Cameroon—as compared to other parts of Africa—for reasons I do not fully grasp. (Possibly one reason is the strict control of the one-party regime over society, especially under Ahidjo.) Recently, authors like Meyer (1995) and Marshall (1991, 1993) have emphasized that Pentecostalist sects especially, with their strong emphasis on the role of the devil and their highly physical purification rituals, seem to be capable of breaking through the circularity of the witchcraft-kinship discourse emphasized above. These authors seem to suggest that Pentecostalism might thus be able to offer a third way, bridging the gap between, on the one hand, local discourse on kinship and witchcraft, with its strong circularity, and, on the other, the modern world of growing individualism and new economic opportunities, which are, however, accompanied by frightening social insecurity.

43. Several informants told us that *kong* witches work with a list. Each time they cross a name off their list by their magic means—for instance, with a finger dipped in a magic potion—this person dies. See also Fisiy 1990a, 1990b; and see Procès-verbal de la gendarmerie nationale, compagnie

d'Ebolowa, brigade d'Olamze, no. 364, 24-12-1985 (I thank Fisiy for having shown me those files).

44. See also Harri Englund's recent (1996) article on the "plurality of witchcraft" in relation to accumulation in present-day central Malawi. Englund relates the different possible articulations of witchcraft notions and new forms of wealth to "the politics of personhood in the morality of accumulation."

45. Cf. a quote from a conversation Warnier had with a Bamileke entrepreneur, where exactly the same contrast is made (Warnier 1993, 90). See also Franqueville (1987, 239, 275) on the contrasts between *le familialisme beti* and the relations of Bamileke migrants to their home village.

46. See de Rosny 1981, 1992. The same emphasis on the continuing link between kinship and witchcraft, despite the modern changes, is to be found in recent literature on many parts of Africa. See, for instance, Meyer (1995) on southern Ghana; Bastian (1993) on eastern Nigeria; Ashforth (1996) on South Africa. Yet in some contexts people seem to believe that this link might be surpassed. The young healers from Kribi were the only ones among my informants who claimed that modern forms of witchcraft were no longer linked to kinship and the family. To them, this was precisely one of the really new aspects of "modern" forms of *sorcellerie*. De Boeck (1996) reports similar ideas among young diamond smugglers in the chaotic boomtown of Kikwit (Zaire). Bastian (1993) also indicates that some Ibo believe that witchcraft can now surpass the framework of kinship. In an impressive, and depressing, radio program, "Congo: La guerre des âges" by Bernard Chenuaud (Radio France, France Culture, 21 November 1995), on fierce actions by youngsters against their elders because of witchcraft in Brazzaville, several informants say as well that *la sorcellerie déborde la parenté*. Especially the Zairean and the Congolese contexts are highly unstable—the violence of the Brazzaville youngsters seems to equal that of the Zairean diamond smugglers. Yet even in these cases the basic link with kinship still seems to be a determinant in witchcraft accusations and therapies. In the Brazzaville case, for instance, it seems that informants refer only to the young men's reactions that, indeed, *débordent la parenté*. The accusations remain enmeshed in the kinship framework.

47. Warnier (1993, 75): "the practice of solidarity according to merit is based on the following principle: only relatives who have proven their worth participate in the networks of solidarity. Relatives support each other, but those who, by their own fault, have not made proper use of the help they received are marginalized." In addition, "the embankment of kinship . . . means that relatives whom one cannot avoid, but who are marginal, are put

to work in a minor enterprise, stable but hardly profitable and sealed from risk-bearing enterprise by an air-tight partition. As a rich entrepreneur said with some cynicism, 'It is there that I place the people from my family: those who keep asking me for a job, the delinquents' " (my translation). See also den Ouden (1987, 18), who makes a distinction between *helping* and *sharing*: "among the Bamileke . . . to give help is quite different from letting others share your prosperity." Another fundamental contrast with the Beti and the forest societies in general is that, in most Grassfields societies, a father's heritage goes to one son only (often the oldest); in most forest societies, on the contrary, all sons share in the heritage, so that it is often dispersed upon the father's death.

CHAPTER 6. THE STATE ATTACKS

This chapter revisits the subject of an article coauthored with Cyprian Fisiy in *Cahiers d'études africaines* (1990). I thank him for allowing me to use certain elements of that publication herein. See also Fisiy 1990a, 1990b; Fisiy and Rowlands 1990.

1. In his last book, de Rosny concludes: "The de-sorcerers have nice days before them since the phenomenon of sorcery continues in the modern world" (1992, 119). He adds that this is as true for European countries as for African cities like Duala.

2. See, for example, Fadika 1975; Kimvimba 1978; Mambou-Pembellot 1985; Mathe 1976; Mboukou 1985; Yombi 1984. It appears that those arguing for more direct state intervention in witchcraft affairs are more often from francophone Africa. In the anglophone countries, interlocutors seem less convinced of the necessity for state intervention in this domain. Doubtless, differences of colonial heritage play a role here. In general, the state is more interventionist in the former French colonies. According to Murray Last (personal communication), similar contrasts can be found in the realm of health care.

3. More recently, similar trials have taken place in other regions (see below), but they remain far less frequent than in the East.

4. I was able to consult these documents thanks to Cyprian Fisiy, who had access to the archives of the Bertua Court of Appeal for the period 1981–84. He uncovered a total of thirty files relating to witchcraft trials (see Fisiy 1990a). All these matters were first treated by one of the four Courts of First Instance of the East Province (Abong-Mbang, Baturi, Bertua, Yokaduma). The files of the Court of Appeal also contained documents con-

cerning trials judged before these Courts of First Instance. In most cases, the Court of Appeal confirmed the judgments of the Courts of First Instance. This chapter is based on twenty-two of these files (eight files were incomplete) and on a series of additional cases I studied in various Maka villages (six of which were highly detailed). I returned to the Maka villages for brief periods during 1987, 1988, and 1991. At these times, I had the impression that judicial action against witches had become more forceful. Élisabeth Copet-Rougier, who returned in 1992 for some time to stay with the Kako (Kaka) in another part of the East Province, confirmed this impression (personal communication).

5. Apparently, this article is derived from a similar one found in the French penal code. There was, then, no change in the law, contrary to the predictions of my Maka friend in 1973, cited above. An existing article sufficed to condemn witches. It is, moreover, striking that this article in no way attempts to define the notion of "witchcraft." It thus lends itself to very wide and variable interpretations. The fact that "divination" is specifically added and that the emphasis is on "taking reward" suggests that this article was to be used especially against "healers" (this was certainly the case under the colonial regime, which pursued healers rather than witches).

6. It seems, however, that lawyers were present at other trials. B. A. Muna, a lawyer in Yaunde, claims that he regularly assisted the accused in witchcraft cases before the court of Bertua during the 1980s.

7. Among the eight accused who confessed before the court, two were children and one was acquitted (even though he confessed) because the acts had been committed ten years prior. (His confession served, nonetheless, to condemn two of his supposed accomplices who, themselves, did not confess.) Six other accused first confessed before the healer or the gendarmes, but they subsequently retracted their statements, insisting that they had been mistreated. Their withdrawals were of no avail: all six were condemned to prison. Therefore, only a minority of the suspects admitted guilt. The question remains, however, as to why these suspects made such dangerous confessions before the tribunal. One explanation might be that, according to local conceptions, a confession is a preliminary condition for being cured. As noted in chapter 1, the *nganga* (healer) can only help someone if the latter admits to nocturnal escapades. If someone is accused in the village but continues to deny the charges even before the healer, he or she is thought to be a particularly dangerous witch. It is only after a confession that the healer can neutralize these troubling forces (on this point, see also Fisiy and Rowlands 1990). The issue of confessions offers a prime example of how the interventions of the courts disturb local discourse; those who confess before

the tribunals are not healed but, rather, are condemned to heavy prison sentences (see Fisiy and Geschiere 1990).

8. It is also surprising that only four of these twenty-two cases took place in urban centers. All the others were village affairs. The number of urban cases is very low considering the proliferation of witchcraft rumors in urban contexts.

9. Among the thirty-eight suspects in our sample, eighteen were men between forty and sixty years of age. It is remarkable that there were only six women among them. In the villages, women are thought to be at least as active in witchcraft as men. The Maka have a proverb: "The women are the first to come out" (that is, to leave their bodies at night and fly to the meeting of witches). Refer also to the myth of the origin of *djambe*, which states that it is a woman—in an act of betrayal similar to that of Eve in paradise— who introduced *djambe* into the village (see chapter 1). One reason why there are so few women among the accused considered here could be that these cases involve supposed attacks against the richer and more "modern" people of the villages. Women do not seem to have a visible role in such affairs.

10. Among the thirty-eight suspects, there were, for example, three men about seventy years old. It is interesting that these three elders were all acquitted after having denied everything.

11. Tribunal de première instance d'Abong-Mbang, jugement no. 1291/COR, 24 June 1983. As in other chapters, I have replaced the names of those villagers who figure in these trials as accused and witnesses with pseudonyms, but I retained the actual names of the healers since they play a public (and crucial) role in the judicial actions against the witches.

12. According to the president of the village committee of the single party, cited as a witness for the prosecution, Nkal had assured him that the heart of the instructor "was already put back." Evidently, Nkal was not very consistent in his statements.

13. To be sure, Nkal seemed obsessed with his relationship to Medumba. He repeated several times to the gendarmes that Medumba was the one who had him "initiated in *sorcellerie*." Before the tribunal, he added that Medumba prevented him from giving back his part of Mr. Mpoam's heart, which he had hidden in the bush. He declared, moreover, that Medumba tried to force him to eat his part of the heart. "He brought me into this project—it was a way to convince me, by eating the same food as him."

14. Cour d'appel de Bertua, doss. 83.4000.968/PG/BE, arrêt no. 75/ COR, 29 November 1983.

15. But often the supposed "gbaticians" are too young to be suspected

of desiring access to women. Another element of these representations, which applies more distinctly to young boys, is the idea that the "gbaticians" are obsessed with the desire to eat meat and fatty foods (which young children normally eat only rarely). In the village, the *onkong* (healers) exorcise the *gbati* by forcing "gbaticians" to eat enormous quantities of meat prepared with a lot of palm oil. They must eat until they vomit; then, they are discharged of *gbati*. In the cases I witnessed, the *nkong* "found" the *gbati* in the boys' vomit, sometimes in the form of bamboo splinters or a cord with knots along it (each knot corresponding to a person whom the "gbaticians" wished to kill).

16. Tribunal de première instance d'Abong-Mbang, jugement no. 02/COR, 5 October 1982; cour d'appel de Bertua, doss. 83.400.250/PG/BE, arrêt no. 145/COR, 29 March 1983.

17. Tribunal de première instance d'Abong-Mbang, jugement no. 1163/COR, 10 May 1982; cour d'appel de Bertua, doss. 83.400.762/PG/BE, arrêt no. 86/COR, 4 October 1983. See also the case cited above involving the attack against the school and the teacher, Mpoam, by Nkal and his companions. In this file, the term *gbati* is not used. One of the accused had a child and, in principle, could thus not possess *gbati*. In other respects, however, the affair corresponds to the *gbati* profile (the ages of the accused, the anti-modern tenor).

18. Aliguéna was a renowned healer in the region of Nguélemenduka, where he resided for some time. He was not a native of the East but an Eton from the Center Province.

19. As indicated above, the Maka term *nkong* is equivalent to the term *nganga*, used more generally in southern Cameroon (and elsewhere in Bantu languages) to indicate healers or witch doctors. In the present chapter, I use *nkong* when discussing a Maka case and *nganga* in more general contexts.

20. Tribunal de première instance d'Abong-Mbang, jugement no. 1196/COR, 17 May 1983; cour d'appel de Bertua, doss. 83.400.971/PG/BE, arrêt no. 81/COR, 6 December 1983.

21. Throughout the region, panther whiskers are thought to be one of the most terrible "medicines" of witches. Some informants add that these whiskers can be used as an effective means to "poison" someone. The pieces of whisker remain so hard and sharp that they pierce the victim's intestines.

22. In other cases, more substantial indemnities were accorded as compensation to healers; for example, 40,000 francs CFA ($100 at the time).

23. The tribunals' uneasiness in relation to the question of how to establish proof for these cases is illustrated by the response a judge in Bertua gave

to Cyprian Fisiy in an interview. The magistrate explained that ultimate proof comes from the "personal conviction" of the judge that witchcraft exists (Fisiy 1990a). This expression is repeated in the files of several of these trials.

24. See, in chapter 1, the portrait of Madame Mendouga, the leading *nkong* during my first stays in the village.

25. In Cameroon, this association is more or less authorized by the government, but it has not yet been legalized as in other African countries (Ghana, Mali, Senegal—see de Rosny 1992, 45; Last and Chavunduka 1986). The official support reflects a general effort made by the government to better control the domain of witchcraft. But it is also an indication of the healers' aspirations for official recognition. The healers themselves often say that their association helps exclude charlatans coming from outside; they especially refer to Nigerian healers who would be ever more active in Cameroon.

26. In the files I consulted at the Court of Appeal, two "modern" healers, Messieurs Baba and Aliguéna, occupy preponderant places. Their testimonies were decisive in seven affairs (of a total of twenty-two); none of the accused in these cases were acquitted. Both men work in the region between Angossas and Nguelemendouka, at the western limit of the East Province. This region is of particular interest: from an economic point of view, it is the most developed part of the province (cocoa cultivation expanded more rapidly and earlier here than elsewhere in the East). Significantly, this is also the area where such modern *onkong* play an important role.

27. Another distinguishing feature of these new *onkong* is that they are predominantly men. In the 1970s, there were at least as many women as men among the renowned *onkong* in the Maka region.

28. De Rosny (1981, 196; 1992, 95) also notes the emergence of these younger and more aggressive *nganga* (healers), who pronounce direct accusations (see also Yombi 1984, who signals a similar development in Ntem, South Province). De Rosny also seems somewhat fearful of these young *nganga*. In general, though, his image of the *nganga* is more positive than mine. The difference stems, perhaps, from a divergent approach. De Rosny concentrates on a few *nganga* with whom he has maintained intense relationships (which, for him, does not preclude a critical perspective). He attempts to demonstrate that their therapies can, in fact, cure. I studied, instead, the role of witchcraft in local communities, thus encountering a wide array of healers, including several with charlatanical airs and often quite aggressive behavior. Of course, I do not wish to ignore the fact that *onkong* can help their clients under certain circumstances. Many have great knowl-

edge of herbs, and others know how to rectify troubled relations. But there are also many *onkong* who act as cunning entrepreneurs, ready to exploit any problem in order to build a reputation. Collaboration with the authorities has increased considerably the *onkong*'s potential for such aggressive entrepreneurial activities.

29. See Chavunduka and Last 1986, 269. These authors describe how the healers' efficiency is linked to the continuity of a "therapeutic community" in the rural context. In more modern contexts, healers must develop new therapies, the efficacy of which are to be appraised. See also Ngubane 1986. And see Last (1986, 14), who refers to the "pervasiveness of the legal idiom"; he adds that today in Africa, in conversations about sorcery, "the diviner is seen as a detective, the witch as a criminal." A much more positive image of the *nganga* emerges from Pamela Reynolds's subtle article (1990) on the role of these healers in healing postwar traumas—especially of children—in Zimbabwe. From her appendix on witch-hunts emerges the familiar image of a *nganga* as a cunning entrepreneur who can hardly be controlled by the ZINATHA (the new Zimbabwe traditional healers' association). But in general, Reynolds emphasizes "the commitment and concern of healers in their handling of troubled children."

30. The tenacity of this stereotype is underscored by the fact that the new president of Cameroon, Paul Biya, repeated Ayissi Mvodo's comment word-for-word while addressing the people of Bertua in 1983.

31. See, for example, *Cameroon Tribune*, 7 August 1992, on the judgment of an affair in Yaunde; Yombi (1984) and Fisiy (1990b) on cases in the South Province; and Mbunwe-Samba (1996) on a case judged by a tribunal at Muyuka (Southwest) in 1989.

32. It would be interesting to inquire as to when exactly appeals to the state are preferred to recourse to the church. Father de Rosny (1992 and personal communication) thinks that, in order to combat the increasing anxiety about witchcraft, a "united front" of state, church, *nganga* (traditional healers), and modern psychiatrists is necessary.

33. Some informants in the East Province suggest, to the contrary, that the state has taken certain initiatives. According to them, in the early 1980s, it was declared in a radio announcement that the tribunals would be prepared to treat future witchcraft accusations, regardless of tangible proof. I could not obtain more details or any further confirmation about this information.

34. It remains to be seen whether the prosecutor's opinion on this point is well founded. According to B. A. Muna, a lawyer based in Yaunde, the Supreme Court already confirmed several verdicts in witchcraft cases heard

by the Bertua Court of Appeal. In his view, the Supreme Court can check only whether the lower courts have respected procedures, but it cannot examine the administration of proof as such.

35. The cases cited by Yombi (1984) and Fisiy (1990a, 1990b) indicate that the government does act with much more reserve in witchcraft affairs in the South. Civil servants, for example, seem to distrust the *nganga* of Bisima (the anti-witchcraft movement mentioned above), which claims to combat *kong* (a new form of witchcraft) in that region. Indeed, the *nganga* do act with great circumspection in this area, always insisting that they will perform only after their clients have asked for government permission. In general, the collaboration between the state elites and the *nganga* seems to be more distanced and less self-evident in this region than in the East. The prosecutor at Kribi also mentioned another reason why the East is especially known for the sentencing of witches. He served there for a short period and was struck by the readiness of the accused to admit to atrocious crimes before the tribunal. According to him, this propensity to admit guilt was specific to the East. However, this observation does not correspond to the low number of accused who confessed, according to the files of the court at Bertua that I consulted.

36. In 1995, I had the opportunity to discuss the preceding case from the Kribi area once more with Mr. Ela, the state prosecutor. This time, the prosecutor was much more sure about how to deal with such affairs. Apparently, he had developed his own strategy since our last encounter. He emphasized that popular pressure on the courts to intervene in witchcraft affairs was even stronger than before. However, he now knew how to deal with such affairs and did not need a *nganga* for this. His strategy was to have the accused arrested—if only for his or her own protection—and then to organize a large court session for which the whole village had to be present. If it was clear that there was no evidence against the accused, he or she could safely return to the village. This is the way he had solved the case in the village of Ntdoua of the seventeen young men who had murdered an old "witch." He had summoned the whole village to a court session. There, he demonstrated that there was absolutely no evidence against the old man. Consequently, the villagers accepted his verdict that the young men should be punished for their deed. They were all sentenced to eight years or more in prison, and at least according to the prosecutor, there was no protest from the village. An editorial in the *Times of Namibia* (21 January 1992) indicates another possible "solution" to the dilemma of how the law has to deal with witchcraft: "A genuine belief in witchcraft, if held by an accused . . . should be taken into consideration in assessing an appropriate sentence, without

creating an impression that belief in witchcraft affords an excuse for criminal conduct." (I thank Jan-Bart Gewald for showing me this article.) Apparently, witchcraft is becoming a thorny issue for judges throughout Africa.

37. Bayart 1993; Warnier 1993.

38. See, for instance, Sulikowski 1993; Elwert-Kretschmer 1995; Tall 1995; see also Elwert 1983.

39. I thank Hugo Soly for directing me to recent publications on studies of witchcraft in Europe.

40. The ideas of "magical equilibrium" and of the "eu-functional" role of witchcraft beliefs are used by the historian Robert Muchembled in his characterization of peasant societies in Europe before the great witchcraft trials. According to him, these trials were triggered by a rapid and large-scale process of "forced acculturation"—perhaps another imprint of functionalist anthropology? (see Muchembled 1978a, 107; 1978b, 218). There is a distinct parallel here with the idea put forth by functionalist anthropologists that African societies were "in equilibrium" or even "harmony" before they were shaken by the acculturation imposed by the West (from this perspective, changes can only come from outside). But, of course, this representation has been severely criticized by African historians. One of the most renowned historians of witchcraft in Europe, Carlo Ginzburg, seems inspired, most notably in his last publications, by another ahistorical anthropological vision: somewhat surprisingly, he seems to opt for the old tenets of evolutionism. He seeks an atemporal substratum underneath witchcraft notions that, at least in Eurasia, supposedly has endured since the neolithic period (Ginzburg 1990). It is certainly surprising that these historians seek their inspiration in anthropological currents of an ahistorical bent.

41. Rowland's contribution (1990) was published in a prestigious collection of historical studies on witchcraft in Europe, edited by B. Ankarloo and G. Henningsen. The editors, both of whom have a reputation in European witchcraft studies, repeat a good part of Rowland's interpretations in their introduction.

42. See, for example, Salmon 1989. Yet, one can wonder how he and other European historians can still maintain that anthropological studies concern "primitive" societies that are not easily compared with the "complex" societies of Europe of the sixteenth and seventeenth centuries. See Rowland 1990; Middelfort 1972; Monter 1976. Evidently, these historians failed to note that almost all anthropological studies of witchcraft refer to societies under colonial rule, which in many respects—infrastructure and communications, labor migration, urbanization—were certainly not less "complex" than European societies studied by these historians.

43. There have been, obviously, some encounters. One might mention, for instance, the conference on "Witchcraft Confessions and Accusations," which took place at Oxford in 1968, on the occasion of the thirtieth anniversary of the publication of Evans-Pritchard's classic monograph, *Witchcraft, Oracles and Magic among the Azande*. In her introduction to the contributions to this symposium, Mary Douglas (1970) notes the gap separating anthropological and historical studies of these phenomena (see the afterword at the end of the present work). It seems characteristic that, in the Douglas volume, the historians (who include Norman Cohn, Keith Thomas, and Alan Macfarlane) are largely inspired by anthropological approaches, while the anthropologists—at least in their written contributions—hardly manifest an interest in the interpretations of their historian colleagues.

44. Muchembled 1978a, 1978b. In a later publication (1981), the author distinguishes yet a third, intermediate discourse of the local judges. The manner in which these discourses are opposed has been criticized by other historians. Rowland (1990) maintains, for example, that this opposition was not so radical; the elite discourse was profoundly influenced by popular notions. However, Muchembled (1981) himself had earlier altered his previous interpretations.

45. These two "micropolitical" studies of sorcery trials in America and France offer at several points interesting comparisons with recent trials in Cameroon. Muchembled, like Boyer and Nissenbaum, relates the abrupt outbreak of these trials to disorder in the judicial organization. (In Salem, there was temporarily no governor in the colony due to a *coup d'état* in Boston; in the Bouvignies case, the region had recently been conquered by the French.) In both cases, the witches' confessions are equally intriguing. One of the strong, and frightening, points of Muchembled's work is that he details how the judges were able to break the resistance of the accused without recourse to torture—how their initial denials were gradually transformed into confessions of supposed misdeeds. Boyer and Nissenbaum (1974, 215) suggest, on the other hand, that accusations spread like wildfire at Salem because the first accused persons refused to confess. They argue that, in these societies, public avowal establishes the possibility for healing and even reintegration into the community. (There is an interesting parallel here with the reasons why some accused confess before the tribunals in Cameroon.) They also remark that all the witches (male and female) who confessed at Salem eventually escaped the executioner (in striking contrast to Bouvignies and other European examples).

A more general point of correspondence *and* difference is the supposed relationship between witchcraft and intimacy. In Western trials, witchcraft is rarely explicitly tied to kinship, but it is often related to the intimacy of neighborhoods. See Muchembled (1981, 174); this is also the central theme in Macfarlane (1970). In Salem, people also believed that witchcraft arose out of close relationships (Boyer and Nissenbaum 1974, 169). But here the practice of accusations differed completely. One of Boyer and Nissenbaum's key arguments is, indeed, that the accusers came, above all, from one neighborhood in Salem-Village whereas the accused belonged to another. Possessed, or "afflicted," girls even began accusing people from other parts of the colony, whom they had never seen. Should this wider scale of witchcraft accusations be ascribed to the more profound impact of Salem-Town and commercial capitalism in this part of the New England countryside? From this perspective, it is striking that in present-day Africa, witchcraft accusations and the intimacy of kinship remain closely related, even in the urban context.

46. See, for example, Mitchell (1956); Turner (1954); Marwick (1965); see also the afterword to this book. The extent to which the historians cited above are directly inspired by these anthropological studies is a point for further examination. Neither Boyer and Nissenbaum (1974) nor Muchembled (at least in his 1981 publication) cite anthropologists. But they refer to Macfarlane (1970), who is clearly influenced by the ideas of the Manchester school.

47. See Asad 1972 and Thoden van Velzen 1973. Boyer and Nissenbaum and also Muchembled are no doubt conscious of the influence of witchcraft notions on their subjects' thinking. But they tend to translate accusations too directly into politico-economic terms. Thus they seem to underrate the inherent force of witchcraft logics and its impact on the accusers' thinking. Refer to the lucid article by Kriedtke (1987), who argues that accusations at both Salem and Bouvignies do not correspond directly to the contours defining the different factions.

48. Briggs 1989; see also Sharpe 1990.

49. Muchembled 1981, 247. Elsewhere (1985), the same author establishes an interesting distinction between "closed" and "open" villages in order to highlight that the villagers' propensity to submit their problems with witchcraft to the tribunals differed strongly per region. This might indeed be an important factor in the explanation of significant regional variations in the increase of trials in Europe (and also in present-day Africa).

50. Bayart 1979. Bayart's interpretation of the "hegemonic project" of the state is based on the Ahidjo regime, but it is equally applicable to the first years following Biya's ascendency to power in 1982.

51. In his 1990 work on the Bertua trials, Cyprian Fisiy (1990a) places special emphasis on this point. He concludes with an eloquent quotation from a judge interviewed at Bertua: "We are all Africans. We should not pretend that witchcraft does not exist. It is very much alive here in the Eastern Province. We cannot allow these primitive villagers to threaten the government agents who are transferred to work here in the East. It is witchcraft which is holding back development in this Province."

52. In one case before the court at Bertua (doss. 84.400.370/PG/BE; arrêt 238/CO, 24 July 1984), one of the accused confessed to being a "sorcerer" but added that his sorcery was used only for hunting and not for killing people. The Maka generally believe that every accomplished hunter must utilize occult forces; otherwise, how could he have such success? But, for the judge in this case, this confession only proved the man's guilt (he was suspected of having killed and eaten a baby); he was condemned to five years in prison.

53. The intriguing title of the book *L'État sorcier* (1985) by Bernard Hours, on public health in Cameroon, suggests another reason to believe that state interventions in this domain will have dubious effects. The author concludes that the state itself is seen as a *sorcier* by both the sick and the hospital personnel. I did not encounter this characterization of the state as a *sorcier* in my informants' statements. But the realm of public health—which Hours justly describes as marked by a permanent lack of means, rude authoritarianism, and arbitrariness—is propitious for such an association. Unfortunately, Hours's book does not make clear who exactly made this association: was it explicitly formulated by his informants or deduced by the author himself?

54. One might add that judicial action, at least when following precedent established in the East Province, furthers the criminalization of witchcraft, especially of commoners. The fact that only the weaker people in society—youth and poorer adult men—appear in court underscores, in the minds of the people, the idea that the state attacks only the witchcraft of small people and not that of the big men.

55. See Rosalind Shaw's question in relation to present-day Sierra Leone: "why are relationships between diviners and contemporary leaders so often ascribed a 'demonic' character today?" (in press, 131).

CHAPTER 7. BALANCE

1. Another crucial change in relation to witchcraft rumors in modern contexts is that women's role seems to be reduced. We saw that, in the local

setting, women are supposed to play a leading role in witchcraft (consider the Maka saying: "Women were the first to 'go out,' but men followed them"; also consider the key role of women as a kind of perfidious Eve in the myth of the origin of *djambe*). But this becomes different when the rumors concern new forms of accumulation in which women are hardly mentioned. It is also striking that there are so few women among the modern *nganga* (healers) who cater to the elites' needs and whose help is invoked by the state courts. But there are exceptions. Mbunwe-Samba (1996, 76) refers to rumors concerning urban associations of rich widows who supposedly have killed their husbands by *ekong* (one of the names for the new witchcraft of wealth) as soon as the latter had accumulated enough money for continuing the familial enterprise ("when he is in the next world, the husband helps to build up what was established for the wife on earth," as Mbunwe-Samba writes with some feeling). The government supposedly has tried to intervene against this association, but the problem was proving that the women really used *ekong*. It may not be accidental that such a rumor comes from the West and the Northwest since it is especially in those provinces that at least some women have succeeded in creating modern enterprises and are running them on their own account. This might suggest that, as soon as women succeed in participating independently in new modes of accumulation, they reappear in rumors about witchcraft and its modern transformations.

2. See Jean-François Bayart 1989; see also chapter 1 and Comparative Interstice 2 of this book.

3. Mbembe (1992, 25): "Recent Africanist scholarship has not studied in detail the logic here of capture and narrow escape, nor the way the traps are so interconnected that they become a unitary system of ensnarement. Yet on making sense of this network depends any knowledge we might have of the logics of 'resistance,' 'disorder' and conviviality that are all inherent in the postcolonial form of authority."

4. See the interview with Mbembe in *Challenge-Hebdo* 79, 22 July 1992, 9. The corresponding view that a political language is needed that relates new inequalities to older, local discourses on power and morality is a central theme of a brilliant recent article by John Lonsdale, with the telling title "The Moral Economy of Mau-Mau: Wealth, Poverty and Civic Virtue in Kikuyu Political Thought" (Lonsdale 1991). The author looks for the "internal architecture" of Kikuyu ethnicity (in contrast to its "external architecture"—that is, the construction of "political tribalism," as Lonsdale calls it, in relation to other groups). He tries to show that the Kikuyu had, and still have, their own discourse on civic morality and virtue. It was in the terms of this discourse that uncertainties about new inequalities were ex-

pressed. (These uncertainties and the concomitant internal tensions would have been the basic cause of Mau-Mau, much more than external pressures.) Lonsdale insists that the present-day crisis of the African state will never be resolved unless new relations of power are connected to these local discourses, which often provide the only "language of accountability" available in the African context (466; see also 317: "African states might do well to remember the unquiet ancestors and their unfinished debates which provide a morally critical and locally resonant tradition for discussing a future nation"). Lonsdale's approach offers fascinating perspectives not only for the study of ethnicity but also for the understanding of the political implications of discourses on sorcery and witchcraft. The preceding may have indicated that these discourses also have to be considered, to borrow Lonsdale's formulation, as "unfinished debates over the morality of the new inequality" (317). And they certainly have a strong "local resonance." However, it is not clear how processes of state formation could relate positively to these discourses. We saw that efforts to do so (for instance, the state courts that started to convict witches in order to protect the population) had highly problematic consequences for both the people and the judges. Moreover, the relation between the occult forces and morality or civic virtue seems to be highly problematic, to put it mildly: the discourses quoted above underlie the basic amorality of any form of power. It is no doubt symptomatic that it is precisely this aspect of local notions on power that retains its relevance in modern contexts. Even in the Grassfields societies, where the chiefs still try to legitimize the power and wealth of the new elites, the association with witchcraft emphasizes the suspect character of new forms of accumulation. The all-pervasiveness of discourses on witchcraft and sorcery in the arenas of modern politics suggests that relating the state to local discourses on power, as Lonsdale advocates, may raise problems. There seems to be a self-evident link through notions on the occult, but they serve to confirm a cynical view of new forms of power.

5. Bill Murphy, oral presentation on "Sorcery and the Public Domain," African Studies Association, 1992, Boston; Shaw in press.

6. Michael Taussig 1993, 85; see also Ashforth (1996), who characterizes witchcraft in present-day Soweto as "both totally secret and yet utterly commonplace."

7. Compare also the solution proposed by the state attorney from Kribi during our second interview with him (see chapter 6, note 36). Apparently, he also felt an urgent need for some sort of new public space to deal with witchcraft. Yet, he was also conscious of the limits of the state's judicial apparatus in this respect. His original solution was that, on the one hand, the state had to arrest people who were accused by their fellow villagers of

being witches (if only to protect them from being lynched). But he insisted, on the other hand, that this did not oblige the court to convict them. He proposed, rather, to organize a court session with as wide an audience as possible. If the villagers could be convinced that there was indeed no evidence against the accused witches, the matter was solved, and the accused could be reinstated in their community. Apparently, in the state attorney's view as well, some sort of public space is needed: if the village itself can no longer organize such an arena, the state has to solve this lacuna by artificially creating such a space.

8. A good reason to be skeptical about the state's ability to effectively intervene in this field is the inherent contradiction between the logics of witchcraft discourses and the basic principles of bureaucratic forms of organization. The witchcraft discourse always tends to personalize relations, but this goes against the grain of the very idea of a bureaucratic and impersonal state (see Kapferer 1983). In this sense, one might conclude that the diatribes of Cameroonian officials against the villagers' *sorcellerie*, as one of the most dangerous forms of subversion, were well founded after all. The personalizing tenor of these discourses can serve only to corrupt the state. However, in this context it is not so much the *sorcellerie* of the villagers—the target of the officials' outburst—that is at stake but, rather, the continuing involvement of the elites themselves with the occult forces that indeed corrupts the bureaucratic project of the state (that is, the principle that the state rules through impersonal relations).

9. See Bierschenk and Elwert (1993) and their emphasis on the lack of *Oeffentlichkeit* as a crucial aspect of Africa's political problems.

10. To continue the admittedly quite adventurous comparison from the preceding chapter with the witch-hunts in early modern Europe: one could suggest that there also the strenuous efforts of state and church to eradicate witchcraft by enforcing a new type of publicity—the imposition of the courts as a new public space for dealing with witchcraft—was not at all successful. There are numerous indications that these beliefs retained their strength in many social circles (and certainly not only at the bottom of society) well into the nineteenth century. It seems, therefore, that in Europe also, it was not direct action by the state and its efforts to unveil witchcraft's secrets that effectively undermined the self-evidence of these representations. Different forms of unveiling—for instance, by the medicalization of society, which imposed its own forms of "publicity"—were much more effective in undermining these beliefs.

11. See also Offiong (1991) and Marshall (1993) on Pentecostalism and the struggle against witchcraft in southern Nigeria.

12. There are important variations within these regional blocs. In the

forest area, for instance, borrowings from elsewhere play an important role. We saw that the Bakweri and the Banyangi bought a powerful juju from Nigeria in order to "domesticate" new forms of wealth—that is, to lift the suspicion that weighed upon them. In Kribi, influences from Gabon—possibly related to the famous *Bwiti-Fang*—play a role. In the West and the Northwest, on the other hand, discourse on the occult seems to be extremely fragmented; even in the terminology, there are fundamental discontinuities between neighboring societies.

13. It is especially important to include in this comparison the Bassa, who live between Edea and Yaunde. In their society, the role of witchcraft seems to be heavily stressed, especially in relation to modern developments. But it also seems that the interaction between occult forces, local forms of authority, and new inequalities follows a particularly complex trajectory here. Unfortunately, I did not find a more detailed study of the relation between *sorcellerie* and modern changes among the Bassa. (Hebga's 1979 book contains highly interesting information concerning the *hu* among the Bassa, but he does not study it in relation to new developments.)

14. Compare the striking image evoked by Goheen (1996), quoted above: the Nso wonder whether the new elites, with their novel titles, will indeed prove to be the new "leopards" of the chief. Will they help him protect the land against the witches? Or will they themselves turn out to be "witches of the night" and corrupt the chief's authority from the inside?

15. There are, of course, other criteria apart from kinship or the role of the chiefs that might help further focus the regional comparison above. An intriguing criterion is the balance, already referred to above, between secrecy and publicity—closure and disclosure—in the role of the witchcraft discourse in these societies (see also Taussig 1993 and Shaw in press). Of interest is that, from this perspective, different regional contrasts emerge. It seems, for instance, that among the Bassa (to the east of Edea) and the Banyangi (near Mamfe)—both in the forest area and both highly segmentary societies—witchcraft seems to be surrounded with a much denser secrecy than in other forest societies. Bassa and Banyangi people express utter amazement at the readiness of people from elsewhere in the forest to bring their witchcraft affairs before the state courts. Indeed, in their areas, this hardly happens. They emphasize that such matters have to be dealt with in secret—certainly not in the openness of the state's institutions—and that they have their own experts to do this. What is even more striking is the fact that precisely the Bassa and the Banyangi have a reputation of great occult cunning in the rest of the country.

16. Compare again the saying, already quoted, of my old Beti colleague

("With us, anyone who ascends must excuse himself constantly to those who do not ascend"); it summarizes very well how heavy the leveling pressure of kinship is in the forest societies.

17. One may regret that anthropological studies of kinship are still so heavily dominated by structuralist preoccupations. Doubtless, it is of great value to analyze formal differences between systems of kinship. But it might be even more valuable to try to relate such formal differences to the varying role of kinship in daily life, especially in relation to contemporary changes. Can these formal oppositions help us understand why, for instance, kinship has a more leveling impact among the Beti than among the Bamileke? It is striking that anthropology has relatively little to say about the modern transformations of themes that have always been preferred topics of anthropology. This applies to witchcraft/sorcery as much as to kinship. See also Meyer (1995, 302).

18. One of the conclusions of the preceding chapters is that, in this context, the relation between urban elites and their respective villages is of strategic importance. We saw that, among the Maka, this relation between *évolués* and villagers played a crucial role in the modernization of witchcraft discourse. It is also through this relation that ideas on witchcraft penetrate easily into new political arenas. The Maka are certainly not exceptional in this respect. Throughout Africa, this relation has become of strategic importance in people's lives (for the elites as much as for the villagers). It is clear that, especially in this relation, kinship norms of solidarity are under heavy pressure—one might say that kinship is stretched almost to a breaking point in order to bridge new inequalities. Yet, it is also clear that this relation does not break: in many parts of Africa, elites still maintain a special relationship with their villages of birth. The tension involved makes this relation a fertile ground for witchcraft rumors: here, witchcraft truly manifests itself as the dark side of kinship. Moreover, regional variations—in the material balance of goods and services, but also in the moral arguments exchanged between elites and villagers—are manifest here. This makes this relation a strategic starting point for comparative studies—for instance, into the day-to-day functioning of ethnic networks, as seen from below, but also into varying patterns in the articulation of national politics with local relations of authority and, consequently, witchcraft (for further information, see Geschiere and Gugler in press).

19. Among the Maka, *nganga* used to follow the same approach. See chapter 2 for a discussion of the ways in which the famous *nganga* Mendouga tried to expose tensions within the family when treating a patient and then tried to appease them.

20. De Rosny 1992, 14; compare also the climax in de Rosny's own initiation as a *nganga*: it was a profound and nearly unbearable realization of the violence around him (1981, 361).

21. This interpretation of witchcraft, reflecting the fear of the family's intimacy, shows again that differences with the West are only relative. The suffocating pressure of kinship—the family as a *noeud de vipères* (snake pit), to quote François Mauriac's famous title—was a central theme in European literature from a period when, in our societies as well, it was hardly possible to escape from kinship ties. Since these links have been loosened, these fears may have become less manifest (they have become rather hidden obsessions to be excavated on the psychiatrist's sofa). But the price of this apparent emancipation is the loneliness of old age—not to say of life in general—that most Africans view as a particularly shocking aspect of the modern Western lifestyle.

22. See the discussion above about the Pentecostalists' success in combating witchcraft. This corresponds to the emphasis on kinship. Typically, Pentecostalism takes a stance not only against witchcraft but also, and sometimes even more insistently, against kinship as a dangerous pull on the true believer (see, for instance, Meyer 1995). This raises the question as to whether their endeavor will ultimately be successful. Meyer (302) also concludes her book by emphasizing the crucial role the family continues to play in people's dealings with witchcraft (or the devil) and modernity.

AFTERWORD

1. See, for instance, Marwick 1965; van Velsen 1964; Douglas 1963a; Middleton and Winter 1963; Mitchell 1956; Turner 1954. For a general overview, see Multhaupt 1990.

2. Compare Fields 1985; see also chapter 6 above.

3. The study of witchcraft as a form of micropolitics was notably developed in a series of monographs on Central Africa by anthropologists such as Mitchell, Turner, van Velzen, Marwick—who, at the time, all belonged to the famous "Manchester school" inspired and commanded by Max Gluckman. This school saw itself as an innovating current in British social anthropology, especially because of its emphasis on conflict. But these anthropologists still studied conflict in relation to the maintenance of social order: it was supposed to function as a *Ventilsitte* (Georg Simmel's expression, who was apparently never quoted by Gluckman), allowing the tension to escape through more or less ritualized conflicts after which the social order could

be reconfirmed. It was this view of a paradoxical equation of conflict and social order that evoked the image, quoted by Mary Douglas, of witchcraft as "tamed" and "domesticated": witchcraft accusations were supposed to allow for a canalized expression of tensions so that social order could be reestablished. (See also Mayer 1954 for a particularly strong formulation of this viewpoint.)

4. A long series of anthropologists have emphasized, since the early 1960s, that the opposition of good and evil is of limited value as a starting point for studying witchcraft and its role in society (for instance, Parrinder 1963; Forge 1970; Dupré 1982; Huizer 1991; Pool n.d.). In his challenging studies on popular movements in present-day Kinshasa, René Devisch appears to see this blurring of good and evil as something new: "the traditional phantasmagory of sorcery escapes the conventional order of meaning and the distinction between good and evil" (1995, 619). It is of interest that for early modern Europe, historians also suggest that the relation between witchcraft beliefs and the good/evil opposition was quite complex. Muchembled (1981, 238, 242) observes that the women stigmatized by the judges as witches (by associating them with the devil through their demonology) were often ambivalent figures for the local community. People certainly feared their secret knowledge, but they were also supposed to be able to use such knowledge in more constructive ways—for instance, to heal or to forestall disasters (see also Thomas 1971, 318, 654, on Tudor and Stuart England). Favret-Saada (1977) shows for a more recent period that healers in the French countryside are still considered to be highly ambivalent figures: they may be healers to their clients who often come from afar, but they are often feared as dangerous witches by the people in their close environment.

5. During my time with the Maka, I was often reminded, as I discussed *djambe*'s endless ramifications, of the characteristic of witchcraft among the Abelam of New Guinea—a society as ferociously segmentary as the Maka— as it was formulated by Anthony Forge (1970, 257): "Supernatural aggression of one type or another is commonly found as an integral and expected part of the political process. This is not to suggest that sorcery and witchcraft are considered good of themselves—indeed their existence is universally deplored—but given that they exist, it is vital for every group to have access to both protective measures against, and active means of, supernatural aggression, with which it can redress the balance and maintain its position relative to other groups."

6. Compare also Meyer (1995, 359, note 15), who expresses a similar uneasiness with the concentration of many anthropologists on formal witch-

craft accusations. Instead, she insists upon more attention to "historical shifts in African witchcraft idioms"—for instance, how they became related to "problems and opportunities of global capitalism." Compare also Austen (1993) for a sophisticated attempt to historicize African ideas on witchcraft by relating them to the evolution of unequal relations with Europe.

7. One may wonder why Augé does not take the trouble to support his interesting criticisms with more detailed references to the studies he criticizes. Is this omission, striking but consistent throughout the book, a consequence of the compelling force of his argument (the ease with which he switches between what his informants told him and the Parisian debates of those days is indeed dazzling); or is this omission, rather, an effect of the topic concerned, proving witchcraft's ability to subvert any code, including codes of science?

8. See also the book by Dozon (1995), comparing the role of such "prophets" in different parts of Ivory Coast. One may wonder whether Augé's analysis of Atcho's role is not too optimistic. It is not clear how Atcho can succeed in reconciling the government's concerns with development, on the one hand, and the preoccupations of his clients, who continue to formulate their problems in terms of kinship, on the other hand. A parallel analysis, but much more pessimistic, is to be found in the fascinating study by Dupré of the Nzabi (Congo), with the eloquent title *Un ordre et sa déstruction*. Dupré links recent reinterpretations of the local witchcraft discourse to the greedy efforts of the elders to appropriate their share of the money their juniors are earning (often it is the young men who profit from new forms of wage labor outside the village). Dupré pays less attention to the role of these notions in the relations to the world outside the village. But his subtle analysis shows clearly how witchcraft has acquired new implications for relations within the village. The elders use their occult knowledge to effect an "overexploitation" of the juniors. This is what Dupré calls *la sorcellerie en liberté*, which seals the "destruction" of the Nzabi order. This somber perspective might be specifically related to the matrilineal structure of this society: the mother's brother commands extensive powers over his sister's son; he can use these powers to protect his nephew but also to harm him. (On the fearsome powers of the mother's brother over his nephews, see also Bonnafé 1988 on the neighboring Kukuya and Hagenbucher-Sacripanti 1973 on the Loango—both in Congo.) Less pessimistic interpretations of new articulations between local witchcraft discourses and modern politico-economic changes are to be found in van Binsbergen 1981 and Hagenbucher-Sacripanti 1989.

9. Compare, for instance, Willis 1970; Fields 1985; and, for a recent

overview, van Dijk 1992. Compare also Hagenbucher-Sacripanti (1989) on the ambiguity of these movements; and Schoffeleers (1992) on their historicity.

10. In his study on Sri Lanka, Kapferer (1983) shows, along similar lines, that beliefs in witchcraft and sorcery are not necessarily a barrier to capitalist penetration; rather, they can become its cornerstone.

11. Compare also van Binsbergen (1991) on the role of the *sangoma* in the urban context in Botswana. The merit of de Rosny's and van Binsbergen's work is that they succeed in relating their experience as an initiate to the role of witchcraft in everyday life. In this respect, they distinguish themselves from the increasing tendency among anthropologists, working on the role of occult forces, to study witchcraft as mainly an esoteric phenomenon. An obvious example of this is, of course, Carlos Castaneda. For Africa, a more recent example is the book by Stoller and Olkes (1987) that is mainly based on the amazing story of Stoller's gradual initiation into the secrets of magicians among the Songhay (Niger). His perseverance is such that, toward the end of the book, he succeeds in putting a spell on a Frenchman who has troubled his friends. Such efforts to penetrate the mysteries of popular knowledge can doubtless lead to fascinating results. However, in his interesting critique of the Stoller and Olkes book, Olivier de Sardan (1988) warns with good reason that the emphasis on esoteric knowledge risks obscuring the omnipresence and banality of witchcraft in everyday life throughout Africa. And it is precisely this triviality that can explain the strong impact of witchcraft in modern politics.

12. Incidentally, this quotation highlights a controversial issue in the more recent literature: the tendency to discuss witchcraft as standing for something else. Several authors have stressed the dangers of reductionism in this respect; they advocate taking witchcraft as a powerful discourse by itself and argue against "reasoning it away" by referring to supposedly deeper layers. It is clear that, in order to understand the cogency of these beliefs, one has to at least start by accepting them at face value, instead of trying to explain them as standing for something else. But it is clear, as well, that the currency of such notions is related to specific contexts.

13. Compare also the fascinating studies by René Devisch and Filip de Boeck on the upsurge of witchcraft rumors as an attempt to signify the chaotic political and economic developments in present-day Zaire (see, for instance, Devisch 1995 and de Boeck 1996). Compare also the already mentioned radio program by Bernard Chenuaud, "Congo, la guerre des âges," on Brazzaville ("France Culture" on Radio France).

BIBLIOGRAPHY

Ahidjo, Ahmadou. 1968. *Ahmadou Ahidjo par lui-même*. Monaco: Paul Bory.

Aletum, A., and Cyprian F. Fisiy. 1987. *Socio-political Integration and Institutions of the Nso Fondom*. Yaunde, Cameroon: MESIRES.

Alobwede d'Epie, C. 1982. *The Language of Traditional Medicine: A Study in the Power of Language*. Thèse d'État, University of Yaunde, Cameroon.

Alexandre, P., and J. Binet. 1958. *Le groupe dit Pahouin (Fang-Boulou-Beti)*. Paris: PUF.

Anderson, Benedict. 1992. "Long-Distance Nationalism, World Capitalism and the Rise of Identity Politics." Wertheim Lecture, University of Amsterdam (CASA).

Appadurai, Arjun. 1986. "Introduction: Commodities and the Politics of Value." In *The Social Life of Things: Commodities in Cultural Perspective*, ed. Arjun Appadurai, 3–64. Cambridge: Cambridge Univ. Press.

———. 1990. "Disjuncture and Difference in the Global Cultural Economy." *Public Culture* 2 (2): 1–25.

Appiah, Kwame A. 1992. *In My Father's House: What Does It Mean to Be an African Today?* London: Methuen.

Ardener, Edwin. 1956. *Coastal Bantu of the Cameroons*. London: International African Institute.

———. 1970. "Witchcraft, Economics and the Continuity of Belief." In *Witchcraft Confessions and Accusations*, ed. Mary Douglas, 141–60. London: Tavistock.

Arens, W. 1979. *The Man-Eating Myth: Anthropology and Anthropophagy*. Oxford: Oxford Univ. Press.

Aronson, D. 1971. "Ijebu Yoruba Urban-Rural Relationships and Class Formation." *Canadian Journal of African Studies* 5:263–79.

Asad, Talal. 1972. "Market Model, Class Structure and Consent: A Reconsideration of Swat Political Organization." *Man* 7:74–95.

Ashforth, Adam. 1996. "Of Secrecy and Commonplace: Witchcraft in Soweto." *Social Research* (winter).

Augé, Marc. 1975. *Théorie des pouvoirs et idéologie: Étude de cas en Côte d'Ivoire*. Paris: Hermann.

Auslander, Mark. 1993. "Open The Wombs!" The Symbolic Politics of Modern Ngoni Witchfinding." In *Modernity and Its Malcontents: Ritual and Power in Postcolonial Africa*, ed. Jean Comaroff and John Comaroff, 167–92. Chicago: Univ. of Chicago Press.

Austen, Ralph. 1977. "Slavery among Coastal Middlemen—The Duala of Cameroon." In *Slavery in Africa: Historical and Anthropological Perspectives*, ed. Igor Kopytoff and Susan Miers, 305–33. Madison: Univ. of Wisconsin Press.

———. 1993. "The Moral Economy of Witchcraft: An Essay in Comparative History." In *Modernity and Its Malcontents: Ritual and Power in Postcolonial Africa*, ed. Jean Comaroff and John Comaroff, 89–110. Chicago: Univ. of Chicago Press.

Balz, Heinrich. 1984. *Where the Faith Has to Live: Studies in Bakossi Society and Religion*. Basel, Switzerland: Basler Mission.

Bastian, Misty L. 1993. "'Bloodhounds Who Have No Friends': Witchcraft and Locality in the Nigerian Popular Press." In *Modernity and Its Malcontents: Ritual and Power in Postcolonial Africa*, ed. Jean Comaroff and John Comaroff, 129–166. Chicago: Univ. of Chicago Press.

Bateranzigo, Léonidas. 1987. "Monographie historique des Maka de l'Est Cameroun, des origines à 1900." Master's thesis, Department of History, University of Yaunde, Cameroon.

Bayart, Jean-François. 1979. *L'État au Cameroun*. Paris: Fondation nationale des sciences politiques.

———. 1981. "Le politique par le bas en Afrique noire." *Politique Africaine* 1:53–81.

———. 1989. *L'État en Afrique: La politique du ventre*. Paris: Fayard.

———. 1990. "L'Afropessimisme par le bas: Réponse à Achille Mbembe, Jean Copans et quelques autres." *Politique africaine* 40:103–8.

———. 1993. "Conclusions." In *The Political Economy of Cameroon: Historical Perspectives*, ed. Peter Geschiere and Piet Konings, 335–44. Paris: Karthala: African Studies Center.

———. 1994. "L'Invention paradoxale de la modernité économique." In *La Réinvention du capitalisme*, ed. Jean-François Bayart, 9–46. Paris: Karthala.

Bayart, Jean-François, Achille Mbembe, and Comi Toulabor. 1992. *Le politique par le bas en Afrique noire: Contributions à une problématique de la démocratie*. Paris: Karthala.

Berman, Bruce, and John Lonsdale. 1991. *The Unhappy Valley: Conflict in Kenya and Africa*. London: Currey.

Berry, Sara S. 1985. *Fathers Work for Their Sons: Accumulation, Mobility and Class Formation in an Extended Yoruba Community*. Berkeley: Univ. of California Press.

Beti, Mongo. 1957. *Mission terminée*. Paris: Buchet-Castel.

Bierschenk, Thomas, and Georg Elwert, eds. 1993. *Entwicklungshilfe und ihre Folgen: Ergebnisse empirischer Untersuchungen in Afrika*. Frankfurt am Main: Campus.

van Binsbergen, Wim M. J. 1981. *Religious Change in Zambia*. London: Kegan Paul; Leiden, Netherlands: African Studies Center.

———. 1991. "Becoming a 'Sangoma': Religious Anthropological Field Work in Francistown, Botswana." *Journal of Religion in Africa* 21 (4): 309–44.

Bockie, Simon. 1993. *Death and the Invisible Powers: The World of Kongo Belief*. Bloomington: Indiana Univ. Press.

de Boeck, Filip. 1996. "Domesticating Diamonds and Dollars: Consumption, Accumulation and Identity in Southwestern Zaire." Paper presented at conference on "Globalization and the Construction of Communal Identities," Amsterdam, March.

Bohannan, Paul, and Laura Bohannan. 1953. *The Tiv of Central Nigeria*. London: International African Institute.

Bonnafé, P. 1988. *Histoire sociale d'un peuple congolais*. Vol. 2, *Posséder et gouverner*. Paris: ORSTOM.

Boyer, P., and S. Nissenbaum. 1974. *Salem Possessed: The Social Origins of Witchcraft*. Cambridge: Harvard Univ. Press.

Brain, Robert. 1970. "Child-witches." In *Witchcraft Confessions and Accusations*, ed. Mary Douglas, 161–83. London: Tavistock.

Braudel, Ferdinand. 1985. *La dynamique du capitalisme*. Paris: Arthaud.

Briggs, R. 1989. *Communities of Belief: Cultural and Social Tensions in Early Modern France*. Oxford: Clarendon Press.

Brown, P., and D. Tuzin. 1983. *The Ethnography of Cannibalism*. Washington DC: Society for Psychological Anthropology.

Buijtenhuijs, Robert. 1995. "De la sorcellerie comme mode populaire d'action politique." *Politique africaine* 59: 133–39.

Bureau, René. 1962. "Ethno-sociologie religieuse des Douala et apparentés." *Recherches et études camerounaises* 7/8.

Burke, Peter. 1978. *Popular Culture in Early Modern Europe*. London: Temple Smith.

Burnham, Philip. 1980. *Opportunity and Constraint in a Savanna Society: The Gbaya of Meiganaga, Cameroon*. London: Academic Press.

———. N.d. "Notes on the Politics of Gbaya Supernatural Beliefs." Unpublished paper, University College, London.

Chaffard, Georges. 1967. *Les carnets secrets de la décolonisation*, vol. 2. Paris: Calmann-Lévy.

Chavunduka, G. L., and Murray Last. 1986. "Conclusions: African Medical Profession Today." In *The Professionalisation of African Medicine*, ed. Murray Last and G. L. Chavunduka, 259–70. Manchester: Manchester Univ. Press.

Chenuaud, Bernard. 1995. "Congo: La guerre des âges." Paris: Radio France, France Culture, November 1996. Audiocassette.

Chilver, Sally. 1989. "Women Cultivators, Cows and Cash-Crops: Phyllis Kaberry's Women of the Grassfields Revisited." In *The Political Economy of Cameroon: Historical Perspectives*, ed. Peter Geschiere and Piet Konings, 383–423. Leiden, Netherlands: African Studies Centre.

———. 1990. "Thaumaturgy in Contemporary Traditional Religion: The Case of Nso' in Mid-Century." *Journal of Religion in Africa* 20 (3): 226–47.

Ciekawy, Diane. 1989. "Witchcraft and Development in Kenyan Politics: Complementary or Conflicting Ideologies." Paper presented at conference of American Anthropological Association, San Francisco.

Clark, S. 1983. "French Historians and Early Modern Popular Culture." *Past and Present* 100:62–99.

Clifford, James. 1988. *The Predicament of Culture*. Cambridge: Harvard Univ. Press.

Comaroff, Jean, and John Comaroff. 1992. *Ethnography and the Historical Imagination*. Boulder, CO: Westview Press.

———, eds. 1993. *Modernity and Its Malcontents: Ritual and Power in Postcolonial Africa*. Chicago: Univ. of Chicago Press.

Copans, Jean. 1991. "No Shortcuts to Democracy: The Long March towards Modernity." *Review of African Political Economy* 50:92–102.

Copet-Rougier, Élisabeth. 1977. "Nguélebok: Essai d'analyse de l'organisation sociale des Mkao Mbogendi." Ph.D. diss., École pratique des hautes études, 5ème section, Paris.

———. 1986a. "Pouvoirs et maladies, devins et guérisseurs dans l'Est du Cameroun." *Cahiers ethnologiques* (University of Bordeaux, France), n.s., 2 (7):74–96.

———. 1986b. "'Le Mal Court': Visible and Invisible Violence in an Acephalous Society—Mkako of Cameroon." In *The Anthropology of Violence*, ed. D. Riches, 50–69. Oxford: Blackwell.

———. 1986c. "Catégories d'ordres et réponses aux désordres chez les Mkako du Cameroun." *Droit et Cultures* 11 : 79–88.

———. 1992a. "L'Altro, l'altro dell'altro e l'altro da sé—Rappresentazioni della stregoneria, del cannibalismo e dell'incesto." In *Lo straniero ovvero l'identità a confronto*, ed. M. Bettini, 155–74. Rome: Laterza.

———. 1992b. "Tu ne traverseras pas le sang—Corps, parenté et pouvoirs chez les Mkako du Cameroun." Paper presented for colloquium on "Corps, parenté, pouvoir," CNRS, Paris, November.

Crick, M. 1979. "Anthropologists' Witchcraft: Symbolically Defined or Analytically Undone?" *Journal of the Anthropological Society of Oxford* 10:139–46.

Das, Veena. 1996. "Rumour as Performative: A Contribution to the Theory of Perlocutionary Speech." Sudhir Kumar Bose Memorial Lecture, St. Stephens College, University of Delhi, India.

Delumeau, Jean. 1978. *La peur en Occident (XVe–XVIIIe siècles): Une cité assiégée*. Paris: Fayard.

Desjeux, Dominique. 1987. *Stratégies paysannes en Afrique noire: Le Congo—Essai sur la gestion de l'incertitude*. Paris: L'Harmattan.

Devisch, René. 1995. "Frenzy, Violence and Ethical Renewal in Kinshasa." *Public Culture* 7:593–629.

van Dijk, Rijk. 1992. "Young Malawian Puritans: Young Born-Again Preachers in a Present-Day African Urban Environment." Ph.D. diss., University of Utrecht, Netherlands.

Dongmo, Jean-Louis. 1981. *Le dynamisme bamiléké (Cameroun)*. Yaunde, Cameroon: CEPER.

Douglas, Mary. 1963a. *The Lele of the Kasai*. London: International African Institute.

———. 1963b. "Techniques of Sorcery Control in Central Africa." In *Witchcraft and Sorcery in East Africa*, ed. John Middleton and E. H. Winter, 123–43. London: Routledge and Kegan Paul.

———. 1970. "Introduction: Thirty Years after 'Witchcraft, Oracles and Magic.'" In *Witchcraft Confessions and Accusations*, ed. Mary Douglas, xiii–xxxviii. London: Tavistock.

Dozon, Jean-Pierre. 1995. *La cause des prophètes*. Paris: Seuil.

Droogers, André, Gert Huizer, and H. Siebers, eds. 1991. *Popular Power in Latin American Religions*. Saarbrücken, Germany: Breitenbach.

Dupont-Bouchat, M. S., Willem T. M. Frijhoff, and Robert Muchembled, eds. 1978. *Prophètes et sorciers dans les Pays-Bas, XVIe–XVIIIe siècles.* Paris: Hachette.

Dupré, Georges. 1982. *Un ordre et sa déstruction.* Paris: ORSTOM.

Ejedepang-Koge, S. N. 1971. *The Tradition of a People: Bakossi.* Yaunde, Cameroon.

———. 1975. *Tradition and Change in Peasant Activities.* Yaunde, Cameroon.

Elwert, Georg. 1983. *Bauern und Staat in Westafrika.* Frankfurt am Main: Campus.

Elwert-Kretschmer, Karola. 1995. "*Vodun* et contrôle social au village." *Politique africaine* 59:102–19.

Englund, Harri. 1996. "Witchcraft, Modernity and the Person: The Morality of Accumulation in Central Malawi." *Critique of Anthropology* 16 (3): 257–81.

Evans-Pritchard, E. E. 1937. *Witchcraft, Oracles and Magic among the Azande.* Oxford: Clarendon Press.

Fabian, Johannes. 1990. *Power and Performance: Ethnographic Explorations through Proverbial Wisdom and Theater in Shaba, Zaire.* Madison: Univ. of Wisconsin Press.

Fadika, M. 1975. "Le droit, les sorciers, magiciens, guérisseurs, féticheurs et marabouts." *Penant* 750:439–50.

Favret-Saada, Jeanne. 1980. *Deadly Words, Witchcraft in the Bocage.* Cambridge: Cambridge Univ. Press. Originally published as *Les mots, la mort, les sorts: La sorcellerie dans le Bocage* (Paris: Gallimard, 1977).

Fernandez, J. W. 1982. *Bwiti: An Ethnography of the Religious Imagination in Africa.* Princeton: Princeton Univ. Press.

Fields, Karen. 1985. *Revival and Rebellion in Central Africa.* Princeton: Princeton Univ. Press.

Fisiy, Cyprian F. 1990a. *Palm Tree Justice in the Bertoua Court of Appeal: The Witchcraft Cases.* Leiden, Netherlands: African Studies Center.

———. 1990b. "Le monopole juridictionnel de l'État et le règlement des affaires de sorcellerie au Cameroun." *Politique africaine* 40:60–72.

———. 1992. *Power and Privilege in the Administration of Law: Land Law Reforms and Social Differentiation in Cameroon.* Leiden, Netherlands: African Studies Center.

Fisiy, Cyprian F., and Peter Geschiere. 1990. "Judges and witches, or how is the State to deal with witchcraft? Examples from Southeastern Cameroon." *Cahiers d'études africaines* 118:135–56.

———. 1991. "Sorcery, Witchcraft and Accumulation—Regional Variations in South and West Cameroon." *Critique of Anthropology* 11 (3): 251–78.

———. 1992. "Sorcery Discourses and the Valuation of People/Things—Examples from Southern and Western Cameroon." Paper presented at conference of African Studies Association, Seattle.

———. 1993. "Sorcellerie et accumulation." In *Les itinéraires de l'accumulation au Cameroon*, ed. Peter Geschiere and Piet Konings, 99–131. Paris: Karthala.

———. In press. "Witchcraft, Violence and Identity: Different Trajectories in Postcolonial Cameroon." In *Postcolonial Identities in Africa*, ed. Richard Werbner and Terence O. Ranger. London: Zed Books.

Fisiy, Cyprian F., and Michael Rowlands. 1990. "Sorcery and Law in Modern Cameroon." *Culture and History* (Copenhagen) 6:63–84.

Forge, Anthony. 1970. "Prestige, Influence and Sorcery: A New Guinea Example." In *Witchcraft Confessions and Accusations*, ed. Mary Douglas, 257–78. London: Tavistock.

Franqueville, André. 1987. *Une Afrique entre le village et la ville: Les migrations dans le sud du Cameroun*. Paris: ORSTOM.

Frijhoff, Willem T. M. 1985. "La culture populaire: Un malentendu? Réflexions à partir du cas néerlandais." *Cahiers de Clio* 1985: 26–38.

Geschiere, Peter. 1980. "Child Witches against the Authority of their Elders." In *Man, Meaning and History: Essays in Honour of H. G. Schulte Nordholt*, ed. Reimar Schefold, J. W. Schoorl, and Hans Tennekes, 268–99. The Hague: Nijhoff.

———. 1982. *Village Communities and the State: Changing Relations among the Maka of Southeastern Cameroun*. London: Kegan Paul; Leiden, Netherlands: African Studies Center.

———. 1983. "European Planters, African Peasants and the Colonial State: Alternatives in the 'Mise en Valeur' of Makaland, South-East Cameroon, during the Interbellum." *African Economic History* 12:83–108.

———. 1985a. "Imposing Capitalist Dominance through the State: The Multifarious Role of the Colonial State in Africa." In *Old Modes of Production and Capitalist Encroachment: Anthropological Explorations in Africa*, ed. Wim M. J. van Binsbergen and Peter Geschiere, 94–144. London: Kegan Paul; Leiden, Netherlands: African Studies Center.

———. 1985b. "The Mode of Production Concept and Its Usefulness in African Studies: Applications of the Lineage Mode." *Canadian Journal of African Studies* 19:80–91.

———. 1989. "Accumulation and Non-accumulation in Agriculture—Regional Comparisons from Cameroon." In *The Political Economy of Cameroon: Historical Perspectives*, ed. Peter Geschiere and Piet Konings, 557–87. Leiden, Netherlands: African Studies Center.

———. 1991. "The Transfer of Knowledge and the Discourse on Occult Forces—The State and New Witchcraft Trials in Eastern Cameroon." Paper prepared for panel on "The Transfer of Knowledge," conference of African Studies Association, St. Louis, November.

———. 1994. "Domesticating Personal Violence—Witchcraft, Courts and Confessions in Cameroon." (Daryll Forde Memorial Lecture, London, March 1993). *Africa* 64 (3): 323–41.

———. 1995a. "Slavery and Kinship in the Political Economy of the Maka." *Paideuma* 41:207–27 (special issue on "Slavery and Slave Trade in Cameroon").

———. 1995b. "Populism, Old and New: Provisional Notes on the Concept 'Popular' in African Studies." In *Popular Culture: Africa, Asia and Europe*, ed. Jos van der Klei, 41–51. Amsterdam: CERES.

———. 1996. "Sorcellerie et politique: Les pièges du rapport élite-village." *Politique Africaine* 63: 82–97.

Geschiere, Peter, and Joseph Gugler, eds. In press. "The Urban-Rural Connection in Africa: Different Trajectories, Different Moralities" *African Rural and Urban Studies* (special issue).

Geschiere, Peter, and Piet Konings, eds. 1993. *Les itinéraires de l'accumulation au Cameroun/Pathways to Accumulation in Cameroon*. Paris: Karthala; Leiden, Netherlands: African Studies Center.

Ginzburg, Carlo. 1990. *Ecstasies: Deciphering the Witches' Sabbath*. London: Hutchinson Radius.

Gluckman, Max. 1955. *Custom and Conflict in Africa*. Oxford: Blackwell.

Goheen, Miriam. 1993. "Gender and Accumulation in Nso." In *Les itinéraires de l'accumulation au Cameroun*, ed. Peter Geschiere and Piet Konings, 241–72. Paris: Karthala.

———. 1996. *Men Own the Fields, Women Own the Crops: Gender and Power in the Cameroon Highlands*. Madison: Univ. of Wisconsin Press.

Gugler, Joseph. 1971. "Life in a dual system, Eastern Nigerians in Town." *Cahiers d'Etudes Africaines* 11 (3): 400–21.

———. 1991. "Life in a Dual System Revisited: Urban-Rural Ties in Enugu, Nigeria, 1961–87." *World Development* 19 (5): 399–409.

Guyer, Jane I. 1985. *Family and Farm in Southern Cameroon*. African Studies Centre, Boston: Boston University.

———. 1986. "Indigenous Currencies and the History of Marriage Payments." *Cahiers d'Études Africaines* 26 (4): 577–610.

———. 1993. "Wealth in People and Self-Realization in Equatorial Africa." *Man*, n.s., 28 (2): 243–65.

Guyer, Jane I., and Samuel M. Eno Belinga. 1995. "Wealth in People as

Wealth in Knowledge: Accumulation and Composition in Equatorial Africa." *Journal of African History* 36:91–120.

Guyer, Jane I., and Achille Mbembe. 1992. "Wealth in People, Wealth in Things." Call for papers for a conference of African Studies Association, Seattle, November.

van Haaren, Wim. 1988. *Nyandong: Een dorp van cacaoverbouwers in Zuidwest Kameroen*. Master's thesis, Department of Anthropology, University of Leiden, Netherlands.

Hagenbucher-Sacripanti, F. 1973. *Les fondements spirituels du pouvoir au royaume de Loango*. Paris: ORSTOM.

———. 1989. *Santé et rédemption par les guérisseurs au Congo*. Paris: Publisud/ORSTOM.

Hannerz, Ulf. 1992. *Cultural Complexity: Studies in the Social Organization of Meaning*. New York: Columbia Univ. Press.

Harms, Robert. 1981. *River of Wealth, River of Sorrow: The Central Zaire Basin in the Era of the Slave and Ivory Trade, 1500–1891*. New Haven: Yale Univ. Press.

Heath, Daniel. 1989. *Lexique mekáa-français*. Yaunde, Cameroon: Société internationale de linguistique.

Hebga, Meinrad P. 1979. *Sorcellerie, chimère dangereuse . . . ?* Abidjan, Ivory Coast: Institut national pour le développement économique et social.

van Hekken, P., and H. U. E. Thoden van Velzen. 1972. *Land Scarcity and Rural Inequality in Tanzania*. The Hague: Mouton; Leiden, Netherlands: African Studies Center.

Horton, Robin. 1967. "African Traditional Religion and Western Science." *Africa* 37:50–71, and 155–87.

Hours, Bernard. 1985. *L' État sorcier, Santé publique et société au Cameroun*. Paris: L' Harmattan.

Huizer, Gert. 1991. "Religious Penetration and Power Struggles in Latin America—Some Historical and Comparative Observations." In *Popular Power in Latin American Religions*, ed. André Droogers, Gert Huizer, and H. Siebers, 26–54. Saarbrücken, Germany: Breitenbach.

Hurault, Jean. 1962. *La structure sociale des Bamiléké*. The Hague: Mouton.

Ittmann, J. 1930. "Der Kupe im Aberglauben der Kameruner." *Der evangelische Heidenbote*, 77–80, 94–95 and 111–13. Basel, Switzerland: Basler Mission.

———. 1963. "Von den Grundlagen der Kameruner Welt- und Lebensanschauung." *Anthropos* 58:661–76.

Janzen, John M. 1982. *Lemba, 1650–1930: A Drum of Affliction in Africa and the New World*. New York: Garland.

Jewsiewicki, Bogumil. 1993. *Naître et mourir au Zaïre: Un demi-siècle d'histoire au quotidien.* Paris: Karthala.

Jewsiewicki, Bogumil, and Henri Moniot, eds. 1988. *Dialoguer avec le léopard? Pratiques, savoirs et actes du peuple face au politique en Afrique noire contemporaine.* Paris: L'Harmattan.

Jewsiewicki, Bogumil, and J. Létourneau, eds. 1985. *Mode of Production: The Challenge of Africa.* Quebec City: Safi. (Also published as special issue of *Canadian Journal of African Studies* 1985, 1.)

Joseph, Richard. 1977. *Radical Nationalism in Cameroon: Social Origins of the UPC Rebellion.* Oxford: Clarendon Press.

Kaberry, Phyllis M. 1952. *Women of the Grassfields.* London: HMSO.

Kaeselitz, R. 1968. "Kolonialeroberung und Widerstandskampf in Süd-Kamerun." In *Kamerun unter deutscher Kolonialherrschaft*, vol. 2, ed. Helmut Stoecker, 11–55. Berlin: VEB.

Kapferer, Bruce. 1983. *A Celebration of Demons.* Bloomington: Indiana Univ. Press.

van Kessel, Ineke. 1993. " 'From Confusion to Lusaka': The Youth Revolt in Sekhukhuneland." *Journal of Southern African Studies* 19 (4): 593–614.

Kimvimba, B. M. M. 1978. "Le juge zaïrois et la sorcellerie." *Penant* 761: 303–15.

Koch, Henri. 1968. *Magie et chasse dans la forêt camerounaise.* Paris: Berger-Levrault.

Koloss, H. J. 1985. "Obasinjom among the Ejagham." *African Arts* 8 (2): 63–65, 98–103.

Kriedtke, P. 1987. "Die Hexen und ihre Ankläger—Zu den lokalen Voraussetzungen der Hexenverfolgungen in der frühen Neuzeit, Ein Forschungsbericht." *Zeitschrift für historische Forschung* 14 (1): 47–71.

Kwayyeb, E. 1967. "Le rapport entre Parti, Gouvernement et Administration." *Ier Conseil National de l'Union Nationale Camerounaise.* Yaunde, Cameroon: Imprimerie Nationale.

Laburthe-Tolra, Philippe. 1977. *Minlaaba, histoire et société traditionnelle chez les Bëti du Sud Cameroun.* Paris: Champion. (Also published as *Les seigneurs de la forêt*, Paris: Publications de la Sorbonne, 1981; and *Initiations et sociétés secrètes au Cameroun*, Paris: Karthala, 1988.)

———. 1986. *Le tombeau du soleil.* Paris: Odile Jacob.

Laclau, Ernesto, and Chantal Mouffe. 1985. *Hegemony and Socialist Strategy: Towards a Radical Democratic Politics.* London: Verso.

Last, Murray. 1986. "Introduction—The Professionalisation of African Medicine: Ambiguities and Definitions." In *The Professionalisation of Af-*

rican Medicine, ed. Murray Last and G. L. Chavunduka, 1–29. Manchester: Manchester Univ. Press.

Last, Murray, and G. L. Chavunduka, eds. 1986. *The Professionalisation of African Medicine*. Manchester: Manchester Univ. Press.

Lattas, Andrew. 1993. "Sorcery and Colonialism: Illness, Dreams and Death as Political Languages in West New Britain." *Man*, n.s., 28: 51–77.

Levin, M. D. 1980. "Export Crops and Peasantization: The Bakosi of Cameroon." In *Peasants in Africa: Historical and Contemporary Perspectives*, ed. Martin Klein, 221–43. Beverly Hills, CA: Sage.

———. 1987. "Family Structure in Bakosi: Social Change in an African Society." Ph.D. diss., Princeton University.

Levine, Victor T. 1964. *The Cameroons from Mandate to Independence*. Berkeley: Univ. of California Press.

Löffler, Irene. 1983. "Hexerei, Staat und Religion in Gabun." *Peripherie* 12 (3) : 77–88.

Lonsdale, John. 1991. "African Pasts in Africa's Future" and "The Moral Economy of Mau-Mau: Wealth, Poverty and Civic Virtue in Kikuyu Political Thought." In *The Unhappy Valley, Conflict in Kenya and Africa*, Bruce Berman and John Lonsdale, 203–19, 315–504. London: Currey.

Macfarlane, Alan. 1970. *Witchcraft in Tudor and Stuart England*. London: Routledge and Kegan Paul.

Mair, Lucy. 1969. *Witchcraft*. London: World University Library.

Malinowski, Bronislaw. [1925] 1954. "Magic, Science and Religion." In *Magic, Science and Other Essays*. New York: Doubleday Anchor Books.

Mallart-Guimera, Luis. 1981. *Ni dos, ni ventre*. Paris: Société d'ethnographie.

———. 1988. *La forêt de nos ancêtres*. *Thèse d'État*, University of Paris X.

Mambou-Pembellot, A. 1985. "La preuve des crimes de sorcellerie devant le juge pénal congolais." *Revue juridique et politique* 1–2 : 124–29.

Marshall, Ruth. 1991. "Power in the Name of Jesus." *Review of African Political Economy* 52 : 21–38.

———. 1993. "'Power in the name of Jesus': Social transformation and Pentecostalism in Western Nigeria Revisited." In *Legitimacy and the State in Twentieth Century Africa*, ed. Terence O. Ranger and O. Vaughan, 213–46. London: Macmillan.

Marwick, Max. 1965. *Sorcery in Its Social Setting: A Study of the Northern Rhodesian Cewa*. Manchester: Manchester Univ. Press.

———, ed. 1970. *Witchcraft and Sorcery*. Harmondsworth, England: Penguin.

Mary, A. 1983. *La naissance à l'envers, essai sur le rituel du Bwiti Fang au Gabon*. Paris: L'Harmattan.

Mathé, M. 1976. "La justice face à la sorcellerie." *Penant* 753:311–27.

Mayer, Philip. 1954. "Witches." Inaugural Lecture, Rhodes University, Grahamstown, South Africa.

Mbembe, Achille. 1989. *La naissance du maquis dans le Sud-Cameroun (1920–1960): Esquisse d'une anthropologie historique de l'indiscipline.* *Thèse d'Etat*, University of Paris I. (Published 1996 by Karthala, Paris.)

———. 1990. "Pouvoir, violence et accumulation." *Politique africaine* 39: 7–25.

———. 1992. "Provisional Notes on the Postcolony." *Africa* 62 (1): 3–38.

Mboukou, J.-H. 1985. "Ethnologie criminelle du Gabon." *Revue juridique et politique* 1–2:178–88.

Mbunwe-Samba, Patrick. 1996. *Witchcraft, Magic and Divination: A Personal Testimony*. Bamenda, Cameroon; Leiden, Netherlands: African Studies Center.

Mbuy, Tatah H. 1989. *Encountering Witches and Wizards in Africa*. Buea, Cameroon.

———. 1994. *African Traditional Religion as Anonymous Christianity*. Bamenda, Cameroon: Unique Printers.

Mebenga, Luc T. 1991. *Les funérailles chez les Ewondo. Thèse de 3ème cycle*, Dept. of Sociology, University of Yaunde, Cameroon.

Meillassoux, Claude. 1975. *Femmes, Greniers et Capitaux*. Paris: Maspero.

Meyer, Birgit. 1995. "Translating the Devil: An African Appropriation of Pietist Protestantism: The Case of the Peki Ewe in Southeastern Ghana, 1847–1992." Ph.D. diss., University of Amsterdam.

Middelfort, H. E. C. 1972. *Witch-Hunting in Southwestern Germany, 1562–1684*. Palo Alto: Stanford Univ. Press.

Middleton, John, and E. H. Winter, eds. 1963. *Witchcraft and Sorcery in East Africa*. London: Routledge and Kegan Paul.

Mitchell, J. Clyde. 1956. *The Yao Village: A Study in the Social Structure of a Nyassaland Tribe*. Manchester: Manchester Univ. Press.

Monter, E. W. 1976. *Witchcraft in France and Switzerland*. Ithaca: Cornell Univ. Press.

Muchembled, Robert. 1978a. *Culture populaire et cultures des élites*. Paris: Flammarion.

———. 1978b. "Avant-propos" and "Sorcières du Cambrésis." In *Prophètes et sorciers dans les Pays-Bas, XVIe–XVIIIe siècles*, ed. M. S. Dupont-Bouchat, Willem T. M. Frijhoff, and Robert Muchembled, 13–41, 155–263. Paris: Hachette.

————. 1981. *Les derniers bûchers, un village de Flandre et ses sorcières sous Louis XIV*. Paris: Ramsay.

————. 1985. "L'autre côté du miroir: mythes sataniques et réalités culturelles aux XVIe et XVIIe siècles." *Annales (Histoire, Sciences Sociales)* 40: 288–305.

Mudimbe, Valentin Y. 1988. *The Invention of Africa: Gnosis, Philosophy and the Order of Knowledge*. Bloomington: Indiana Univ. Press.

Multhaupt, Tamara. 1990. *Hexerei und anti-Hexerei in Afrika*. München: Trickster Wissenschaft.

Ndjio, Basile. 1995. "Sorcellerie, pouvoir et accumulation en pays bamiléké: Cas du *Ngru*." Unpublished paper, Yaunde, Cameroon.

Ngoa, H. 1968. "Le mariage chez les Ewondo, étude sociologique." *Thèse de 3ème cycle*, Dept. of Sociology, University of Yaunde, Cameroon.

Ngubane, H. 1986. "The Predicament of the Sinister Healer." In *The Professionalisation of African Medicine*, ed. Murray Last and G. L. Chavunduka, 189–205. Manchester: Manchester Univ. Press.

Nicod, Henri. 1948. *La vie mystérieuse de l'Afrique noire*. Paris: Payot.

Niehaus, Isaac A. 1993. "Witch-Hunting and Political Legitimacy: Continuity and Change in Green Valley, Lebowa, 1930–1991." *Africa* 63 (4): 498–529.

————. 1995. "Witches of the Transvaal Lowveld and their Familiars: Conceptions of Duality, Power and Desire." *Cahiers d'études africaines* 25 (2–3): 513–41.

Nkwi, Paul N. 1976. *Traditional Government and Social Change: A Study of the Political Institutions among the Kom of the Cameroon Grassfields*. Fribourg, Switzerland: Fribourg Univ. Press.

Nomo, N. N.d. *L'Evu dans la tradition eton*. Yaunde, Cameroon (published with the help of MESRES).

Nyamnjoh, Francis B. 1985. *Change in the Concept of Power amongst the Bum*. Master's thesis, Dept. of Sociology, University of Yaunde, Cameroon.

Nyamnjoh, Francis, and Michael Rowlands. In press. "Elite Associations and Political Identities in Cameroon." In "The Urban-Rural Connection in Africa: Different Trajectories, Different Moralities," ed. Peter Geschiere and Joseph Gugler. *African Rural and Urban Studies* (special issue).

Offiong, Daniel A. 1991. *Witchcraft, Sorcery, Magic and Social Order among the Ibibio of Nigeria*. Enugu, Nigeria: Fourth Dimension.

Olivier de Sardan, Jean-Pierre. 1988. "Jeu de la croyance et 'je' ethnologique: exotisme religieux et ethno-égo-centrisme." *Cahiers d'études africaines* 28 (3–4): 527–40.

————. 1992. "Populisme développementaliste et populisme en sciences sociales: idéologie, action, connaissance." *Cahiers d'études africaines* 30 (4): 475–93.

————. 1993. "L'espace wébérien des sciences sociales." *Genèses* 10: 146–60.

Ombolo, J.-P. 1990. *Sexe et société en Afrique noire: L'anthropologie sexuelle beti*. Paris: L'Harmattan.

————. 1995. *Anthropologie et développement: Essai en socio-anthropologie du changement social*. Paris: Karthala.

Ongolo, Adrien. 1986. *Fondement rationnel de l'idée d'evu eton. Thèse d'État*. University of Grenoble, France.

Ortigues, C., and E. Ortigues. 1966. *Oedipe africain*. Paris: Plon.

den Ouden, Jan. 1987. "In Search of Personal Mobility: Changing Interpersonal Relations in Two Bamiléké Chiefdoms, Cameroon." *Africa* 57 (1): 3–27.

Parrinder, Geoffry. 1963. *Witchcraft: European and African*. London: Faber and Faber.

Parry, Jonathan, and Maurice Bloch, eds. 1989. *Money and the Morality of Exchange*. Cambridge: Cambridge Univ. Press.

Péan, Pierre. 1983. *Affaires africaines*. Paris: Fayard.

Pels, Peter. 1993. "Critical Matters: Interactions between Missionaries and Waluguru in Colonial Tanganyika, 1930–1961." Ph.D. diss., University of Amsterdam.

Pool, Robert. 1994. *Dialogue and the Interpretation of Illness: Conversations in a Cameroon Village*. Oxford: Berg.

————. N.d. "Witchcraft and Western Anthropological Discourse." Unpublished paper, University of Amsterdam.

Pradelles de Latour, Charles-Henry. 1991. *Ethnopsychanalyse en pays bamiléké*. Paris: EPEL.

Rey, Pierre-Philippe. 1971. *Colonialisme, néo-colonialisme et transition au capitalisme*. Paris: Maspero.

————. 1973. *Les alliances de classes*. Paris: Maspero.

Reynolds, Pamela. 1990. "Children of Tribulation: The Need to Heal and the Means to Heal War Trauma." *Africa* 60 (1): 1–38.

Riches, D., ed. 1986. *The Anthropology of Violence*. Oxford: Blackwell.

de Rosny, Éric. 1981. *Les yeux de ma chèvre: Sur les pas des maîtres de la nuit en pays douala*. Paris: Plon.

————. 1992. *L'Afrique des guérisons*. Paris: Karthala.

Rowland, R. 1990. "'Fantasticall and Devilishe Persons': European Witchbeliefs in Comparative Perspective." In *Early Modern European Witch-*

craft, Centres and Peripheries, ed. B. Ankarloo and G. Henningsen, 161–91. Oxford: Clarendon Press.

Rowlands, Michael. 1987. "Power and moral order in precolonial West-Central Africa." In *Specialization, Exchange and Complex Societies,* ed. E. M. Brumfield and T. K. Earle, 52–63. Cambridge: Cambridge Univ. Press.

———. 1993. "Economic Dynamism and Cultural Stereotyping in the Bamenda Grassfields." In *Les itinéraires de l'accumulation au Cameroun,* ed. Peter Geschiere and Piet Konings, 71–99. Paris: Karthala.

———. N.d. "The Domestication of Modernity in Cameroon."

Rowlands, Michael, and Jean-Pierre Warnier. 1988. "Sorcery, Power and the Modern State in Cameroon." *Man,* n.s., 23:118–32.

Ruell, Malcolm. 1969. *Leopards and Leaders.* London: Tavistock.

Salmon, J. H. M. 1989. "History without Anthropology: A New Witchcraft Synthesis." *Journal of Interdisciplinary History* 19 (3): 481–86.

Schatzberg, Michael G. 1993. "Power, Legitimacy and 'Democratisation' in Africa." *Africa* 63 (4): 445–61.

Schoffeleers, J. Matthew. 1992. *River of Blood: The Genesis of a Martyr Cult in Southern Malawi, c. a. d 1600.* Madison: Univ. of Wisconsin Press.

Seur, Hans. 1992. *Sowing the Good Seed: The Interweaving of Agricultural Change, Gender Relations and Religion in Serenje District, Zambia.* Ph.D. diss., University of Wageningen, Netherlands.

Shanklin, Eugenia. 1988. "Witchcraft Accusation and Labelling in a Matrilineal Society." Unpublished paper, Trenton College, Trenton, NJ.

Sharpe, J. 1990. "Witchcraft and Persecuting Societies, Review and Commentary." *Journal of Historical Sociology* 3 (1): 75–86.

Shaw, Rosalind. In press. *The Dangers of Temne Divination: Ritual Memories of the Slave Trade in West Africa.* Chicago: Univ. of Chicago Press.

Siret, M. 1946–49. *Monographie de la Région du Haut-Nyong.* Yaunde, Cameroon: Archives IRCAM/MESIRES.

Stephen, Michele, ed. 1987. *Sorcerer and Witch in Melanesia.* Melbourne: Melbourne Univ. Press.

Stoller, Paul, and C. Olkes. 1987. *In Sorcery's Shadow: A Memoir of Apprenticeship among the Songhay of Niger.* Chicago: Univ. of Chicago Press.

Sulikowski, Ulrike. 1993. "'Eating the Flesh, Eating the Soul': Reflections on Politics, Sorcery and *Vodun* in Contemporary Benin." In *L' Invention religieuse en Afrique: Histoire et religion en Afrique noire,* ed. Jean-Pierre Chrétien, C. H. Perrot, G. Prunier, and F. Raison-Jourde, 379–91. Paris: Karthala.

———. 1995. "The Cakatu and the President—An Inquiry into 'Rituals of Politics' in Benin 1989–1995." Unpublished paper, University of Vienna.

Tall, Emmanuelle K. 1995. "De la démocratie et des cultes voduns au Bénin." *Cahiers d'études africaines* 137:195–209.

Taussig, Michael. 1980. *The Devil and Commodity Fetishism in South America*. Chapel Hill: Univ. of North Carolina Press.

———. 1987. *Shamanism, Colonialism and the Wild Man: A Study of Terror and Healing*. Chicago: Univ. of Chicago Press.

———. 1993. *Mimesis and Alterity: A Particular History of the Senses*. London: Routledge.

———. 1995. "The Sun Gives without Receiving: An Old Story." *Comparative Studies in Society and History* 37 (2):368–98.

Tempels, P. 1949. *La philosophie bantoue*. 2d ed. Paris: Présence africaine.

Thoden van Velzen, H. U. E. 1973. "Robinson Crusoë and Friday: Strength and Weakness of the Big Man Paradigm." *Man* 8:592–612.

———. 1977. "Staff, Kulaks and Peasants." In *Government and Rural Development in East Africa*, ed. Lionel Cliffe, J. S. Coleman, and Martin Doornbos, 219–50. The Hague: Nijhoff.

———. 1996. "Dangerous Creatures." Paper presented at conference of European Association of Social Anthropology, Barcelona, July.

Thoden van Velzen, H. U. E., and W. van Wetering. 1988. *The Great Father and the Danger: Religious Cults, Material Forces and Collective Fantasies in the World of the Surinamese Maroons*. Dordrecht, Netherlands: Foris.

Thomas, Keith. 1971. *Religion and the Decline of Magic: Studies in Popular Beliefs in Sixteenth- and Seventeenth-Century England*. London: Weidenfeld and Nicolson.

Turner, Victor W. 1954. *Schism and Continuity in an African Society: A Study of Ndembu Village Life*. Manchester: Manchester Univ. Press.

———. 1964. "Witchcraft and Sorcery: Taxonomy versus Dynamics." *Africa* 34 (4):314–25.

Vansina, Jan. 1990. *Paths in the Rainforests: Toward a History of Political Tradition in Equatorial Africa*. Madison: Univ. of Wisconsin Press.

van Velsen, Jaap. 1964. *The Politics of Kinship: A Study in Social Manipulation among the Lakeside Tonga*. Manchester: Manchester Univ. Press.

Warnier, Jean-Pierre. 1985. *Échanges, développement et hiérarchies dans le Bamenda précolonial (Cameroun)*. Stuttgart: Steiner.

———. 1989. "Traite sans raids au Cameroun." *Cahiers d'études africaines* 113:5–32.

———. 1993. *L'esprit d'entreprise au Cameroun*. Paris: Karthala.

Warnier, Jean-Pierre, and Dieudonné Miaffo. 1993. "Accumulation et ethos de la notabilité chez les Bamiléké." In *Les itinéraires de l'accumulation au Cameroun*, ed. Peter Geschiere and Piet Konings, 33–71. Paris: Karthala.

van Wetering, Wilhelmina. 1973. "Hekserij bij de Djuka: Een Sociologische Benadering." Ph.D. diss., University of Amsterdam.

White, Luise. 1993. "Vampire Priests of Central Africa: African Debates about Labor and Religion in Colonial Northern Zambia." *Comparative Studies in Society and History* 35 (4): 746–72.

Willis, Roy. 1970. "Instant Millennium: The Sociology of African Witch-Cleansing Cults." In *Witchcraft Confessions and Accusations*, ed. Mary Douglas, 129–41. London: Tavistock.

Wirz, Albert. 1972. *Vom Sklavenhandel zum kolonialen Handel, Wirtschafts-räume und Wirtschaftsformen in Kamerun vor 1914*. Zürich, Switzer-land: Atlantis.

Yombi, A. B. 1984. "La répression de la sorcellerie dans le Code pénal ca-merounais: Le cas du Kong dans le Ntem." *Jahrbuch für afrikanisches Recht* 5:3–12.

INDEX

accumulation. *See* witchcraft, and accumulation

Ahidjo, Ahmadou, 5, 37, 104, 115–20, 248 n.13, 248 n.14, 248 n.20, 260 n.42; and hegemonic project, 271 n.50; and politics of regional equilibrium, 100

ambition. *See* equality vs. ambition

anti-witchcraft movements, 165, 184, 220, 253 n.18, 260 n.42. *See also* Obasinjom; Bisima

Appadurai, Arjun, 227 n.16, 257 n.31

Appiah, Kwame A. 231 n.33, 232 n.37

Ardener, Edwin, 65, 143, 146–51, 230 n.28, 241 n.10, 241 n.11, 253 n.13, 254 n.20, 255 n.24

Arens, W., 235 n.11

Aronson, D., 246 n.3

Asad, Talal, 271 n.47, 274 n.6

Ashforth, Adam, 223, 226 n.11, 232 n.35, 261 n.46

association of elites. *See under* elites, new

association of traditional healers. See *Nganga*

Augé, Marc, 219–20, 280 n.7

Auslander, Mark, 223

Austen, Ralph, 222, 227 n.15, 279 n.6

Baba, Denis ("modern" witch doctor), 177–83, 266 n.26

Baka ("Pygmies"), 23, 107, 120–22

Bakossi, 151, 152, 155–58, 166, 255 n.22, 255 n.24

Bakweri: and Germans, 146–47; and *liemba* (witchcraft), 65, 241 n.11; and *nyongo* (witchcraft of new riches), 143, 146–51, 156, 166, 254 n.20, 257 n.31, 275 n.12

Balz, Heinrich, 155–57, 255 n.22, 255 n.24

Bamenda, 11, 18, 66, 151, 158, 206–11

Bamileke: and compartmentalization of witchcraft discourse, 206–11 ; economic success,